The Attlee Years

Moon cartoon]

[Reproduced by courtesy of the "Sunday Dispatch"

IF THE GOVERNMENT GOES INTO THE HOLIDAY CAMP BUSINESS

The Attlee Years

Edited by Nick Tiratsoo

Pinter Publishers
London and New York

First published in Great Britain in 1991 by
Pinter Publishers Limited
25 Floral Street, London WC2E 9DS

British Library Cataloguing in Publication Data
A CIP catalogue record for this book is available from the British Library
ISBN 0 86187 822 1

For enquiries in North America please contact
PO Box 197, Irvington, NY 10533

Library of Congress Cataloging-in-Publication Data
The Attlee years / edited by Nick Tiratsoo.
p. cm.
Includes bibliographical references and index.
ISBN 0-86187-822-1
1. Great Britain—Politics and government—1945–1954. 2. Great Britain—Politics and government—1936–1945. 3. Attlee, C.R. (Clement Richard), 1883–1967. I. Tiratsoo, Nick, 1952–
DA588.A83 1991
941.082—dc20

91–27196
CIP

Typeset by Florencetype Ltd, Kewstoke, Avon.
Printed and bound by Biddles Ltd of Guildford and Kings Lynn

Contents

List of tables

List of contributors

Steve Fielding is currently a Lecturer in the Department of Cultural Studies, the Polytechnic of East London, having previously taught at Lancaster University and the University College of Swansea. His book *Class and Ethnicity. The Irish in Britain 1880–1939* will soon be published by the Open University Press.

Anthony Gorst is a Lecturer in History at the Polytechnic of Central London and a Research Fellow of the Institute of Contemporary British History.

Lewis Johnman is a Senior Lecturer in Economic History at Thames Polytechnic and a Visitor at the Business History Unit, London School of Economics. He is currently working on industrial policy and economic reconstruction during and after the Second World War.

Tony Mason is a Senior Lecturer at the Centre for the Study of Social History, University of Warwick.

Helen Mercer lectures in Economic History at the University of Leeds. Her book *Constructing a competitive order: the hidden history of British Anti-trust* is to be published by Cambridge University Press in 1992.

Nicholas Owen read Philosophy, Politics and Economics at Christ Church, Oxford, from 1985 to 1988. He is now a research student at Nuffield College, Oxford, working on British decolonisation.

Bill Schwarz teaches in the Department of Cultural Studies at the Polytechnic of East London where he chairs the MA in Cultural Studies: History and Theory, and is on the editorial collective of *History Workshop Journal*. His history of British Conservatism will be published by Verso.

Ian Taylor has been a Lecturer in Government at Aston University since 1978, having taught previously at Bristol Polytechnic and Exeter University.

Peter Thompson is a doctoral student at the Centre for the Study of Social History, University of Warwick, producing a thesis on the resettlement of ex-servicemen and women after the Second World War.

Nick Tiratsoo teaches at the Centre for the Study of Social History, University of Warwick, and is currently researching economic policy 1945–51 and the popular politics of the late 1960s.

Jim Tomlinson is Reader in the Economics Department, Brunel University and Fellow of the Business History Unit, London School of Economics. He has recently published *Public Policy and the Economy Since 1900* (Oxford University Press 1990) and *Hayek and the Market* (Pluto Press 1990) and is currently working on the economic policies of the Attlee Government.

Acknowledgements

I should like to thank Terry Gourvish, Lewis Johnman, Anthony Seldon and my current and ex-colleagues at the Centre for the Study of Social History, the University of Warwick—especially Richard Coopey, Steve Fielding, Tony Mason, Jim Obelkevich and Peter Thompson—for encouragement and advice during the compilation of this volume. The collection is dedicated to the memory of the late George Hodgkinson.

1 Introduction

Nick Tiratsoo

In recent years, the literature about Attlee's administrations between 1945 and 1951 has grown enormously, encouraged by a range of factors such as the release of the relevant state papers and the controversies of current politics.[1] However, advances in this historiography have been rather uneven.[2] Much has been written on the detail of the period's high politics, policy and administration. Against this there is far less on the framework within which decision-making was occurring—the full complex of constraints which shaped policy formation. Consequently, some of the overall judgements on the Attlee years are, on close inspection, more than a little partial: Labour is evaluated not in terms of real possibilities, but against various sets of either left-wing or right-wing a priori and ahistorical standards. The result, as Hennessy notes, is a situation where 'ideological distortion distilled from prejudice and hindsight' all too often masquerades as real historical analysis.[3]

The idea of this new collection of essays is to provide a corrective to such literature by focusing on policy very much within its context. The aim, in short, is to examine the variety of economic, social and political impediments that faced the governments of 1945–51, and analyse how these fashioned the choice and implementation of objectives. The hope is that this, in turn, will contribute to a more accurate appreciation of Labour's record and, indeed, the whole post-war period.

These are, of course, bold words, and they clearly require some further elaboration. The rest of this brief introduction attempts to fulfil this requirement, starting with a discussion of the existing historiography and its limitations, and then moving on to indicate what each of the authors gathered here is arguing. A final section tries to draw out some general conclusions which are suggested by the detailed material.

The current historiography of the Attlee governments is of three distinct types. Left-wing critics of Labour—Miliband, Blackwell and Seabrook,

Saville[4]—argue that the party was elected on a dramatic, popular and radical upsurge in 1945; subsequently enacted some reforms, but was mostly concerned with restabilizing the capitalist system; and ended by being rejected at the polls in 1951 because of disenchantment at this betrayal amongst its erstwhile supporters. The conclusions reached are, therefore, very unflattering to Labour. Blackwell and Seabrook offer this observation on the party's place in Britain's post-war reconstruction:

> The role of Labour . . . was two-fold. First of all, to provide illusions that the new beginnings actually represented a radical break with the past, the will to create a new society which would articulate the hopes and desires of their own people; and secondly, and more prosaically, to provide a scaffolding of welfare services which would both support and shroud the restoration of the old structures.[5]

A second kind of historiography has been offered by those with a more sympathetic viewpoint, such as Morgan.[6] Here, Labour's triumph in 1945 is explained in terms of a broad consensus for change that had developed during the war; while its record in office, far from being belittled, is seen as decisive and particularly noteworthy, given the country's precarious international trading and currency position. The picture is of a united party with a coherent programme, in step with public opinion, and making a break with the past over issues from welfare to the Empire. Labour eventually fell, in this version, because it ran out of steam, but a measure of its historic impact, it is suggested, can be seen from the imprint it left on the following years. Morgan puts this latter point in the following way: 'In large areas of policy, the Attlee government had a clear record of achievement and of competence, which acted as a platform for successive governments, Conservative and Labour, throughout the next quarter of a century.'[7]

Finally, there are a number of more right-wing interpretations, such as that recently offered by Barnett.[8] These often accept the broad conclusions of the Morgan view, yet set them in a very much more pessimistic light. Thus, Barnett agrees that Labour's aims were supported by a majority of the electorate in 1945, but explains this in terms of the malignant influence wielded by a group of unrepresentative, middle-class reformers. Similarly, he has no doubts about the decisive shift in Britain's social and economic development that had occurred by 1951. Nevertheless, this is seen as having been disastrous, since the emphasis on welfare, which was Labour's alleged priority, sapped the country's longer-term ability to solve its economic problems. For the Right, then, the country took the wrong fork in 1945, and Labour must bear much of the responsibility. It was not until 1979 that some of the damage could begin being repaired.

As this brief review indicates, therefore, historians have reached very different conclusions about the successes and failures of the Attlee years. However, if characterizations of the administrations' performances vary, there is at least some agreement about where an explanation of the outcome should be sought. For Labour, in all three kinds of account, appears as very much responsible for its own fate. The point to emphasize, according to taste, is its 'class-collaborationist ideology', or its 'realistic democratic socialism' or its 'unrealistic New Jerusalemism'. On the other hand, constraints limiting or confusing action were, it is commonly agreed, of somewhat less importance. All recognize that the country faced grave economic problems. Nevertheless, against this, the argument runs, Labour had many blessings. Left-wing critics emphasize, amongst other things, the scale of popular radicalism, which opened up the way for a real shift in power relations even if Labour was not prepared to follow it.[9] Barnett, at the opposite extreme, is equally struck by the country's mood in the late 1940s, and notes how few stood out against the corrupting 'New Jerusalemism'.[10] Finally, the idea of a benign environment also occurs in more balanced and scholarly accounts. Addison and Morgan both recognize that opposition to Labour was very pronounced at certain points between 1945 and 1951, but each is more struck by the degree of consensus Attlee enjoyed. Addison has argued that the government began its work 'at a unique moment in social history, when working-class unity was at its height'.[11] Morgan makes a similar point, stressing that Labour was secure in its proletarian base, and also that the wider political mood 'seemed relatively friendly':

> The Conservatives remained shell-shocked for at least two years. The Civil Service was uniquely anxious to plan and innovate. The City was sullen but docile. The Lords usually gave little trouble. Press and people voiced much of the passion for social change inherited from wartime years.[12]

There was, in short, an overwhelming urge that a peoples' war should be followed by a peoples' peace, a situation that the Attlee government was perhaps uniquely placed to respond to and ultimately benefit from.

Clearly, then, the idea that Labour was operating in a relatively favourable environment—the economic situation excepted—has a widespread appeal, and is accepted by authorities of very different political persuasions. However, on close examination what is being argued here is perhaps less convincing than it at first sight appears. Much of the historiography of the Attlee period is, as has been pointed out, essentially about 'high' politics and policy, and uses sources appropriate to those spheres. On the other hand, the complexion of 'low' politics and the nature of social life are often assumed, with relevant bodies of evidence rarely fully used. Thus, a whole range of important issues—the composition of public opinion, the attitudes of the trade unions, Labour and private industry—remain largely unstudied in the current literature. The study of Labour in office has been, all too often, the study of Labour at Westminster,[13] with all that this implies about the nature of the conclusions that have then been offered.

The present collection of essays is an attempt to begin to correct this bias. The various authors were charged with re-examining the whole question of constraints, within their particular field of detailed expertise. The idea was not to create a new homogeneous orthodoxy, but rather to explore a range of issues which previous surveys have tended to ignore or assume away. This, it was hoped, would generate a fresh body of evidence with which to re-evaluate the major controversies thrown up by the existing historiography.

The three opening chapters in the book survey various aspects of the wartime period, in order to provide some background on Labour's election to power. Taylor, one of the few scholars to have worked on the Labour Party in the war, provides an accurate and detailed view of how Labour's programme evolved during the conflict, and what influences lay behind *Let Us Face The Future*. Johnman focuses on industrial politics, in order to see how far Labour's objectives in this area were shared by the Civil Service and the business community. He shows that leading employers were very pessimistic about reconstruction, and determined in their insistence that a return to unfettered private enterprise must occur once the war had been won. Attitudes in the Board of Trade were more complex, though in 1944 and 1945 there was increasing worry about the short-term balance of payments position. Neither kind of attitudes augured well for a party committed to planning and industrial modernization. Finally, Mason and Thompson survey the popular political situation as it developed during the hostilities. Most accounts stress the public's drift to the Left during these years, but Mason and Thompson paint a rather different picture, in which radicals are outnumbered by those who yearn for little more than a swift return to peacetime normalcy. This provides an important corrective to the view, propagated by the playwright Trevor Griffiths amongst others,[14] that by 1945 the British working class had become openly insurrectionist.

The second part of the book looks at various aspects of what actually happened once Labour had achieved power. Mercer examines how Labour coped with private industry, a previously neglected subject. It has generally been assumed that the Attlee government had no real policy for the industries it did not contemplate nationalizing, but Mercer shows that this is far from true. Labour was interested in modernization and pursued this via a number of strategies (including the creation of Development Councils). It achieved relatively little, however, because of opposition from the industrialists themselves—opposition which Mercer shows to have been more coherent and sustained than has previously been suspected. Tomlinson follows this with an overview of government–trade union relations. He examines three key policy areas—the administration's concerns over 'undermanned' industries, productivity, and the level of wages in relation to export objectives—and can find little evidence of union obstruction. Nevertheless, he emphasizes that this conclusion must be seen in context. Government objectives were often rather conservative. Moreover, antagonistic attitudes towards official goals were sometimes more evident amongst the rank and file.

The following three chapters deal with aspects of the national political situation. Fielding surveys public opinion over the Attlee years and highlights not the extent of radicalism, but rather the degree of apathy. 'The public', he writes, 'was disengaged from a system preoccupied with issues felt to be all too remote from their everyday concerns.' Whether or not this was a constraint on Labour's strategists is, however, debatable. As Fielding stresses, the party was committed in theory to building a participatory society, but its specific endeavours in this area usually remained fairly vague and hesitant. Tiratsoo examines the often ignored local dimension of Labour's ascendancy, looking in particular at efforts to rebuild the bombed city of Hull between 1945 and 1951. The Labour city council, the author points out, had a visionary plan for reconstruction, but little of this was actually carried out, because of opposition from local vested interests and indifference in Whitehall. The case of Hull, Tiratsoo concludes, contradicts Barnett's well-known contention about the triumph of 'New Jerusalemism'. Lastly, Schwarz provides an accomplished overview of the Conservative opposition in the second half of the 1940s. He argues that the election defeat in 1945 was traumatic for the Tories, but goes on to show that the Conservative recovery was fairly swift, hastened not only by initiatives from within (both organizational and ideological), but also by broader developments in a larger—global and imperial—context (particularly those related to India and the Cold War). The upshot of this, as Schwarz shows, was that Labour found itself increasingly outflanked by a party better able to respond to, and perhaps transform, a range of key popular concerns.

The final two pieces in the collection deal with aspects of Labour's foreign policy and defence records. Owen surveys how the Attlee government dealt with the India question. This is often told as a heroic story, in which the granting of independence is seen as a well-planned crowning achievement, executed by a wise and far-seeing government. However, as Owen shows, this is far from the truth. There was no linear progression to independence, nor any wealth of high-minded idealism, but rather muddle and indecision, and a range of constraints shaped as much, or more, by narrow political calculation as by altruism. In conclusion, Gorst focuses on how Labour dealt with the defence issue over this period. The party came into office with an ill-defined desire to cut expenditure on defence, but was never able to achieve this objective. As Gorst points out, this was not only because of opposition from the armed forces' lobby, but it also has to be seen as in part a consequence of Labour's growing commitment to fighting the Cold War.

Taken together, therefore, the pieces in this collection provide a reasonably comprehensive map of the political realities and possiblities faced by the Attlee administrations. They show that Labour's room for manoeuvre was more tightly constrained than many have subsequently allowed. The extent of the war-time consensus has been exaggerated. Some Labour policies were clearly never acceptable either to the majority party in Parliament or to many key civil servants. Moreover, a large slice of the electorate remained indifferent: assessments of the war's impact on the contours of political consciousness differ (compare Schwarz and Mason and Thompson in this volume) but it appears increasingly difficult to support a mass radicalization hypothesis. After 1945, the Labour Party enjoyed some definite advantages, of which a close relationship with the trade union movement was the most obvious. None the less, it also found itself opposed —and vehemently opposed at that—by a number of influential pressure groups as well as a rejuvenated Conservative Party, and subject to widespread public indifference or hostility. All in all, this was certainly a very bleak environment in which to try and plant the seeds of socialism.

This conclusion casts doubt on some of the wilder critiques of the Attlee governments, which assume that the administrations had a virtually free hand. However, it also opens up interesting questions about Labour's own attitude to the constraints. Although accepting that the situation was difficult, might not more have been done to transform adversity, rather than simply suffer under it? This issue has most usually been addressed from within a rather stale debate on Labour's socialist credentials, where the canons of the Great Men of the Left are given preference, regardless of the historical actuality. Superseding this kind of approach means taking Labour at face value, as a party engaged in electoral politics, and evaluating its strengths and weaknesses accordingly. It is to be hoped that this book will provoke further research on these lines.

Notes

1. Reassessments of the recent past have, of course, been especially prevalent on the political Right, since a key belief amongst Thatcherites has been that a decisive break with the alleged post-war consensus founded by Attlee is vital for Britain's future. See on this point, K.O. Morgan *The People's Peace*, Oxford, 1990, pp.437–8.
2. For a recent survey of the current historiography, see K. Laybourn, *The Rise of Labour*, 1988, pp.107–38.
3. P. Hennessy, 'The Attlee governments, 1945–1951' in P. Hennessy and A. Seldon (eds), *Ruling Performance*, Oxford, 1989, p.50.
4. R. Miliband, *Parliamentary Socialism*, 2nd edn, 1970, pp. 272–317; T. Blackwell and J. Seabrook, *The Politics of Hope*, 1988, esp. pp.24–5; and J. Saville, *The Labour Movement in Britain*, 1988, pp.82–121.
5. Blackwell and Seabrook, op.cit., 25.
6. K.O. Morgan, *Labour in Power*, Oxford, 1984.
7. Ibid., 494.
8. C. Barnett, *The Audit of War*, 1986.
9. See e.g. Saville, op.cit., 4 and 82–6.
10. Barnett, op.cit., 19 and 37.
11. *New Statesman*, 17 and 24 December 1982.
12. *New Statesman*, 23 February 1984.
13. A point made by E.P. Thompson in *The Guardian*, 3 March 1984.
14. See his 'Country: "A Tory story"' in T. Griffiths, *Collected Plays for Television*, 1988, pp.233–98.

Notes on sources

Monographs cited in Notes are published in London unless otherwise stated. References beginning with the letters BT, CAB, DEFE, ED, HLG, INFII, LAB, PREM, T and WO relate to files in the Public Records Office, Kew.

2 Labour and the impact of war 1939–45

Ian Taylor

Most of the literature dealing with the Second World War refers to the role of the Labour Party in the Coalition and in particular the contribution of leading Labour politicians to the war effort. The most useful books deal with the impact of war on British society and domestic policy. For example, Arthur Marwick in *Britain in the Century of Total War* (1968) argues that both world wars helped to break up traditional patterns in British politics and society. Both Angus Calder in *The People's War* (1969) and Henry Pelling in *Britain and the Second World War* (1970) show that the war in itself was not particularly innovative as a catalyst for change because the social structure and ownership of wealth remained largely unaffected afterwards. Paul Addision in *The Road to 1945* (1975) argues that a consensus developed during the war, which hastened the introduction of a reformed style of capitalism. This consensus helped Labour to victory in 1945. Lawrence Harris in *The War Economy: State socialism and state monopoly capitalism* (1984) claims that the war inaugurated a form of state monopoly capitalism. T.D. Burridge's *Britain's Labour and Hitler's War* (1975) considers the role of the Labour Party in war-time foreign policy-making. The author's doctoral thesis 'War and the development of Labour's domestic programme 1939–45' (1977) studies the impact of the war on the party's domestic policy, focusing on the policy documents issued by the party's reconstruction organization. When pieced together they provided a picture of the background to Labour's reconstruction programme for post-war Britain.

The picture that emerges is that the war was a catalyst in creating a greater role for the state in social provision and economic management. However, many of the controls over financial institutions and industry were designed to be short-term, for the duration of war only. Consequently, Labour's social welfare, agriculture and physical planning policies were enhanced by wartime developments whilst proposals for changing or at least controlling the distribution of wealth remained much the same: limited and unclear.

In keeping with many figures on the Left,[1] Labour politicians agreed that the Second World War was the consequence of competition within and between nations, and the lesson of war was that co-operation must predominate in the post-war world. The war represented the end of a social order that had outlived its usefulness and presented a challenge to the party to win the peace. During its early stages rhetoric abounded. Many leading figures in the party, notably Harold Laski, Arthur Greenwood and Clement Attlee,[2] called for radical reform whilst the war was in progress. Labour's policy documents reflected this, none more so than the Interim Report *The Old World and the New Society* (1942), which called for the nation to make use of wartime progress in planning for peacetime.

> We have learnt in the war that the anarchy of private competition must give way to ordered planning under national control. That lesson is no less applicable to peace. The Labour Party therefore urges that the nation must own and operate the essential instruments of production, their power over our lives is too great for them to be left in private hands.[3]

The Report was the work of the party's Central Committee on Reconstruction Problems, which had been set up in 1941 at the instigation of Hugh Dalton, and Harold Laski, who was sceptical about the role of the government's own Reconstruction Committee established under Arthur Greenwood's chairmanship in 1940. He wanted Labour to offer counter-proposals of a more radical nature.[4] In fact, the Reconstruction Committee had little power, being more of an instrument of co-ordination between departments. As Paul Addison[5] has argued, one of its main objectives was to show the government's concern about the post-war world and make some recommendations for the future. Labour's Committee consisted of twenty-four members, including Emanuel Shinwell as Chairman and Laski as Secretary. Many members were MPs and leading trade unionists, reflecting the dominance of the Parliamentary Party and National Council of Labour in policy-making. The reconstruction organization comprised a number of subcommittees dealing with various policy areas, which were charged not only with drawing up plans for post-war Britain, but also monitoring and reviewing wartime policies and, wherever relevant, incorporating them into Labour's policy proposals for the Central Committee, Policy Committee and the National Executive to consider. The party's leaders, Attlee, Dalton, Morrison and Greenwood, were all ex-officio members of the subcommittees, but Laski expressed concern that as members of the Coalition government they should not be overburdened with extra work![6] Consequently, the subcommittee proposals tended to be more adventurist than the leaders might have liked. This is clearly reflected in the way in which official policy documents sometimes fell short of policies advanced by the subcommittees. The recommendations of the subcommittee influenced the party's official policy statements, which in turn determined the content of Labour's 1945 programme contained in the election manifesto *Let Us Face the Future*. The manifesto closely resembled the 1937 policy document *Labour's Immediate Programme*, which represented what a future Labour government hoped to implement during a single term of office. Whilst this implies that the impact of war on Labour Party policy was insignificant, this was not so in most policy areas. In order to appreciate the impact of war it is necessary to consider the work of the reconstruction subcommittees and the way in which Labour formulated its policies for post-war Britain.

The Second World War proved to be a catalyst in social policy and provision. The Beveridge Report,[7] the 1944 Education Act, and White Papers advancing proposals for a comprehensive unified system of social insurance and a national health service bear testimony to this. Many of the reformist documents of wartime were aimed at peace and had relatively little impact on wartime policy, although they were triggered by the war, which put a tremendous strain on the social services and in particular the hospital and allied services.

Evacuation highlighted serious social problems such as substandard housing, inadequate health and education, and in some cases malnutrition. This, combined with the immediate need to create and maintain a healthy population to bring the war to a successful conclusion and reward those who were making sacrifices led to better provision whilst the war was in progress. Improved pensions, free school meals and milk for children, improved maternity benefits and the more effective co-ordination of social services were products of wartime. Under the Emergency Medical Service (EMS) the government took partial control of all hospitals. The service was more egalitarian than anything that had existed previously because it was rendered on the basis of need. Advances were made in preventive medicine and there were improvements in the maternity and child welfare services. General practitioners were called upon to utilize more specialist skills in special centres and hospitals which were under severe pressure dealing with war casualties. The need to establish on a permanent basis a comprehensive range of services and overhaul the social insurance system and health service led to the setting up of the Committee on Social Insurance and Allied Services under Sir William Beveridge. The Beveridge Report of November 1942 became a focal point of post-war reconstruction policy and *the* symbol of better things to come.

Labour regarded the Beveridge Report as of extreme importance, so much so that the party pressed for its immediate implementation, voting *en bloc* against the government's decision to delay, the only time that the Parliamentary Party took such action during the lifetime of the Coalition. Following these events, both Morrison and Bevin lost popularity in the party,[8] Bevin having accused the Parliamentary Party of disloyalty.[9] According to Alan Bullock,[10] the dispute over the Beveridge Report and debate precipitated a quarrel between Bevin and a group of Labour MPs which had been simmering for some time and led to an estrangement between him and the Parliamentary Party which lasted until the summer of 1944. The National Council of Labour was given responsibility for assessing Beveridge and adjusting Labour's proposals in the light of the report, which it accepted with few reservations, applauding the universality principle which characterized many of Beveridges's recommendations. These included the unification of social insurance in respect of contributions and administration, the suspension of the existing system of Approved Societies giving unequal benefits for equal compulsory contributions, the separating of medical treatment from the administration of cash benefits, the setting up of a comprehensive medical service for all, and the recognition of housewives as a distinct insurance class of occupied persons with benefits adjusted to their special needs. The Council also welcomed the scheme for Children's Allowances, to be granted to each child when the parent was in receipt of any benefit or pension and for each child after the first in all other cases. The assimilation of benefit conditions for unemployment and disability into the same scheme and recommendations for administrative changes, notably the creation of a single Ministry of Social Security, were particularly welcome.[11]

The actual benefits proposed by Beveridge were not particularly generous and were certainly less so than those put forward by Labour, the TUC, and the Fabian Society both before and after the report's publication. However, they adhered to the principle of a national minimum which was widely supported throughout the Labour movement. The White Paper *Social Insurance*[12] did not. In proposing a new unified social insurance scheme to cover the whole population, incorporating family allowances, sickness and unemployment benefit, training allowances, retirement pensions, and married women and widows' provision, the government departed from the Beveridge Report. Benefits would not be distributed on a subsistence basis. Maurice Bruce has written: 'So much for the hopes that went back to the Webbs, and all the careful work that Beveridge, with Keynes's assistance, had put into his estimates.'[13] Contribution levels proposed by the government were lower than Beveridge's but so were benefits. On the other hand, the government's White Paper on workmen's compensation[14] was more radical. Compensation would in future be treated as a social service, not an aspect of employer liability law and would cover everyone above school-leaving age under contract schemes. Liability would reside with a Central Fund from which benefits would be paid.

Labour's own social insurance proposals lacked clarity in terms of details of administration and benefit levels although they were as purposeful as the Beveridge Report. In fact, a number of proposals along the lines of Beveridge had been produced before the report's publication and were an extension of pre-war party policy.[15] On the other hand, Labour's proposals for a National Health Service which predated Beveridge by half a century (in principle if not in substance) were clearer than ever before. In this policy area at least, Beveridge had little impact on Labour's plans. Several wartime reports recommended a complete overhaul of the service. The policy document *A National Service for Health* (1943) called for a state service covering all aspects of health including prevention, cure, maintenance of optimum health, education and rehabilitation. GPs would be full-time, salaried and subject to fixed hours of service. Local authorities would provide maternity and child welfare schemes. The hospital service would be unified and publicly controlled. Local authorities were to have full responsibility for all hospitals and would be required to pool resources and unite into a regional administrative structure. Voluntary hospitals would be required to adhere to government plans and local authority control. The service would be funded partly from national taxation and the rates. Overall control would rest with the Ministry of Health, with democratically elected Regional Health Authorities empowered to appoint Health Committees for each region. What was particularly noteworthy about Labour's proposals apart from their comprehensive nature was the extent of local authority involvement in future health provision.

Labour's proposals for a national health service remained unchanged until the end of the war, and there were reservations about the Government's scheme which in many respects was similar to that proposed by the party. *A National Health Service* (1944)[16] reflected Beveridge's recommendation that medical benefits should be removed from health insurance (which would be a cash benefit scheme), that a state service should be part of a social welfare system, and that it should be comprehensive and free at the point of delivery. However, concessions to the medical profession, in particular the proposal that each doctor should be contracted to a Central Medical Board rather than a local authority, were criticized by Labour. The Socialist Medical Association supported the Labour Party and called for an end to the panel system for GPs, and for the redistribution of doctors proportionately according to population. Along with the TUC, the Association was concerned that when legislation was drafted, the proposals of the White Paper would not be diluted at the very least.[17]

One of the great legislation landmarks not only of the war but arguably of the twentieth century was the 'Butler' Education Act of 1944. The act was the culmination of two main initiatives, the Norwood Report (1943)[18] and the White Paper *Educational Reconstruction*.[19] Norwood assumed three kinds of abilities amongst children and recommended three types of school to accommodate them, grammar, technical and modern. In addition, the report proposed an end to the School Certificate examination system. The White Paper supported Norwood's approach and proposed a diversified form of secondary schooling based on a competitive examination at 'eleven plus', due to the limited number of grammar school places. The school-leaving age would be raised to fifteen and there would be increased provision for adult education and easier access to the universities. The ensuing Education Act set out the framework for reforming the law relating to education in England and Wales. Its objective was to *facilitate* a national policy for education based on state schools run by local authorities under ministerial control. This was designed to eliminate the dual system of voluntary (non-provided) and state (provided) schools which had hitherto existed side by side. The Act's provision for a secondary education system, free and open to all, was certainly consistent with Labour's own policy. It is important to stress that the Act's aim was to reform the framework. It did not set out or prescribe forms of schooling to be adopted, although it was widely assumed that the types of schools referred to in the White Paper would be established.

During the early years of the war, the Labour Party's Education

Subcommittee turned its attention to the nature of education. There was much support for the common multilateral school through which all children would pass, rather than a multiplicity of secondary schools, and no support for a competitive examination at 11 years.[20] However, Labour's official policy document 'Labour's Educational Policy' failed to clarify the objectives of the party and did not adhere to the proposals of the subcommittee. Less attention was paid to secondary school provision than the machinery for education administration. There was clearly a division of opinion over the form secondary education would take. According to Rodney Barker,[21] supporters of the multilateral system saw it increasingly as an alternative to the tripartite system proposed in the White Paper. At no stage did the party officially advocate the outright abolition of private schools, although a subcommittee report somewhat optimistically called for the conversion of boarding-schools like Eton, Rugby and Winchester into universities or schools for post-certificate children, for whom specialist teaching was unavailable at local secondary schools.[22]

Clearly, supporters of the multilateral school on the subcommittee such as Alice Bacon and Harold Clay had little influence when it came to Policy Committee decisions. *Let Us Face the Future* focused on the 1944 Act, confirming a future Labour government's intention to implement it in full. The Act left much scope for interpretation since it offered both local authorities and parents the ability to influence education provision. *Arguably*, the war and the Act in particular had a major impact on Labour Party policy since a framework for education was provided, a skeleton to which the substance of education could later be added. However, Labour's inability to adopt a formula for the substance of education should be regarded as a major failing.

As with education, Labour's housing policy was not clearly defined. In view of the problems associated with rebuilding blitzed areas and the increasing attention paid to town and country planning, this was hardly surprising. The 1944 (Temporary Accommodation) Act, which set out the government's policy for the emergency provision of dwellings after the war, and the 'Housing' White Paper[23] were supported by Labour. Both dealt predominantly with the short-term crisis, during which exceptional measures would have to be introduced to meet the shortage. Overall, Labour was dissatisfied with the government's failure to establish effective controlling and planning agencies for housing, although it should be stressed that emergency house-building remained the party's overriding priority. More generally, housing was incorporated into Labour's proposals for planning and land control, which were also influenced by wartime developments.

The devastation of urban areas by enemy bombing exposed the lack of planning of Britain's towns and cities and brought to the attention of the government the need to control the future development of land and building in urban areas. In turn, this raised questions about landownership and land use as well as building priorities and cost and availability of building materials. In response, the government created the Ministry of Town and

Country Planning in 1943 and set up the Uthwatt and Scott Committees to consider questions of planning, land control and utilization in urban and rural areas. Physical planning became a key issue for the government's Reconstruction Committee, and involved the Cabinet in regular discussions, especially in the light of the Uthwatt and Scott recommendations.

The Uthwatt Report[24] criticized the inadequate powers of central government to control urban development and land. It advocated the creation of a Central Planning Authority, along the lines proposed by the Barlow Report on industrial location. The Authority's task would be to assist the government to control the rebuilding of blitzed areas, the future location of industry, house-building, the provision of open spaces, and the development of public utility services. It would also play a role in the overhaul of the transport system, the decongestion of built-up areas and slum clearance. Although Uthwatt ruled out land nationalization for practical reasons, the committee recommended increased governmental powers to control and compulsorily purchase land whenever necessary.

Overall, the recommendations supported a massive increase in the role of the state in physical planning and were met with enthusiastic support from the Labour Party. Labour called on the government to accept them as a matter of urgency, especially proposals empowering local authorities to acquire reconstruction areas at prices not exceeding those of March 1939. Other priorities included the creation of a Central Planning Authority, and state ownership of undeveloped land required for future development.[25]

The Scott Report[26] was also welcomed. Set up by Lord Reith in October 1941, the Committee on Land Utilisation in Rural Areas recommended the creation of a Central Planning Authority to develop and administer a national scheme to enable central government to plan the use of land and transfer the execution of policy to regional and local authorities. It recommended control over industrial location and close collaboration between the Ministry of Agriculture and other government departments concerned with housing and town and country planning. Most of Scott's recommendations reflected the view that stricter state control over land use and development was required after the war. Like Uthwatt, Scott stopped short of advocating outright nationalization, which remained a major objective of the Labour Party but not a priority. The party was more concerned that the state should assume compulsory purchase powers over land.[27] Uthwatt and Scott offered ready-made alternatives to nationalization, which was pushed into the background as an immediate policy issue as the war progressed.

In putting together its reconstruction plans, Labour made full use of the Scott and Uthwatt proposals, and Labour members of Churchill's government argued against the introduction of measures which would compromise the establishment of long-term controls.[28] The Town and Country Planning (Interim Development) Bill was one such measure. The Bill aimed to strengthen local authority control over planning but not to create a Central Planning Authority, and there were doubts over the powers conferred on the new Minister. These were strengthened and the Bill became law in 1943, to be superseded by the Town and Country Planning Bill (1945). This too was criticized by Labour on the grounds that it failed to establish effective control and co-ordinating machinery, failed to grant sufficient powers to the Minister and gave too many concessions to landowners over compensation. In spite of the party's abstention on the second reading, the government remained unmoved. Labour attached extreme importance to town and country planning and land. In spite of the legacy of Scott and Uthwatt and criticisms of the government there were surprisingly few plans for the future. The setting up of a Central Planning Authority was not new. It was part of Labour's 1937 programme. Once again, it could be argued that expert opinion caught up with Labour during the war, once the potential for state control of, and involvement in, physical planning was realized.

Agriculture was one of the great success stories of the Second World War. Unlike in relation to sections of industry which were geared up for war production, the object of wartime agricultural policy was to produce more food. This approach could be transferred directly to peacetime with few modifications. During the war, agriculture was radically reorganized, as the Ministries of Food and Agriculture exercised effective control over the production, distribution and price of food. One of the key initiatives of the war was the creation of sixty-one County War Agriculture Executive Committees under the control of Executive Officers, permanent officials of both Ministries and specialist officers. The committees, which had extensive powers over land management and use, cultivation, livestock and feedstuff, brought together civil servants, farmers, agricultural workers, veterinary surgeons, technicians and educationalists. Compulsion, allied to co-operation in what had been traditionally a conservative industry, generated and sustained a sense of urgency and involvement in agriculture, which continued to be supervised locally by those closest to farming and the countryside. The government subsidized essential foods, stabilized the price of food and fertilizers and in general ensured that the burden of higher prices was passed on to the Exchequer, not the consumer. There was considerable assistance for farmers in the form of grants towards disease eradication, improvement of the quality of livestock, husbandry methods and drainage. Acreage payments were issued for certain crops and there were grants to expand hill sheep and cattle.[29]

In spite of these advances, the government's own post-war proposals were vague and noncommital, a factor which led to rifts in the Cabinet from May 1943 until the end of the war, although Attlee pressurized his Conservative colleagues into making concessions which ensured that fixed prices and agreed markets would continue for not less than two years after the war.[30] By contrast, Labour was committed to extending wartime controls well into peacetime and to maintaining the wartime administrative structure of the industry. County Committees were the key to future policy, acting as agents for a Ministry of Agriculture which would take over the functions of the Food Ministry.[31] During the war, many of Labour's traditional agricultural objectives were implemented. They included guaranteed prices for producers, price controls for the consumer, the control of domestic and overseas supplies of food, the control of market operation, control over the distribution of charges, and a minimum wage for agricultural workers. For the first time land was controlled in the public interest. During the war

Labour's policy advanced from the 1930s without any fundamental rethinking. If the comment of Michael Foot that the 'best example that I've seen of Democratic Socialism operating in this country was during the Second World War'[32] means anything, it can surely be applied more to agriculture than to any other policy area.

During the 1930s the Labour Party's fiscal policy was aimed specifically at the regeneration of industry and employment. This was to be achieved through a high level of central governmental direction of investment into areas vulnerable to economic recession. Policy documents advocated the establishment of a National Investment Board with the power to license and direct investment into specific concerns and mobilize available financial resources. The Board would prepare annual estimates of the National Income and co-ordinate all capital expenditure of central and local government. Effectively the Board would be the focal point of the state-managed economy. With the Bank of England nationalized and under Treasury control, a future Labour government would be able to formulate a financial plan and control industrial location and development. This would ensure that government would help to maintain high levels of employment through fiscal planning.[33]

The war went a long way to fulfilling many objectives of Labour's financial policy. Under the Emergency Defence Regulations, the government was empowered to implement any financial measures deemed necessary. Correspondingly, the role of the Treasury expanded. Through the Treasury, the government could obtain all acquisitions of foreign exchange, demand the surrender of all residents' holdings of gold and foreign currencies, fix the bank rate, enforce selected interest rates, influence the direction of bank loans and demand the preparation of investment plans by central government departments, local authorities and public utility companies. In effect it could finance the budget deficit as it saw fit.[34]

Keynes's influence on fiscal policy was considerable. In *How to Pay for the War*[35] he advanced proposals eventually incorporated into Treasury thinking and policy. The need to reconcile the demands of war with the claims of private consumption led to a partial withdrawal of earnings from expenditure and immediate consumption, using rationing and encouraging savings. The Kingsley Wood Budget of 1941 was responsible for some of the most important financial measures of the war. It increased income tax, overhauled the excess profits tax, promoted the principle of deferred pay (to be offset by post-war credits) and proposed the stabilization of prices by extending subsidies introduced early in the war.[36]

If the measures to take the profit out of the war, reduce consumption and encourage saving were immediate objectives, the fact that Treasury control was so extensive in directing investment into key areas of production was not lost on the Labour Party, nor indeed on Churchill's government. The 1944 White Paper *Employment Policy*,[37] described by Arthur Marwick as 'the most revolutionary document of the whole war period',[37] was drafted by the Ministry of Reconstruction. The thrust of the White Paper was to encourage private enterprise to plan capital expenditure in accordance with government policy, to maintain a stable public investment programme, maintain the national income and pursue a policy of budgetary equilibrium to secure the confidence necessary for healthy industry. When coupled with Dalton's Distribution of Industry Bill,[39] which proposed the extension of Board of Trade powers to secure a balanced distribution in industry, the White Paper showed the concern of the government in taking advantage of wartime thinking and recommendations in considering post-war reconstruction. More generally, the principle of state involvement in the generation of full employment was widely supported. It became the number one reconstruction priority. However, the White Paper had its critics. Beveridge[40] claimed that the White Paper put forward a public works policy rather than a full employment policy, arguing that it was too inhibited with regard to central finance and the need to maintain total expenditure. Although Bevin supported the White Paper in the Commons, several Labour MPs were concerned that the government would have too little control over the capital expenditure of industry if companies remained in private hands.[41] In other words, public ownership and rigorous controls over the private sector should form the central part of a full employment strategy.

Labour's response on this issue was the policy document *Full Employment and Financial Policy*[42] which advocated the extension of wartime financial policy into peacetime. The proposed National Investment Board would play a key role in controlling the export and issue of capital. It would co-operate with the Treasury and government departments in making estimates. Other reports recommended the extension of Treasury power to fix and control interest rates,[43] a more progressive taxation system[44] and the continuation of exchange controls. Overall, the impact of the war on Labour's financial policy was quite limited. However, it strengthened the party's determination to control finance to stimulate employment and regenerate industry. This was entirely in keeping with pre-war policy. *Let Us Face the Future* reflected on the significance of the National Investment Board but dropped nationalization of the Joint Stock Banks, on the surface a significant deviation[45] from the *Immediate Programme* (1937), although given effective levels of government control over banking during the war, perhaps not so surprising. The relationship between governmental financial controls such as fixing interest rates, influencing the lending policy of banks, controlling capital issues and investment become more widely understood during the war. That Labour's approach stayed much the same was due in part to the fact that Dalton, Douglas Jay, Evan Durbin, Joan Robinson and their supporters were already Keynesians and had advanced these policies for a considerable time. In a sense, Treasury thinking caught up with the party during the war.

During the war the government controlled industry and finance to create high employment levels, and in so doing turned its attention to the maintenance of full employment during peacetime. The Barlow Report led to proposals for controlling the future distribution of industry. The White Paper *Employment Policy* advanced the need for state control over finance and industrial development, reflecting the influence of Keynes at the Treasury and, more generally, the widely held belief that the mass unemployment experienced during the 1930s should never return. The war led to levels of control which had more in common with socialist command economies than capitalist economies. Practically all of the country's resources were utilized to the full. The state became the principal source of new capital, almost the sole customer of heavy industry and the chief supplier of raw materials. With luxury goods at a premium and manufacturing aimed at supplying the factories and armed services, scope for domestic consumption was severely restricted.

The Ministry of Supply, set up in 1939, was at the centre of wartime administration. Responsible for the provision and co-ordination of supply, and sponsoring the labour and raw materials supply for many industries, the Ministry was granted considerable powers with respect to acquisition, manufacture and disposal of goods as well as their prices.[46] The Ministry of Production co-ordinated war industry, providing a link between strategy and production. The Board of Trade controlled civil industry and trade through licensing and consumer rationing. One of its main functions was responsibility for the concentration of production scheme. Introduced in 1941, the scheme was designed to prevent wastefulness in the use of resources in civilian industry and to free factory space for war purposes.[47] Employment policy was determined by the Ministry of Labour and National Service. Under the Essential Work Order of 1941, sometimes harsh controls over employers and the movement of labour were exercised by the Ministry, and Ernest Bevin as Minister argued persistently that it would be necessary to maintain the order after the war during the transition to peace.[48]

As far as economic policy was concerned, manpower budgeting became a key instrument for determining the balance of the war economy. After 1940, the government utilized the manpower budget to direct the allocation of physical resources to different sectors of the economy. By 1942 it had become the main instrument of governmental planning, and according to Bullock,[49] had replaced the fiscal budget as the means of directing the country's resources. These were the main instruments of control during the war. The Labour Party regarded the machinery as a useful vehicle through which to implement both industrial and fiscal policy in the interim period between war and peace. In spite of general approval of controls there were criticisms,[50] and Herbert Morrison in particular came under pressure to persuade his Cabinet colleagues to commit themselves to the extension of controls into peacetime. As peace drew nearer, there was increasing suspicion that the Conservatives in the government could not be trusted and that Labour members of Churchill's administration would compromise over controls. In spite of this, the party's own industrial policy remained unclear. There was no organization in the party set up to deal with the post-war control of private industry. Consequently, there were no specific proposals for post-war industries other than those designated for nationalization. The Social and Economic Transformation in Great Britain Subcommittee published occasional articles on industrial controls, one of which was written by industrialist Samuel Courtauld, Director of the British Rayon Corporation. Courtauld argued that industrialists were more prepared to accept controls as a result of wartime patriotism which had reawakened their consciences: 'They ask themselves what they have done to earn past privileges and what they are doing in return for them today.'[51] Understandably the Left opposed the publication of Courtauld's article. The weekly *Tribune*[52] denounced it wholeheartedly as a proposal to retain the 'paternal class-state'.

Although Morrison and Bevin emphasized the need to control industry in general and monopolies in particular, it was not a conception of control with which the Left agreed. The fact remained that Labour was significantly divided throughout the war, and consequently failed to develop an agreed policy of its own. Articles by Austin Albu[53] and Ian Mikardo[54] called for a wider recognition that there had been a shift of responsibility in industry from owners to managers under state direction, and argued that ultimately more central control over industry would be necessary after the war. The TUC's *Interim Report on Post-War Reconstruction*[55] called for the setting up of Industrial Boards under government control to examine questions of internal organization and the policies of industries. Although vague and open-ended with regard to controls, at least the report offered some proposals. The lack of a specific controls policy was recognized by the party's Policy Committee in 1945 and the Mikardo resolution at the party's 1944 Annual Conference, which called for a much more extensive list of industries to be nationalized, had probably as much to do with the lack of a policy for private industry as the restricted list of industries designated for nationalization.

Labour's policies for the public ownership of industry were certainly clearer, even if there remained little in the way of a nationalization strategy. The party's Central Committee on Reconstruction Problems and subcommittees dealing with fuel, power and transport examined closely the wartime performance of those industries designated for nationalization in Labour's 1937 *Immediate Programme*. These were coal-mining, gas, electricity and the railways. As the war progressed, inland waterways, road transport, civil aviation and iron and steel came increasingly under the spotlight. Labour's pre-war nationalization plans reflected Morrison's view that inefficiency and lack of co-ordination were important reasons for nationalizing transport and heavy industry. The war put heavy industry and all forms of transport to the test, and highlighted many deficiencies in their organization, notably the lack of co-ordination and planning that one hundred and fifty years of haphazard development had created.

There had never been effective fuel, power and transport policies until the Second World War, so the relative success of wartime policy made nationalization a more viable, practical and electoral proposition. In 1942 the Ministry of Fuel and Power was set up as a co-ordinating department. This was an innovatory measure which brought coal, gas and electricity under the control of a single ministry for the first time. The new Ministry was partially successful in ensuring that priority industries received adequate supplies of fuel and that wasteful competition was eliminated as far as possible.[56] In spite of this initiative, the coal-mining industry posed serious problems of inefficient management, poor labour relations and high absenteeism throughout the war, strengthening Labour's demands for the immediate nationalization of the industry.[57] Labour's official post-war document on fuel and power referred to the importance of a co-ordinating Ministry to oversee the production of coal, gas and electricity. It recommended the creation of a National Coal and Power Corporation to own the industries and supervise their administration, with separate boards for each industry responsible for their day-to-day management. Regional and district organizations would be responsible for operational matters and would report to each board.[58] These proposals amounted to nothing new. There remained no rational *plan* for nationalization and Labour's compensation policy was not clarified. The much-repeated words of Labour's post-war Minister of Fuel and Power confirmed the lack of progress made during the war:

> I was optimistic enough to believe that, after twenty five years of talking about nationalisation at least an outline of a plan would have been available at Labour Party headquarters. Nothing existed beyond a few pamphlets for party workers and the public, and copies of resolutions passed at party conferences.[59]

During the war, Labour's Post-War Transport Subcommittee was charged with the task of drawing up plans for the post-war organization of all forms of transport in the light of wartime developments. The most important outcome of the committee's work was an extension of the 1937 nationalization list to include not only the railways but significant sections of road transport, canals and civil aviation.

As was the case with the fuel and power industries, the government set itself the task of co-ordinating all forms of transport. According to the official historian, by the end of 1943 'the Government exercised powerful and extensive control over the four branches of inland transport',[60] and for the first time in the country's history there was a fully planned system of inland transport with a high level of co-ordination of all forms of transport by land and sea. However, there were organizational problems throughout the war as the Ministry of War Transport was handicapped by the many different powers of control over various forms of transport, some retaining more autonomy than others. Given the number of operatives within each transport system, this was hardly surprising. The most successful controls were exercised over the railways through the Railways Executive Committee, which reduced the autonomy of the individual companies, and the Road Haulage Association, which was partly staffed by civil servants. This ensured that this highly individualistic section of the transport system complied with government policy. These were significant developments as far as Labour was concerned, but none more so than the establishment of a co-ordinating Ministry of War Transport, whose ultimate success cut short Labour's demands that transport should be nationalized as part of the war effort.

A Research Department report, 'The Post-War Organisation of British Transport',[61] called for the transfer from private control to public ownership, although in the case of road haulage nationalization would be a gradual process. A National Transport Control Authority would be set up, with a Board appointed by and accountable to the Minister, with the creation of single boards for the various forms of transport. Whilst this did not represent a departure from pre-war policy, the need for co-ordination was confirmed by the success of the Ministry of War Transport. Labour also considered the future of shipping which would remain under control after the war to prepare the way for public ownership.[62]

Civil aviation, which was discussed by the War Cabinet more than any other transport concern from 1943 onwards, was the subject of a far-reaching futuristic policy document published by Labour, *Wings For Peace*.[63] During the war, the use of new technology for military purposes and new production techniques raised the possibility of the massive expansion of the industry. There were divisions in the Cabinet over the 1945 White Paper *British Air Transport*,[64] with Brendan Bracken and Lord Beaverbrook abstaining from this compromise between nationalization and unlimited competition, and Stafford Cripps having to bear the brunt of his party's criticism in the House of Commons for defending what was described as a 'reactionary' White Paper.[65] Labour's document was adopted by the Annual Conference of 1945. It called for the international control of civil aviation through a World Air Authority which would represent the main trunk air lines of the world and own all trunk routes, airports, and ground organization. This reflected advances made during the war in international co-operation in the planning of routes and essential services. In the event of failure to reach international agreement, the party would, in any case, nationalize Britain's air services. Civil air transport would be entrusted to an Air Department of the Transport Ministry. BOAC would be strengthened and its role extended, and a new organization for Europe, 'Europa Airways', would be established under a Board appointed by the Minister under parliamentary control.

As was the case with the fuel and power industries, the public corporation with a board appointed by a minister would form the organizational structure of nationalized transport concerns. Questions of efficiency as well as the need to control the commanding heights of the British economy were equally important in the case of transport, which was why priority was given to the railways, sections of road haulage, and road passenger transport above shipping and aviation. Wartime controls and co-ordination would continue until nationalization had been achieved. However, in common with the fuel and power industries, there were neither detailed plans nor a strategy for public ownership.

There were several reasons why steel nationalization was included in the nationalization list of 1945. Steel was the epitome of a powerful monopolistic industry which had hitherto thwarted government plans to control its activities, particularly during the 1930s. Many industries depended on steel, a major reason why the party's leadership came under strong pressure to include its nationalization in the manifesto. The TUC's *Interim Report on Post-War Reconstruction*[66] argued that steel nationalization was next in priority after fuel and power and transport, and the fact that the Mikardo resolution called for the nationalization of heavy industry was a factor that had to be taken into account by the Labour Party's Policy Committee.

During the war the steel industry was brought under state control, although this was not always effective. The steel owners, represented by the British Iron and Steel Corporation, became the commercial instrument of the newly created Iron and Steel Control. The Control was responsible for the day-to-day running of the industry under the Ministry of Supply. The ambiguous relationship between the control and employers led to a lack of governmental influence over the industry, which, according to G.W. Ross,[67] clung to its old traditions and pre-war pricing policies. In spite of this, Labour's only wartime report on the industry offered limited criticisms of the control,[68] and the Iron and Steel Union's Secretary, John Brown took a similar line.

In view of the importance of the iron and steel industry to the economy, it would have been surprising if its nationalization had been omitted from Labour's post-war plans. Yet its inclusion was in doubt until 1944, and it was not until 1945 that it assumed importance as an item for debate in the party. Dalton's reference[69] to the preparedness of Morrison and Greenwood to back down on nationalization disclosed the disunity and indecision which beset the party's leadership and guaranteed that steel would not be the first nationalization priority when peace came. Furthermore, there was no plan for the future of state control over the industry, let alone a strategy for public ownership.

Labour's reconstruction objectives were set out in *The Labour Party and the Future* (1943), modified by the Policy Committee in 1944[70] and laid down in *Let Us Face the Future*, the party's 1945 election manifesto. Labour's programme for a full term of office partially reflected the efforts of the reconstruction policy committees but was on the whole limited and cautious. The path to the drafting of the manifesto was consequently by no means smooth. The party leaders in Churchill's government were increasingly pressurized to justify and defend their role in the pursuit of what were widely regarded as compromise policies. There can be little doubt that some lack of faith in the leadership—suspicion that there was too little commitment to nationalization as well as too few concrete plans for either nationalization or control over industry—contributed to the NEC's defeat at the 1944 Annual Conference. Mikardo's resolution calling for the nationalization of land, building, heavy industry, all forms of banking, transport, and fuel and power was carried, in spite of Shinwell's attempts to reassure the delegates of the commitment of the leadership to public ownership.[71] Nevertheless, even after the Executive's defeat, only steel was added to the 1937 nationalization list of fuel and power and transport, and the public ownership of the joint stock banks was omitted altogether. The manifesto reflected the priorities of the leaders in general and Morrison in particular, who had been made Chairman of the Special Campaign Committee formed in January 1945. In his autobiography Morrison wrote: 'My feelings in drafting the programme were inspired by one major factor: the changed nature of the electorate. I knew that victory would go to the party which recognised and served this mature and thoughtful public'.[72]

Let Us Face the Future focused on the justice of wartime controls on profits and the benefits of operating industry and transport in the public interest. The rationing of food and price controls had contributed to fairer shares for all. 'Drastic' policies of replanning were required, as well as a programme of modernization which would include re-equipping homes, factories, schools and domestic social services. More specifically, the manifesto committed a future Labour government to a policy of full employment through the control and direction of investment, controls over private industry, the maintenance of wartime agricultural policy, and a housing and building programme with more state controls. A new Ministry of Housing and Planning would combine the Ministries of Health and Town and Country Planning. Labour would bring the 1944 Education Act into practical effect and move towards land nationalization. The manifesto committed the party to the extension of social insurance to all and the establishment of a National Health Service, traditional objectives which the Beveridge Report had already made popular and essential prerequisites for any post-war reconstruction plans. This reflected the fact that much of the groundwork for social reform had been laid during the war and it appeared that the objectives of the leaders were not so much how to win the peace for socialism as how not to lose it for a limited form of social democracy.

Quite clearly the war had influenced the content of policy and to some extent the priorities of the party leaders, who had to convince the electorate that the great reform proposals of the war years were more likely to be implemented by Labour than the Conservatives. On the domestic front the war brought to the attention of government and citizens the often appalling state of the inner cities, a decaying housing stock, lack of educational opportunity and inadequate health and social services. Full employment highlighted the wasted years of the 1930s and was a spur to the adoption of Keynes's economic theory as well as many of the reformist documents of the war period. Above all, the role of the state expanded massively during the war. In a few years the state assumed control over the economy, manpower, finance, industry, the social services and agriculture. It had a major stake in policy decisions at all levels. Whether or not this marked a lasting change in the role of the state is an important question. The collectivist theories and policies of Liberals, Socialists and even Conservatives since the late nineteenth century had already pre-figured a more interventionist role for the state in society. Whether or not wartime intervention constituted a breach of the accepted limits to state intervention in a capitalist society or indeed, complimented advanced capitalism in crisis, invites valid speculation about wartime public enterprise. During the 1930s the Left argued that nationalization would provide a serious challenge to ruling class interests. Taking into account the level of state control over society and the economy during the war, the state had superseded and greatly extended its hitherto restricted interventionist role, although control over industry stopped short of nationalization. The extension of the role of the state had for long been a central objective of the Labour Party, an essential pre-requisite for the implementation of a wide range of policies designed to create a more egalitarian society. The extension of state power, or rather the maximum use of potential power to provide comprehensive social services, direct industrial production and control of the economy symbolized a more egalitarian approach to public policy. An important issue is whether or not wartime Britain approximated to what democratic socialists believed socialism to be. Certainly, the war was regarded as a catalyst throughout the Labour Movement, not only because of state provision but also because it was believed that there could be 'no going back'. The war was regarded as something to build upon. However, one of Labour's main fears was that if the Coalition government continued into peacetime, the state would concede its gains to the private sector. Given the party's emphasis on extending the role of the state to control and plan the economy and redistribute wealth through social service provision and public ownership, the British war economy was regarded as a significant advance, lying somewhere between capitalism and socialism. However, industry and the financial institutions remained in private hands, and although the state was directly involved in the productive process in the public interest, the purpose of its involvement can be said to have been one-dimensional in that the overriding objective was the defeat of the enemy and all that entailed. It should be stressed that democratic socialism viewed the state in essentially neutral terms, not as an instrument of class rule or oppression but as a means to an inconclusive and infinite end. The state was seen as the only effective means through which society could be transformed, whether it was through state education, the provision of state social services or state control over the economy. Whilst a large number of objectives were realized during the war, or their potential established through the publication of reformist reports, White Papers and legislation, for the majority of committed democratic socialists *public ownership* represented the difference between capitalism and socialism and presented the major challenge for the Labour Party.

The failure of the Labour Party to produce proposals for post-war industry, in spite of the state controls instituted during the war was due to a number of factors. The nature of war production was not really conducive to the sort of scrutiny which would have been necessary in order to put forward specific policies for industry in the light of wartime developments. Industry was geared to production for war purposes and was obviously going to require major adjustments during the transition to a peacetime economy. Fiscal controls and manpower budgeting were favoured as the instruments for reconstructing industry. There were no plans to establish new state machinery to maintain or extend industrial controls. This was largely in keeping with Labour's pre-war policy. Plans for private industry were vague before the war also. The main difference was that by 1945 all industrial production was controlled by government departments. The key point was that the effectiveness of state control over industry was related directly to war production, and specific wartime targets. When demand and markets expanded, the relevance of government was likely to diminish. Only by laying down proposals for developing state machinery for controlling industry in the transition could Labour have approached industrial control policy with any confidence. This the party failed to do. The emphasis on nationalization which preoccupied the policy committees, the National

Executive and Annual Conferences throughout the war, diverted attention from control policy. In spite of this emphasis, Labour's public ownership proposals hardly changed. The only real significance of the war was that it highlighted the inadequacies of vital industries and services, notably the fuel and power industries and transport. Labour's nationalization proposals for these industries and services incorporated wartime developments such as the establishment of co-ordinating government departments. The party still opted for the public corporation as the most appropriate body for the day-to-day running of nationalized industries. The addition of steel to the nationalization list did not receive whole-hearted support. It was an obvious economic contender for public ownership to the Left, because it was of symbolic importance and remained a relatively healthy and therefore powerful capitalist bastion. During the war, shipbuilding, textiles and sections of the construction industry were shown to be in need of state support, and it is surprising that they were not included in Labour's nationalization plans.

Taking into consideration the importance attached to nationalization, why were Labour's objectives not bolder? Certainly there was a credibility gap between Labour's general policy statements of the early war years and the party's post-war objectives, although it should be remembered that the proposals of the 1937 programme also offered limited nationalization objectives. In spite of the opportunities for radical change that the war seemed to offer, translating these opportunities into electoral advantage and realizable objectives remained the principal tasks of the leaders of the party, many of whom had been active members of the Coalition government. The adoption of more radical policies required support from a sizeable group of left-wing MPs as well as left-dominated policy committees. Whilst there were influential Leftists on the National Executive Committee, such as Laski, Bevan and Bacon, they were in a minority. The major policy committees were representative of a wide cross-section of the Labour movement. The Parliamentary Party was small and trade union dominated, as was the National Council of Labour. Both were unlikely sources of left-wing pressure within the party. The electoral truce dampened open hostility to the government and the majority of Labour MPs were fully occupied in considering a wider range of policy options and responses to wartime policy and administration. As social policy (rather than industrial policy) became the focal point of post-war planning and reconstruction, so Labour politicians, policy-makers, and activists turned their attention to the Beveridge Report and its implications, rather than the complex and controversial issues associated with nationalization and the extension of state control over industry in the peace.

In the broad category of social policy, wartime reports and White Papers left their mark on Labour's policy, in particular the Barlow, Beveridge and Uthwatt Reports. They presented Labour's policy-makers with formulas for dealing with a wide range of social problems so that the subcommittees of the Central Committee on Reconstruction Problems, the Policy Committee and the National Executive could utilize their recommendations and revise them if necessary. As a result, the party's social insurance proposals were considerably more detailed and coherent than before the war. This was not merely the result of Beveridge because by 1942 a number of statements had already been issued by the party's policy machinery. War forcused attention on the need to reform the social services as a matter or urgency and the party responded accordingly. The war did not radicalize opinion in the party but it did make Labour's social insurance and social services policies more acceptable. Uthwatt's impact on Labour's policy was almost as significant as that of Beveridge. The Uthwatt Report stressed the need to plan the use and development of land and co-ordinate the services on which both urban and rural dwellers depended. The Report's advocacy of a central planning authority was pre-empted by Labour's pre-war proposals. Its importance lay in the recognition that the state should play a leading role in planning and development. On the other hand, it could be argued that wartime innovation had the reverse effect upon Labour's educational policy. There were few plans to reform radically the educational system except those offered by the 1944 Education Act, which was in any case concerned with the structure rather than the form of education, and virtually ignored establishing educational priorities. It could well have been the case that the Butler Act encouraged compromise, in spite of the significant support in the party for the multilateral school and the abolition of the private sector.

Thus, the prospects for the new Labour government elected in 1945 were mixed. On the one hand Labour's ambitions were, as before, restricted by political and economic constraints, both at home and abroad. In spite of a plethora of state controls, social reform proposals ready-made for adoption and implementation, politicians with experience of national office and a relatively united party organization, the incoming Labour government had the unenviable task of guiding Britain from a wartime to a peacetime economy in a world which was transformed and disfigured by five years of total war. On the other hand, never had the mood for change been greater or more clearly voiced. The prospects for improving the standard of living of the British people by the establishment of a comprehensive welfare state had never been better. Capitalism had been forced to limit its profit motive in the public interest, at least for the duration of war. The prospects for maintaining the expanded level of state intervention in the economy were high, given the widespread acceptance of Keynesian economic theory.

On balance, it could be argued that the war focused attention on so many problems and immediate issues that less attention was paid to transforming society than to practical short-term reforms. Early on, rhetoric abounded, but later the party's policy-makers were concerned with immediate objectives and learning lessons from the wartime experience of state intervention and management of economy and society. Since the reform of society through the state was the primary objective of the leaders, it was sufficient for them to be able to focus upon how to utilize the state to improve standards of living generally and provide vital services wherever they were needed. War confirmed that Labour was a programmatic party, whose limited idealism had found a renewed outlet for expression during the years of conflict and uncertainty. In the light of the war, Labour's objectives seemed modest, but if ever there was a time when the opportunities to instigate radical change appeared to be greater than they actually were, it was probably in 1945.

Notes

1. See, for example, J. Strachey, *A Faith to Fight For*, 1941; J.B. Priestly, *Postscripts*, 1940; J. Huxley, *On Living in a Revolution*, 1944.
2. H. Laski, *The Labour Party, The War and the Future and Reflections on the Revolution of Our Time*, 1943; A. Greenwood, *Why We Fight: Labour's case*, 1940; C.R. Attlee, *Labour's Peace Aims*, 1939.
3. Labour Party, *The Old World and the New Society*, 1942, p.13.
4. Memo by H. Laski in Labour Party NEC Minute 291, 4 February 1941.
5. P. Addison, *The Road to 1945*, 1975, p.168.
6. Labour Party Archive [hereafter LPA], National Council of Labour Minutes July 1941–April 1943. Memorandum from Laski.
7. Cmd.6405, *Social Insurance and Allied Services*, HMSO, 1942.
8. See B. Donoughue and G.W. Jones, *Herbert Morrison*, 1973, p.315.
9. A. Bullock, *The Life and Times of Ernest Bevin*, 1967, p.230.
10. Ibid., 233.
11. NEC Report on NCL Report in Labour Party, *Annual Conference Report for 1943*, pp.23–4.
12. Cmd.6650, *Social Insurance Part 1*, HMSO, 1944.
13. M. Bruce, *The Coming of the Welfare State*, 1961, p.280.
14. Cmd.6651, *Social Insurance: Workmen's compensation Part II*, HMSO, 1944.
15. See for example, LPA, Labour Party Social Insurance and Assistance, Family Allowances Subcommittee RD 39/1941, 'Social insurance and assistance in the post-war world'.
16. Cmd.6501, *A National Health Service*, HMSO, 1944.
17. LPA, Labour Party Public Health Advisory Committee Minutes 13 March 1944; and TUC, *Report of the Sub-Committee to examine the government's White Paper* A national health service', 1944.
18. *Report of the Committee of the Secondary Schools Examination Council on Curriculum and Examinations in Secondary Schools*, 1943.
19. Cmd.6458, *Educational Reconstruction*, HMSO, 1943.
20. See LPA, Labour Party Education Subcommittee RDR 88/1942, 'Secondary education'; and RDR 139/1942, 'The junior school'.
21. R.S. Barker, *Education and Politics 1900–1951*, 1972, p.79.
22. LPA, Labour Party Education Subcommittee RDR 165/1942, 'Public and private schools'.
23. Cmd.6609, *Housing*, HMSO, 1945.
24. Cmd.6386, *Report of the Expert Committee on Compensation and Betterment*, HMSO, 1942.
25. LPA, Labour Party Policy Committee, 'Comments on Research 51', 1943.
26. Cmd.6378, *Report of the Committee on Land Utilisation in Rural Areas*, HMSO, 1942.
27. See for example, LPA, Labour Party Land and Agricultural Land Reorganisation Subcommittee RDR 229/1943, 'Labour's post-war policy for British agriculture'.
28. War Cabinet Memorandum W.M. (43) War Cab 51 (43), 9 April 1943.

29. For an account of wartime agriculture, see K.A.H. Murray, *Agriculture*, HMSO, 1955.
30. War Cabinet Minutes War Cab 55 (43), 15 April 1943.
31. War Cabinet Minutes War Cab (WC 146 (43)), 27 October 1943.
32. *The Guardian*, 6 December 1982.
33. Labour Party, *For Socialism and Peace*, 1934; and *Labour's Immediate Programme*, 1937.
34. For an account of wartime financial policy, see R.S. Sayers, *Financial Policy*, HMSO, 1956.
35. J.M. Keynes, *How to Pay for the War*, 1940.
36. Sayers, op.cit., 58–93.
37. Cmd. 6527, *Employment Policy*, HMSO, 1944.
38. A. Marwick, *Britain inthe Century of Total War*, Oxford, 1968, p.136.
39. The Bill reflected a number of recommendations of the Barlow Report, Cmd. 6153 on the *Distribution of the Industrial Population*, HMSO, 1940.
40. W. Beveridge, *Full Employment in a Free Society*, 1944, pp.262–73.
41. *Hansard*, vol.401, cols 217–396, 20 June 1944.
42. LPA, Labour Party Post-War Finance Subcommittee, 'Full employment and financial policy', 1944.
43. LPA, Labour Party Post-War Finance Subcommittee RDR 172/1942, 'War-time control of the rate of interest'.
44. LPA, Labour Party Post-War Finance Subcommittee RDR 222/1943, 'Notes on post-war taxation policy'.
45. LPA, Labour Party Post-War Finance Subcommittee, 'Exchange control', 1943.
46. See J.D. Scott and R. Hughes, *The Administration of War Production*, HMSO, 1955; and M.M. Postan, *British War Production*, HMSO, 1953.
47. See H.M.D. Parker, *Manpower*, HMSO, 1957.
48. Churchill College Cambridge, Bevin Papers 2/4. Note dictated by Bevin on 'Demobilisation', 10 December 1943.
49. Bullock, op.cit., 47.
50. See Labour Party, *Annual Conference Report for 1941*, pp.141–5 and . . . *for 1943*, pp.127–33.
51. S. Courtauld, 'An industrialist's reflections on the future relations of government and industry', *The Economic Journal*, vol.51, no.205 (April 1942)1, considered by the Labour Party Social and Economic Transformation Subcommittee as RDR 92/1943.
52. *Tribune*, 13 April 1942.
53. See A. Albu, *Management in Transition*, 1942.
54. See I. Mikardo, *Centralised Control of Industry*, 1943.
55. TUC, *Interim Report on Post-War Reconstruction*, 1944, pp.12–15.
56. For an extensive account of the coal industry during the war, see W.H.B. Court, *Coal*, HMSO, 1951.
57. *Hansard*, vol.392, cols 773–86, 12 October 1943.
58. Labour Party, *Coal and Power: Labour's post-war policy*, 1944.
59. E. Shinwell, *I've Lived Through It All*, 1973, p.192.
60. C.I. Savage, *Inland Transport*, 1957, p.568.
61. LPA, Labour Party Transport Subcommittee RDR 266/1944, 'The post-war organisation of British transport'.
62. LPA, Labour Party Research Memo 23, 'Post war shipping policy', 1942.
63. Labour Party, *Wings for Peace*, 1944.
64. Cmd. 6605, *British Air Transport*, HMSO, 1945.
65. *Hansard*, vol.1409, cols 686–99, 20 March 1945.

66. TUC, *Interim Report*, op.cit., 9.
67. G.W. Ross, 'The Labour party and the iron and steel industry', unpublished Masters dissertation, University of London, 1964.
68. LPA, Labour Party Social and Economic Transformation Subcommittee RDR 111/1942, 'Steel control'.
69. M. Dalton, *The Fateful Years*, 1957, pp.432–3.
70. LPA, Labour Party Policy Committee RDR 271/1944, 'Short term programme . . .' with NEC Minutes 16 April 1944–12 December 1944.
71. Labour Party, *Annual Conference Report for 1944*, pp.161–7.
72. H. Morrison, *Herbert Morrison*, 1960, p.232.

3 The Labour Party and industrial policy, 1940–45

Lewis Johnman

There exist two well-known assumptions concerning the Labour Party's membership of the wartime Coalition government.[1] The first assumption is that during the war consensus developed around a broad range of issues which were ultimately favourable to the election of a Labour government. As Paul Addison has noted : 'When Labour swept to victory in 1945 the new consensus fell like a bunch of ripe plums, into the lap of Mr Attlee.'[2] The second assumption is that the balance of payments position proved a major constraint on a range of Labour policy options.[3] Perhaps the most vivid enunciation of and attack upon the idea of consensus has come from Correlli Barnett in *The Audit of War*.[4] Barnett has claimed that 'there is evident throughout Whitehall debates and reports and eventual policy decisions on 'reconstruction' up to the end of the war a conflict between two contrasting and competing priorities—New Jerusalem versus a realistic national "corporate strategy".'[5]

To Barnett the reasons why such a national corporate strategy failed are clear. In party political terms he blames the Labour Party, which had 'been committed to New Jerusalem ever since the Labour movement was born',[6] so that there was a forceful New Jerusalemist lobby within the wartime Coalition government.[7] In industrial terms the fault lies with British industrialists and exporters who are excoriated for 'not . . . [having] . . . got the root of the matter in them.'[8] This criticism in turn leads to an attack on government and in particular the key department within government responsible for industry, the Board of Trade, where efforts to develop an industrial strategy are described as 'tinkering'.[9] The attack is then widened to include most of the wartime British establishment because of their non-industrial background and approach 'to the question of industrial strategy', which 'was rooted in a Victorian mercantile conception of a myriad firms competing in the market place'.[10]

It is the contention of this chapter that on all of these issues the views of Barnett and others are in need of serious qualification. Whilst it is undoubtedly the case that no consensus was achieved over industrial policy, this has little to do with a national corporate strategy being sacrificed to New Jerusalem. As this work will seek to demonstrate, both the Labour Party and the Board of Trade had developed highly credible industrial strategies which had become homogenous by 1944. Between 1942 and 1944 it appeared as if the major employers' organizations had moved towards supporting at least some version of these strategies. Between 1944 and 1945, however, and contingent on the developing balance of payments crisis, crucial groups of civil servants and businessmen became opposed to what in particular the Labour Party wished to do with regard to industry. Ultimately, therefore, it was the combination of the balance of payments situation and the weight of vested interests ranged against Labour Party policy which caused the failure of any national corporate strategy, and not the countervailing pressure of New Jerusalem.

Consideration of industrial policy took place in the context of discussions on post-war reconstruction which began in 1940. It involved a nexus of politicians, officials (temporary and permanent), businessmen, academics and trade unionists, and this needs to be comprehended if the process itself is to be understood.[11] The main themes to be considered below are the Board of Trade's examination of British industry and its analysis of what should be done; the views of British industry on the positions of both Labour and the Board of Trade; and what industrialists themselves wanted from the process of reconstruction. The chapter is structured in four sections with consideration being given in turn to the development of thinking within the Labour Party, the Board of Trade and organizations of industrialists, and then the impact of the balance of payments problem on the issue of industrial reconstruction.

Throughout the 1930s and during the war the Labour Party made a consistent attempt to formulate an economic and industrial strategy. The Society for Socialist Inquiry and Propaganda (SSIP) and the New Fabian Research Bureau (NFRB) were both established in 1931 by G.D.H. and Margaret Cole to 'ginger up' party activity and thinking.[12] The Labour Party's own policy-making machinery was overhauled, primarily by Hugh Dalton, with the establishment of the Finance and Trade Committee (FTC), chaired by Dalton, and the Reorganization of Industry Committee (RIC), chaired by George Latham, in 1931. Dalton also established the 'secret' XYZ Club of Labour sympathizers in the City of London in 1932.[13] Through these fora a number of economists, intellectuals and journalists, many of whom would play important roles in the attempt to formulate an industrial policy during the war years, began the work of overhauling Labour's economic and industrial policy. This group included the economists Hugh Gaitskell, Evan Durbin, James Meade and Colin Clark, the financial journalists Douglas Jay and Nicholas Davenport, and the journalist Robert Fraser. Both Gaitskell and Jay entered the wartime Civil Service, initially as assistants to Dalton at the Ministry of Economic Warfare, and were between 1942 and 1945 Principal Assistant Secretaries to him at the Board of Trade. Gaitskell became a Labour MP in 1945, and Jay, after being personal assistant to the Prime Minister, Attlee, between 1945 and 1946, also became an MP. Meade joined the Central Economic Information Service, the forerunner of the Economic Section and the Central Statistical Office, in 1940 and was in the Cabinet Office between 1944 and 1946. Durbin was in the Economic Section between 1940 and 1942 and served as personal assistant to the Deputy Prime Minister, Attlee, between 1942 and 1945 before becoming a Labour MP in 1945. From these individuals and groups a huge range of proposals and ideas emerged which 'filled the Party's "live pigeon hole" of unofficial and official memoranda on economic policy';[14] as Elizabeth Durbin has commented, 'it is impossible to do justice . . . to the richness and diversity of the industry studies undertaken by the NFRB.'[15]

The keystone of the Labour Party's economic policy as it was worked out in the 1930s was planning. The basis of planning would be the socialization of the major industries and utilities and the control of finance. These measures were outlined in a number of party publications throughout the period and in studies by its major thinkers such as Dalton, Cole and Jay.[16] By the late 1930s the party envisaged the nationalization of monopolies, utilities, inefficient and essential industries, reinforced by a range of physical controls which would embrace a nationalized Bank of England and control boards for National Investment, Credit and Foreign Exchange.[17]

The exigencies of war brought about the realization of a number of aspects of Labour's pre-war programme. The Bank of England came under Treasury control and the Emergency Powers Acts of 1939 and 1940 subjected foreign exchange to government direction. The Capital Issues Committee was established to regulate issues over a certain amount. Industry was also directly controlled with a system of licensing for manufacturing and construction and the direction of labour. These measures gave Labour planners first-hand experience in the operation of a planned economy. Evan Durbin noted that the workings of the economy were 'laid bare' while another of Labour's pre-war planners observed that almost 'every one' of Labour's 'ideas' had become a reality during the war.[18] As *Labour's Aims In War and Peace*, published in 1940, made clear:

> The Labour Party . . . demands now, that wartime organization shall be undertaken in the full knowledge that there can be no going back; that after the war, the national war effort must be turned to the building of a new Britain.
> While planning for the war, the Government must plan for the peace and a new society. Instead of regarding each item of state control as a temporary infringement of the normal, the occasion should be seized to lay the foundations of an efficient economic system.[19]

Or as Attlee told the House of Commons in 1939, 'If you want to win this war you will have to have a great deal of practical socialism. While planning for the war, we have to plan for peace.'[20]

Labour policy development continued throughout the war years when the National Executive Committee established the Central Committee on the Problems of Post-War Reconstruction with its eleven subcommittees. These bodies were responsible for a public restatement of the commitment to post-war planning in *The Old World and the New Society* (published in 1942),[21] but, more importantly, they added to the analysis of industry which the SSIP, NFRB, FTC, RIC and the XYZ had all contributed to earlier. For example, the Coal and Power Subcommittee met sixteen times between late 1941 and 1944 and produced a micro-economic analysis of the coal industry. As Barry Supple has noted, the sheer weight of material available to Shinwell, to whom as Minister of Fuel and Power fell the task of nationalizing the industry in the post-war period, gives the lie to Shinwell's claim that he 'had to start on a clear desk'.[22] Although those Labour supporters who had become temporary civil servants and the party at large were confident that wartime controls could be retained and utilized in the post-war economy, the party's thinking remained dynamic during the war and was a good deal more sophisticated than the stock response that controls 'worked' and therefore should be retained. Various elements of Keynesian thinking were adapted to Labour's purposes. To conclude that the party had become Keynesian would be a dramatic overstatement,[23] but the success of Keynesian budgetary techniques convinced many Labour planners that fiscal policy and deficit financing could be used in the stimulation and control of national income and expenditure and against unemployment. They also believed that wartime control of inflation through budgetary techniques meant that inflation need no longer be a problem in the post-war period.[24] Keynesian economics were viewed as useful adjuncts to planning and physical controls.

In perhaps Labour's most important policy document of the war years, 'Full employment and financial policy', published in 1944, the maintenance of full employment was envisaged through investment and a sustained level of purchasing power to be achieved by 'following the same principles in peace-time that have served us well in war . . . the principal war-time financial controls'.[25] This document modified the party's views on public ownership whilst revealing increased faith in the efficacy of controls. It retained the view that industries and utilities controlled by private monopoly were either inefficient or essential to the economy and therefore should be nationalized. Wholesale public ownership for its own sake, however, was now discounted in favour of control. As a report by the TUC Economic Committee made clear in 1944: 'Whilst it would be impossible for this country to bring more than a limited number of industries under complete public ownership within any reasonable future period, no industry should, after the war remain free from public regulation.'[26] Full employment could be maintained by a combination of strict controls on the economy and industry together with budgetary demand management.

Although there was no full internal consensus in the Labour Party over the issues of nationalization and full employment,[27] the manifesto of 1945, *Let Us Face the Future*, reaffirmed Labour's faith in nationalization, economic controls and planning. The nearer Labour came to a general election, however, the more difficult it became for the party to gain the support of key groups for its policies. The vast majority of industrialists and the Civil Service—rapidly losing its significant numbers of important Labour sympathizers who had entered it during the war years—viewed controls as, at best, temporary measures which would ease the difficulties of post-war economic transition, not as permanent features of an economic and industrial policy, and so were opposed to what Labour wanted to achieve. With respect to industrial policy, therefore, Paul Addison's view that the consensus fell 'like ripe plums' into Mr Attlee's lap needs to be severely qualified. There was no industrial consensus because key vested interests—industrialists and the Civil Service—had moved away from Labour.

It was the Board of Trade (BOT) which had the most direct contacts with industry both before and during the war and consequently it was this department within which most of the debate on industrial reconstruction during the war years was conducted.[28] Board of Trade officials therefore were very important figures in the dynamic process of that debate. This was all the more important in that it was to the BOT that a significant group of Labour's pre-war planners—in particular Dalton, Gaitskell and Jay—went in 1942. The temporary officials were highly critical of the restrictionist nature of the economy in the 1930s, characterizing the main features of the period as monopoly, oligopoly, price and output fixing to keep up profits, and rationalization leading to the destruction of capacity. The temporary officials tended to take a very firm line against the practices of the past and argued for radical remedial measures.[29] The permanent officials, whilst no less critical of the industrial situation, were more conservative in their approach, fearing that consideration of radical legislation in the war period could only lead to a deflection of industry's contribution to the war effort. Although neither the temporary nor permanent officials exactly shared views of what industrial reconstruction should entail, they did have reasonably firm views about what they were opposed to. They shared the opinion that the kind of post-war dislocation that occurred in 1920–1 and the inherent restrictionism of British industry in the inter-war period should be avoided after the Second World War. As a consequence of this many officials reacted adversely to the conservative stances being taken on reconstruction by the main employers' organizations. Both the Federation of British Industries (FBI) and the British Employers' Confederation (BEC) published reports on reconstruction in 1942, and A.S.J. Baster, the economist to the Minister without Portfolio, summed up the tone of the two reports by quoting *The Economist*'s conclusions about the documents:

> The point is that these businessmen have thrown up the sponge. They see the world economy as physicists see the world, running down. The background of the FBI's proposals is a tragic picture of Britain in decline—a debtor country assisted by overseas industrialists, with dwindling assets, a declining, ageing population, and war damaged equipment. . . . It would be a pity if this despair went on record as the voice of Britain. . . . Hardly once do these reports from British industry mention the need for greater technical efficiency either in Britain or abroad, the need for more output per head, or the development of new techniques and industries. They assume

the worst. They forecast a Britain brooding like an aged miser in the twilight over a dwindling treasure.[30]

This was a conclusion with which many BOT officials would have agreed.

What officials were particularly worried about was the stress being placed on the self-government of industry and the total maintenance of private enterprise. The BOT officials argued that private enterprise—which was taken to mean a system involving minimum government intervention—would only be acceptable if it was associated with price competition and thereby afforded the consumer some protection against exploitation. The danger was that self-regulation through trade associations—the common factors of the FBI and BEC reports—could destroy competition which would bring the state in to protect consumers. In this sense the more industrial self-government was pushed, the more scope there would be for state intervention and, the officials argued, the 'nearer will be the end of private enterprise'.[31] The BOT's minimum demand therefore was the promotion of efficient competition—hardly an extremist measure.

Criticisms of industrialists' attitudes took shape as the Board of Trade Reconstruction Committee began to receive replies to a series of questionnaires which it had issued to trade associations in 1942.[32] The results tended to confirm the conservative stance which had been taken by the FBI in its report. In the responses there was a general assumption that the post-war world would not differ from the pre-war world. On the issues of compulsion to join trade associations or for representatives of the state, consumers or labour to contribute to the associations, there was little support. Most bodies replied that they were waiting to see what the final shape of government post-war policies would be before they committed themselves to a clear direction, suggesting at least a very tame reaction by industrialists to reconstruction at this level.[33]

In response to this situation, from early 1943 the BOT began to take a more pro-active approach to industry on a range of issues. This would produce two results: first, it would give the Board a more direct line to individual industries than that necessarily represented by the various umbrella organizations; and second, it would make civil servants acutely aware of the deficiencies in some parts of the British industrial structure. The Board wanted to discover, first, the main obstacles which would confront industry at the end of the war, how these could be overcome and how full activity in the industry could be restored; second, the likely condition of capital equipment at the end of the war; and third, which technological improvements and which new products had or were being introduced.[34] The Board agreed that its main aim was to remove all obstacles to the full development of production, and work towards minimizing unemployment. The very scale of these problems necessitated careful planning but it recognized that 'the speed of transfer of production from one form to another is clearly a matter on which guidance must be obtained from manufacturers' and that this was the rationale for a large-scale inquiry.[35]

On the basis of this approach the Regional Controllers of the BOT began to prepare a series of reports.[36] In general, co-operation between the BOT and industrialists was good, but what came through strongly in the vast majority of reports was a widespread fear of re-emergent unemployment. Indeed the Regional Controller for the Midlands reported that industrialists in the region all believed that it was essential that there should be full employment or 'we shall be faced with serious disturbances from the working people'.[37] In this region the reconversion of the motor-car industry from war to peace was the key problem and if this could be achieved smoothly there was little fear of unemployment. Other regions were even more pessimistic about the transition. The Controller for Wales made the obvious point that pre-war Wales had suffered heavy unemployment because of the depression in its basic industries and lack of development of new industries. This problem had been alleviated in the war because of the expansion of the basic industries, but it was now envisaged that these would return to their pre-war employment levels and that high levels of unemployment would again emerge. The reports for Scotland, the northern region, the north-west and that area of the south-east dominated by government contracts envisaged that they would all face either pockets of heavy unemployment or be chronically depressed, and it was suggested that the government sponsor the setting up of new industries.[38]

This and a number of other developments contributed to the discussion on full employment policy, but they also prompted the BOT officials to begin considering the general problem of war-expanded industries. The problem was twofold as between those industries which produced the same as they would do in peacetime (e.g. coal and shipbuilding) and other industries producing solely for war (e.g. parts of engineering). The major problem for the first category of industry was the likelihood that it would fail to utilize its wartime capacity in the peace and that the future of the industries rested on the strength or otherwise of demand for their products. For the industries in the second category it was felt that two options were possible: first, the adaptation of planning and production (e.g. from military to civil aircraft); and second, outright scrapping, although this was not favoured. Even here it was thought unlikely that adaptation and conversion would absorb all wartime capacity. In this case 'no industry suffering from excess capacity was to absorb more capital'.[39] The BOT admitted that the most orderly elimination of excess capacity would be done by monopolies but felt that this could lead to abuse, and conceded that where redundancy was lightest, orderly elimination was the most problematic.

Conscious of the problems posed by inter-war rationalization, the Board was beginning to face up to the problem of monopoly. The BOT felt that the solution to the problem might be gleaned from examining the difficulties of rationalization between the wars. The Board defined surplus in terms of the fixed assets of an industry up to the point at which the revenue earned was just balanced by the cost of working these assets (exclusive of any return on the fixed capital employed), assuming that from the country's point of view any new investment made should be considered as a sunk cost. On this basis it would be expected that owners earning no profits would try to use their plant for different products, that depreciation funds would be invested in new plant and that this process would gradually reduce capacity to a size at which profits could be earned. The inter-war period, however, was redolent of a different type of experience. In cotton and steel production vast amounts of capital had been used to enable companies to finance businesses which carried heavy loan charges due to the borrowing which had been undertaken to finance expansion between 1914 and 1918 and to keep such concerns afloat in the drastically changing conditions of the 1920s. Such capital should have been used for new trades and had effectively been wasted. Furthermore, wage reductions had helped delay readjustment. The quality of labour, plant and management had deteriorated in a depressed and defensive atmosphere. Most insidiously of all, industries had resorted to price agreements and output quotas to maintain profits, and this had the simple effect of sustaining high unit costs as all plants had worked well under capacity. Rationalization had resulted in oligopolistic practices.

In the light of this experience the BOT argued that any post-war rationalization scheme had to meet a number of conditions: the least efficient units must be closed; voluntary rationalization schemes that had tended toward oligopoly and thus industrial self-government must be eschewed; no new capital should be available for rationalization; and schemes should be introduced as quickly as possible and as soon as it became clear that a long-term problem existed.[40] In this sense at least, the BOT was convinced that there could be no decontrol of industry as there had been after the First World War and no return to the industrial self-government and protectionism which had been characteristic of the 1930s. At this stage and on these issues the BOT shared many of the criticisms of industry which Labour critics had been advancing throughout the 1930s, and it was now that the BOT began making its most trenchant criticisms concerning industry and the attitude of industrialists. Gaitskell, as Principal Assistant Secretary to Dalton at the BOT, found the attitude of industrialists infuriating:

> One of the alarming things I notice is the very great gap between what I believe is the popular attitude to postwar—which is now much more socialistic, and the attitude of the businessmen we have to deal with which is for the most part reactionary and capitalistic . . . there is such a very real struggle for industrial *power* . . . the Director class . . . are really much less concerned with maximising profits than just exercising arbitrary power. They regard shareholders as a bore . . . and . . . the state as a menace. *They* want to be allowed to decide for themselves what is in the public interest.[41]

A special subcommittee of the Reconstruction Committee went so far as to recommend the setting up of a government-backed British Institute of Management on the grounds that most firms seemed 'self-satisfied about the quality of their management'.[42] The BOT reiterated its criticism that there was 'no doubt that many British industries are lagging behind their competitors and that efficiency must be increased if they are to have a full share of the benefits of an expansionist policy'.[43] Many of these criticisms would be collated and amplified in the production, in June 1944, of the BOT memorandum on 'The long term prospects of British industry'.[44]

This document was a full summary of all the research which the BOT had conducted into British industry during the war. It criticized the 'hazily optimistic assumption' that Britain would secure, almost as a matter of right, a 50 per cent increase in its export trade after the war. The Board's view was that as far as two-thirds of manufacturing industry was concerned, little appreciable improvement in the import/export position could be expected and indeed some worsening might occur. It was directly critical of the attitude of industry to this situation, commenting that 'few seem to be contemplating any considerable increase of production or export trade, and many are apprehensive about foreign competition.' The desire for protection of the home market remained high, few industries seemed to be contemplating extending their plant (by taking over government factories) and few manufacturers contemplated 'any change of production or selling methods, or the development of new products. . .'.[45] The Board also felt that the position with respect to the newer industries (specifically citing wireless, television, rayon, nylon and plastics) was little better. The only solution here was to increase British industrial efficiency: 'If we achieve the American standard of efficiency we can, on British wages, look to the future with some confidence. But if we fail, we cannot.'[46] The report concluded with a detailed examination of thirteen industries, which revealed that machinery and electrical goods had good export prospects in the post-war world, that vehicles and chemicals could 'possibly' do well, but for the rest (including textiles and iron and steel) improvement was unlikely. The President of the Board of Trade, Dalton, concluded that 'the prospects thus revealed look pretty bleak' and that 'vigorous and varied action must be taken if we are to realise our post-war hopes and make good our promises.'[47]

Turning to the second group under consideration, it is evident that early indications of the attitudes of industrialists to the post-war world were that this group was clearly against any state intervention in industry. At a meeting of members of trade associations held in 1940 under the aegis of the FBI to discuss the institution of rationing and, by extension, the limitation of production and consumption, no businessman defended or supported the position of the government. Indeed, one speaker referred to the 'cynical attitude of the officials in regard to industries having to close down'. 'The result of the Board of Trade measures,' he argued, 'must end in destroying industry.' The speaker asserted that the structure of industry was a delicate mechanism which would be a matter of life and death in the post-war period. In this sense Board of Trade insistence on reform now would preclude co-operation later. Lest this be viewed as selfishness in the face of the national interest, it was noted that every effort must be made to win the war but that in 'the long view . . . our efforts must be dedicated to forestalling more vigorous restrictions'.[48]

By 1942 the main employers organizations had all produced reports on reconstruction.[49] The major body, the FBI, published its report in May 1942.[50] This was an essentially conservative work seeking to delineate the extent of post-war change. The report recognized that the post-war world would be essentially 'new' and that the aim should not be to recreate pre-war conditions, although a complete break with the past was rejected and continuity appealed to. The report envisaged a British Empire–American trade network—with government-sponsored encouragement for the development of the colonies and China—the retention of import and export quotas and essentially bilateral trade systems. It also argued that protection of the home market should continue and supported the retention of rationing to restrain pent-up consumer demand. The report was bleak about the prospects for the British economy. It envisaged a static and ageing population, with industry no longer providing the main expanding channel for employment, viewing this as being provided by the tertiary sector. It also argued that current tax policy did not allow industry to build up resources for the future and was worried that future taxation policy might prove inimical to investment.

In terms of the direct relationship between industry and the state the report was also conservative. It accepted that the war necessitated the government assuming wide powers over industry but insisted that such control should not be perpetuated in the post-war period. It did allow that controls in the transition period would be essential—on the premise that the post-First World War situation must be avoided—but insisted that they should be strictly limited to easing the transition. The report conceded that government regulation had existed before the war, but warned against any decisions being made on the basis of 'political theories of government' or 'control for the sake of control', envisaging the 'stifling of individual and private enterprise'. Although the FBI accepted that trade associations had been successful—and remained in favour of voluntary association—it insisted that the future organization of industry should be left in the hands of industrialists. Having laid out this conservative ground, the report concluded that government regard industry 'as a partner in the national life, and not as an interest which must be regarded with mistrust and suspicion'.[51]

There were, however, some industrialists who dissented from this 'official' view. Samuel Courtauld wrote to Sir William Jowitt, the Paymaster-General, in June 1942, declaring that there was a predominating volume of progressive opinion among employers—an estimation which he left deliciously vague—which, if collated by government, 'could be forged into a most valuable weapon'.[52] Accepting that the FBI report was the nearest thing to an 'official' view from British industry, he recommended that the government explore exactly how representative of industry the organization was, the implicit criticism being that it was not. He also included the notes of a speech he had made at the Engineers' Club in Manchester, where he deplored the conservative attitude of businessmen towards change and argued that employers had to be prepared to give labour a share in the management and control of industry 'from top to bottom'. Courtauld envisaged worker directors; a government-appointed director on the board of every company reporting to the government and exercising special powers; complete control over new industrial development, labour, technical education; and a newly formed central body to represent industrial employers.[53] It was, however, an adaptation strategy because, as he put it, 'Unless the men in possession are prepared to adapt themselves and compromise, there is no alternative to a complete socialist revolution.' It was a strategic move aimed at conceding 'control' whilst retaining 'power':

> If the Government, though armed with overriding control, did not in fact interfere with the day-to-day running of business any more than shareholders now do, I believe that the best business executives from the top down would not object to the change. With the same proviso, some of them would not really object to Government ownership.[54]

Further dissent from the FBI line came in the form of *A National Policy for Industry* (NPI)—a manifesto by 120 industrialists under the nominal chairmanship of Lord McGowan of ICI—which stated the duties of industry to the community, advanced a charter for labour and analysed the organization of industry.[55] This document, however, marked the reappearance of the 1930s Industrial Reorganization League (IRL) in another guise. The IRL, headed by Lord Melchett—the son of Sir Alfred Mond and a key signatory of the NPI document—had introduced a bill into Parliament in the 1930s, seeking 'self-government in industry' to 'enable redundant effort and uneconomic competition to be progressively eliminated', the avowed aim being to 'defend industry from the dislocating consequences of overproduction, weak-selling, and the maladjustment of supply to estimated demand'. The main provisions of the Bill would have allowed the majority of producers in any industry to set up an organization with compulsory powers over any minority which opposed it.[56] The FBI pointed out that the NPI was representative only of individuals, and neither companies nor trade associations, and a memo noted that of the signatories some 60 were FBI members and that 103 different firms were represented.[57] Sir Guy Locock, the FBI Director, wrote to the district secretaries pointing out that a large number of prominent businessmen had been asked to sign the report but 'refused to do so for various reasons'.[58] Locock declared that the NPI statement with regard to industry's responsibility to the community represented a 'death-bed repentance of people connected with the big combines who were trying to save what they could in the present circumstances'. The charter for labour, he argued, simply reflected the ability of monopolists to pay higher wages and would make the task of negotiating with labour 'impossible' after the war. The NPI's views on the organization of labour amounted, according to Locock, to 'compulsion over the individual and the operation of something which certainly approximates towards the Fascist co-operative state', so that publication of the report was 'most unfortunate'.[59]

By the end of 1942 therefore the views of industrialists were ranged across a wide number of options, depending upon their particular constituency, with one thing in common, the desire for industrial self-government. Conservatism was perhaps best summarized by the FBI Report with its declaration that reconstruction should be left to industrialists. How far this simply represented an ultra-conservative, defensive negotiating position is unclear, but much of it seems framed to limit what some industrialists regarded as the more extreme measures of control or nationalization. A good deal of the 'progressive' posture may have been presaged on the basis that some form of government control was inevitable and that the best policy was to concede this and negotiate on the basis of strength. What the 'progressive' stance amounted to was a form of voluntary corporatism, incorporating the state and labour, the aim of which was to forestall nationalization. What was common to all industrial thinking was a desire to return to the 1930s, the retention of cartelization, monopoly and oligopoly, and fear of foreign competition.

Fear of nationalization prompted a discussion within the FBI about the efficiency of industry, with the Federation realizing that the issue of efficiency was something of a lacuna in its thinking. Sir Charles Bruce-Gardner, who had been industrial adviser to the Governor of the Bank of England in the 1930s and was now on the National Production Advisory Council, declared that 'there was a need for efficient association to cover all the major industries, among other things as a safeguard for private enterprise.'[60] Perceived inefficiency was viewed as a major 'threat' to private industry in the post-war period. As Bruce-Gardner commented on the report of the inquiry established by the FBI to examine the Working of Export Groups, 'it had become clear that on one side was the pitfall of chaos and on the other the Corporative State.'[61] Given the FBI's statement of position one year earlier, this represented something of a change. The report stated that it would be impossible not to concede the need for some form of organization which would provide for official contact between industry and government, and that each branch of industry should assist the government in a consultative and administrative capacity in dealing with post-war problems. So great was the change that one member felt that 'the activity of the State gave little cause for complaint',[62] whilst another opined that the solution would be 'typically English' as some industries would be forced by circumstances towards closer integration between industry and the state whilst others would not, a result which was ascribed to 'the English temperament'.[63] Bruce-Gardner again commented that industry had to be more strongly organized, more critical, more suggestive, improve the standard of its performance and ensure leadership, rather than have these imposed by government.[64] At this stage it may have been the case that the FBI was worried that the government would adopt the suggestions made in the *National Policy for Industry* document and that this would undermine any influence the FBI had. Perhaps it was a recognition that its original report was too conservative and perhaps even that this had provided a successful basis of negotiation on the grounds that it at least looked dynamic. Whatever the case, the formation of the Reconstruction Joint Advisory Council (RJAC) in January 1943 must have helped the process. This tripartite body provided a forum for both the main employers' organizations (FBI and BEC) to meet the TUC and government ministers and officials. In particular it allowed the employers to realize that the TUC was not adopting a 'nationalize everything' stance, and that the government had some way to go before it formulated a policy on industrial reconstruction. The employers realized that they could have a major role in influencing this process.[65]

Just how far attitudes had changed can be seen by the type of contact now emerging between industrialists and government. Locock, for example, wrote to Jowitt to report a speech he had made to Bradford FBI members, where he had advocated the need for new equipment and taken 'the opportunity of stressing the point you raised at our last meeting of the inevitability of control for some time after the war'.[66] He stated that he had received assent on the issue. He went further at a later meeting in Manchester by insisting that members there should accept control and not be lulled into demands for its removal at the first sign of any easing of post-war pressures.[67] In a similar vein, Lord Dudley Gordon, from the FBI executive, speaking at the FBI AGM in 1943, stressed the 'vital importance of government control in the post-war period', and specifically played down the fear that control was merely the precursor to nationalization.[68] Lords McGowan and Melchett added their voices to this trend.[69] Lindsay of Morgan Crucible remarked on the excellent work being done by government in helping industry make more effective use of manpower, commented on the large degree of ignorance in British industry with regard to modern industrial methods and looked forward to a 'suitable blend of private enterprise and regimentation' in the post-war period. H.L. Bostock of Lotus argued that 'direction if not control' would have to be continued 'if we are to avoid the mistakes that led to the disastrous slump that followed the last war'.[70] The British Employers' Confederation contacted the BOT to assure the Board that it had not been niggardly in its approach to the RJAC, with Forbes-Watson of the BEC commenting that 'the Council was a most excellent body and had given an insight to its members into general Government attitude and plans.' He wrote that he would regret its discontinuation for any reason and indeed looked forward to it becoming more important.[71] Thus industrialists had moved into exactly the type of arrangements which many of them had been deprecating in 1942—and even a manifestly pro-private enterprise declaration by the FBI President, Sir George Nelson, could not disguise this fact.[72]

This stance would change again in 1944 following the publication of the full employment White Paper and the growing realization that the balance of payments and therefore exports would be a major policy issue (see pp. 44–6 below). Concern over exports was underlined by the publication in October 1944 of the FBI report on *The Organisation of British Industry*. This accepted that in the post-war period there would be a need to maintain full employment and a proper balance between imports and exports and that this would necessitate close co-operation between government and industry. Co-operation would also be required for the success of any export drive. These factors raised the question of the type of organization which industry would need to meet these challenges. Once again the favoured solution was industrial self-government through trade associations. The view of the FBI, what it termed 'the ideal from the national point of view', was that the government should confine itself to producing a general framework of national policy and leave the detailed working out of the policy to organizations provided by the industries themselves.[73] The FBI report was a recognition that much of the pressure it had been under between 1942 and 1944 was now deflected, and that satisfactory policy towards trade associations and the fulfilment of the government's ambitions with respect to exports could well serve to prevent any extension of state control.

The FBI's position was sharpened in the early months of 1945 as the war in Europe appeared won and the Coalition began to show signs of breaking up. The end of the Coalition meant that a general election could not be long delayed and industry began to fear that a Labour victory would mean full-scale nationalization. This was heightened by a public speech by Sir Stafford Cripps in which he declared that 'we must . . . lay the foundations of a great changeover of control, and ultimately ownership, from the individual enterprise to the State.'[74] Predictably enough the FBI responded with horror to this, with Sir George Nelson declaring before the President's Advisory Committee of the FBI that he was anxious to secure from colleagues how best to put before the public the case for private enterprise rather than nationalization. The Federation recognized that it was on shaky ground with respect to monopolies, utilities and lame ducks, and there was some complaint that neither the press nor the Conservative Party were wholeheartedly in support of private enterprise. It was felt that some form of manifesto and continual campaign in support of free enterprise would be necessary, and Sir Guy Locock commented that he had been in touch with Conservative Central Office in an effort to get someone to draw up a statement of the case.[75] This was not exactly to say that an anti-private enterprise tide was running. The FBI praised the 'good work' done by the Economic League which between January and April 1945 had held 2,255 meetings, reached an audience of 300,209 people and distributed some 870,160 leaflets.[76] The FBI resolved to offer J.C. Johnson of the *Daily Telegraph* £500 to draft a report on private enterprise to be used as anti-nationalization propaganda and to contact Colonel Baker White of the Economic League to prepare a leaflet dealing with the principles of private enterprise. The FBI/BEC decided to pay the League's expenses in this regard although it was recognized that it was not in the interests of the League to be seen to be in the pay of the employers' organization.[77]

Sir Clive Baillieu, the new FBI President, also launched a spirited defence of private enterprise at a Chamber of Commerce lunch. On relations between private enterprise and government, he declared that:

> Attempts to substitute one for the other over the whole field must result in acute social strife and may end in disaster. This is also what is involved in any scheme to maintain, in peace, Government Expenditure at about wartime levels, and indefinitely to keep in being the whole system of wartime controls. Regimentation, control, the perpetuation of all the trappings of total war, is the price we must pay if we listen to this siren song. In other words we would be accepting the creation of the Servile State. That, I believe, to be repugnant to the deepest instincts of Britishers throughout the Commonwealth. I believe Britishers everywhere, once they see the issue will never allow the mighty stream of British freedom to perish in the bogs and sands of doctrinaire socialism and bureaucratic control. Whilst we would agree that

there must be an orderly devolution of the control, let us remind our political leaders that we have not fought this war to impose on ourselves a form of Neo-Fascism nor to forge forever on our backs the fetters of war-time control.[78]

Although the FBI was counselled to accept the result of the general election and work for the success of the nationalized industries on the grounds that employer obstruction of the programme would simply intensify the demands for the extension of control, it was argued that resistance should involve critically analysing the results of the nationalized industries, propounding the successes of private enterprise and developing 'a positive philosophy in support of private enterprise'.[79] A Labour Government and a nationalization programme further shrunk an ever-diminishing ground for industrial consensus.

Indeed the conjunction of nationalization and the balance of payments crisis (see pp. 44–6 below) served to marginalize the critique which the Board of Trade had advanced of industry between 1942 and 1944. Industrialists returned to their 1942 stance of defending private industry and its efficiency. The FBI *Statement of Policy* rallied against nationalization for precisely the deleterious effects which it would have on turning the economy around: the government should avoid the 'spread over wider fields of industry of the mentality which must accompany the prospect of being brought out'. Controls and taxation should be reduced, personal incentives increased, partly through increasing personal consumption and partly through restoring market discipline, and government should refrain from criticising private industry.[80] The moral was clear: private industry could only play its part in restoring the country's economic fortunes in an atmosphere which was conducive to it. The denouement came at a conference of employers to discuss the economic situation in March 1946. Government ministers addressed the conference and stressed the need for a production and export drive and the co-operation of government and industry to achieve this. The same theme was reiterated by Attlee, Dalton, Cripps, Bevin and Isaacs. In reply to this battery of urgings and exhortation the President of the FBI, Sir Clive Baillieu required the government to attend to three fundamental points: the promotion of genuine co-operation, the removal of current uncertainties with regard to production and the cessation of attacks upon private industry. Co-operation, he stated, would require the government to reconcile its own party and programme to private industry:

Industry knew that this co-operation, so essential to the country's needs, would not be achieved if attacks continued on the personalities, principles and practices of industry. The leaders of industry were not out-of-date dyed in the wool, selfish reactionaries, and profits were the criterion of a healthy vigorous industry and not of capitalist greed. The restrictive practices so often alleged against industry were largely a figment of the imagination. Few men responded to a mixed diet of kicks and threat, innuendoes and misrepresentations. There was no question of sabotage or disloyalty; it was a matter of human nature. The Government had emphasised the existence of a common task and they should understand the great bulk of production would inevitably come from private enterprise and that the salvation of the country and the Government in their respective spheres operated on the basis of an alliance. If this were done, the Government and the country would reap a rich reward.[81]

The message was that the government should limit its nationalization programme and cease its critique of private industry: without clear delimitation of the government's programme the awesome short-term problems of the balance of payments position could not be overcome.

The employers' change in position had been predated by a deep split within the BOT over future policy. The issue on which this division occurred, in the spring of 1944, was the balance of payments situation. In many respects the BOT position on industry remained consistent:

In the past eighteen months the Board of Trade has discussed with every industry and virtually every Trade Association its plans and prospects for the post-war period. These discussions provide no solid grounds for believing that British industry is approaching its peace-time problems with the energy, imagination and inclination to take risks which will be needed if we are not to sink to the position of a third class industrial power. Few industries are thinking in terms of anything more than a return to their pre-war value of exports. Little enthusiasm is shown for the introduction of new machines, methods and processes. The general disposition is to return to the methods of marketing, the industrial organisation and the procedures for design which were, before the war, progressively revealing their weaknesses. Such views are perhaps, in some measures, merely a reflection of the single sighted pre-occupation of British industry with the task of winning the war. But they also indicate a deep-seated conservatism particularly in some of the long-established industries which must be broken down if the level of our export trade and our standards of living are to be raised.[82]

One commentator at the Board even went so far as to state that official confidence in the prospects of industry seemed to vary inversely with the contact between the official and the industrialist: 'the more the contact the less the confidence'.[83]

These views were in line with the BOT's declared policy position as epitomized by the memorandum on 'The long term prospects of British industry',[84] which was submitted to the Cabinet Reconstruction Committee in June 1944. This document, however, occasioned a major split within the BOT. A series of responses from elsewhere within the BOT described the memorandum as 'special pleading', and although its aims of drawing lessons from the past and dispelling complacency were accepted, it was criticized on the grounds that it was far too pessimistic and open to misunderstanding. Of the memorandum's major conclusion, that increased efficiency in industry was vital, one official commented that 'This kind of thing has been said over and over again but unless some new factor emerges, such as the energetic application of Government policy to stimulate efficiency, nothing will be done'.[85] Even here though, there were real dangers that government measures which aimed at improving industrial efficiency might actually make matters worse. The government's desire to strengthen trade associations (a desire shared by the FBI and BEC) might simply tend to perpetuate current organizational methods and thinking, and in any case government support tended to be given to existing (declining) industries rather than to emergent new industries. It was argued that the greatest stimulus to efficiency remained the forces of competition, particularly foreign competition, and much play was given to the fact that although civilian industry had been 'cribbed and confined to every sort of control', its outstanding feature had been 'its extreme responsiveness to changes in demand'. The pessimistic tone of the original memorandum was harshly criticized as being conducive only to despair:

> Farewell! A long farewell to all our greatness. The quicker we confess to a cut in home rations and a catastrophic fall in real income (but with longer working hours), the better. Not to mention bilking on our current debts. The inner intention seems to be to invoke a spirit of realism: as presented, however, the paper will invoke complete defeatism.[86]

In this sense the defeatist attitude of one section within the BOT simply reflected that of industrialists, and whilst it was true that they were organizing themselves defensively to hold their own position and privileges, there was little in the BOT's attitude to change their views. The memorandum concluded:

> This is what the report should bring out—export or die. And be, at least, moribund and poor to the extent we can't export. With this choice clearly put before them, Ministers may settle policy in the right direction, which at least would be keeping us more alive than the draft would have us. . . The home market should be held back in the transition and immediate post-war years in order the better to be satisfied in the future. . . . The whole apparatus of propaganda for an export drive should be started and defeatism kept out. It is 'export or die' but who wants to die. . . . I think the whole report and the spirit informing it must be attacked and killed.[87]

It was in this area that the real dichotomy of reconstruction opened up. Essentially the argument was between short-term and long-term objectives. Much of the BOT's efforts had been directed towards British industry avoiding the restrictionist growth paths which it felt had been so inimical to British interests in the 1930s. In this sense it blamed both the structure of the economy in the 1930s and the attitude of industrialists, whom the BOT saw as settling for lower, but still perfectly acceptable profit rates, whilst the economy as a whole failed to confront the challenges posed by its major competitors. It was this situation which many in the BOT wished to break. However here was another wing of the BOT establishing a different priority—the country's short-term balance of payments position—and arguing that the long-term strategy was a luxury which the country (almost literally) could not afford. As the realization of the gravity of the country's balance of payments position grew (throughout 1944 and 1945) so too would the attraction of the pragmatic short-term strategy. This was a situation which industrialists would seek to exploit on the basis that British industry could not be expected to fulfil an immediate export drive to overcome balance of payments problems if it were engaged in longer-term restructuring. The short-term strategy allowed industry a way of offsetting the critiques of both the BOT and the Labour Party and of returning to the more familiar and safer ground of their 1942 position.

The extent to which the short term gained the ascendancy during 1944 and 1945 can be witnessed in the lexicon of reconstruction. True, all of the major reconstruction committees continued to meet, but their agendas were dominated not by the wider consideration of reconstruction policy or reports from the Industrial Controllers in the field but by the pragmatic consideration of the 'export problem'. 'Reconstruction' would increasingly become 'reconversion', which would become 'the transition period', which would become the 'export problem'. The draft of the President of the Board of Trade's paper 'Proposals on industrial and export policy' was considerably altered to reflect these changed priorities and its two opening sections given over to 'Rapid transfer to productions for Export' and 'Export markets'.[88] The policy choice was again sharply delineated by the BOT. Referring to the differences in emphasis between the short and long-term strategies, the Board observed that:

The immediate significance of this . . . is that if the level of exports in the transition period is inadequate markets will be lost which it will be difficult to regain in the period when our capacity is less restricted. And, more immediately, any increase in our adverse balance of payments gives rise to a debt which must be repaid in later years.[89]

In other words adoption of the longer-term strategy would have drastic short, medium and long-term implications. To some extent the need for an export drive (and by implication the adoption of the shorter-term strategy) had been made in the White Paper on Full Employment. Discussing the same issues the authors of this document had made the point that 'An export drive is thus of paramount importance and hence demand whether for consumption goods or capital expenditure must not be allowed to divert the resources needed for exports.'[90] In June 1944, the Chancellor of the Exchequer opined that the real problem with industry was that it was unsure whether the government desired an expansion of exports, while the Minister of Reconstruction argued that if an export drive was announced industry would respond vigorously.[91] Accordingly, by the following month Dalton had produced a paper on 'Measures to promote exports and industrial efficiency'. All of the BOT's efforts were targeted on increasing exports whilst not harming efficiency and improving efficiency to increase exports.[92] Obviously exports were a crucial element of industrial health and, indeed, a performance indicator of many problems, but now, however, there was no discussion on what the medium or long-term objectives, requirements or capabilities of British industry would be. The future had been sacrificed to the present.

Labour's victory in 1945 presented the party not with a 'ripe plum' of consensus over industrial policy but a rather acidic bunch of sour grapes. What is clear is that the party had not engaged in 'tinkering' with respect to industrial matters but had developed a thoroughgoing critique of industry. Labour believed that the long-term future of industry required a wholesale revamping, the tools to achieve which would be planning, controls and nationalization—a set of policies which had been considerably enhanced by the success of planning and controls during the war. To Labour, reconstruction would be achieved by 'following the same principles in peace-time that . . . [had] . . . served well in war' using the 'principal war time financial controls'.[93] The problem was that from mid-1944 onwards, controls, planning and nationalization had increasingly less constituency outside the Labour Party. The Conservatives, the Civil Service and industrialists were prepared to accept controls and planning only as a means whereby the economy could be eased from war to peace. On these issues there was no consensus. Although nationalization was a more complex issue, Labour had pressed during its period in the Coalition for nationalization of the railways and substantial reorganization of the steel, coal, cotton and electricity industries, only to meet stiff opposition from Conservative ministers and industrialists.[94] The crucial factor in weakening Labour's ability to formulate the type of industrial policy which it desired was that the key groups—the BOT and the employers' organizations—which had moved towards Labour between 1942 and mid-1944, had moved away thereafter.

Nor can the BOT be justly accused of 'tinkering' with respect to industrial strategy. It was no coincidence that many of the influential figures—especially those acting as temporary officials—had been identified with Labour in the 1930s. Between 1940 and 1944, however, the BOT spoke with one voice on industrial matters and had a clear vision of what it did *not* want to happen, namely that the restrictive practices of the inter-war years had been, were and would be, inimical to industrial efficiency. The BOT strategy as it evolved moved closer to Labour—it was interventionist and opposed to the voluntarism of the past—and shared some of the party's commitment to physical controls and planning. In this sense the BOT, like Labour, had a long-term view of industrial policy. Such a view was effectively marginalized by the BOT's second voice, which advanced a short-term strategy designed to deal with the immediate problems of the economy, most notably the balance of payments position, and this proved a crucial restraint on Labour's ability to formulate an industrial policy. Between 1940 and 1944 the party and the main department of state responsible for industry shared wide-ranging grounds for the analysis of and prognosis for British industry. From 1944 onwards the BOT's stance changed from one of sympathy with Labour to one which industrialists would find far more conducive to their interests.

The shared themes in the employers' organizations' reports on reconstruction were a variety of conservative stances aimed at retaining and enhancing the self-government of industry and the desire to keep the state at arm's length. These bodies did recognize, however, that they were open to criticism with respect to the recent past and consequently moved into a more accommodating position between 1942 and 1944. Whether this was because they had been persuaded of some of the virtues of the critique which the BOT and Labour Party had advanced (which is unlikely, given later events), or because they feared that striking too conservative a position would perhaps result in far more draconian measures later, is difficult to be absolutely certain about. What is clear is that their position did change, from a relatively conservative to a more dynamic stance between 1942 and 1944, with a return to the conservative position between 1944 and 1945. Here, too, the ground on which industrial consensus could be achieved was narrow in the extreme.

On at least one issue Correlli Barnett may be correct. As he stated in *The Audit of War*: 'Had all the most powerful groups and institutions in . . . society been willing enthusiastically to throw themselves behind the process of transformation, it would still have been difficult enough to achieve, given the scale of the inherited problems.'[95] However, this was exactly the problem: the most powerful groups and institutions were not willing to do so. From mid-1944 onwards key groups were moving away from the Labour Party and were opposing what the party wished to achieve on the industrial and economic fronts. This left Labour in a dire quandary. The party was committed to policies of democratic socialism and in industrial terms could only operate by persuading or forcing industry to change its methods. There were, however, clear limits to the amount of force that could reasonably be employed, and the government faced the constant threat that industry would withdraw its support for the export drive and thus further weaken the balance of payments position if Labour pushed too hard for change. Thus Barnett's favoured option of 'scruff of the neck intervention in industrial change'[96] was never a realistic possibility. His positive vision of a national corporate strategy failed not because of countervailing pressures from 'New Jerusalem' but because the business community wanted little or nothing to do with any such policy. Ultimately if both the major department of state responsible for industry and the Labour government were reduced to 'tinkering as an industrial strategy', then the fault was not theirs but that of the industrialists.

Notes

1. Research for this study was made possible by an award from the Social Sciences Small Grants Scheme of the Nuffield Foundation, SOC/181 (1953) and I should like to thank the Trustees for this assistance. The work was conducted in the Business History Unit of the London School of Economics and I should like to thank the director, Dr Terry Gourvish, for his kindness. I am also grateful to Roy Campbell, Helen Mercer, Catherine Schenk and Jim Tomlinson who read and commented on an earlier draft, and in this respect I am also especially grateful to Nick Tiratsoo. Thanks are also due to Patricia Knight, Mavis James, Norma Phayer and Pat Williams of the School of Social Sciences, Thames Polytechnic, who rendered the text legible. All errors remain my own.
2. P. Addison, *The Road to 1945*, 1975, p. 14.
3. A. Cairncross, *Years of Recovery*, 1985, pp. 3–17, 61–87; G.D.N. Worswick and P.H. Ady (eds) *The British Economy, 1945–50*, 1952, pp. 1–2, 62–71 and 476–549; and J. Tomlinson 'Labour's Management of the National Economy 1945–51', *Economy and Society*, vol. 18, no. 1 (February 1989) 1–12.
4. C. Barnett, *The Audit of War*, 1986.
5. C. Barnett, *The Audit of War*, 1987 edn, p. 238.
6. Ibid., 36.
7. Ibid., 238.
8. Ibid., 266.
9. Ibid., 265–75.
10. Ibid., 275.

11. For the purposes of this chapter, I am not considering the impact on the reconstruction debate of academic bodies such as Nuffield College or the Trades Union Congress. Although this input was important, space does not permit any analysis of it here.
12. E. Durbin, *New Jerusalems: The Labour party and the economics of democratic socialism*, 1985, pp. 79–83.
13. Ibid.
14. S. Brooke, 'Revisionists and fundamentalists: the Labour party and economic policy during the Second World War', *The Historical Journal*, vol. 32, no. 1 (1989) 159.
15. Durbin, *op. cit.*, 121.
16. See, for example, the Labour Party, *Labour's Financial Policy*, 1935; *Why Banks Should be Nationalised*, 1936; *Labour's Immediate Programme*, 1937; H. Dalton, *Practical Socialism for Britain*, 1935; G.D.H. Cole, *Principles of Economic Planning*, 1935; D. Jay, *The Socialist Case*, 1937.
17. Labour Party, *Labour's Immediate Programme*, 1937.
18. S. Brooke, 'The Labour party during the Second World War', in A. Gorst, L. Johnman and W. Scott Lucas (eds) *Contemporary British History 1931–1961: Politics and the limits of policy*, 1991, pp. 13–14.
19. Labour Party, *Labour's Aims in War and Peace*, 1940, p. 144.
20. Quoted in Brooke, 'The Labour Party during the Second World War', *op. cit.*, 5.
21. Labour Party *The Old World and the New Society*, 1942.
22. Quoted in B. Supple, *The History of the British Coal Industry*, vol. 4, Oxford, 1987, pp. 629–632.
23. Brooke, 'Revisionists. . .', *op. cit.*, passim.
24. Ibid.
25. Labour Party Archives RDR 265 April 1944: 'Full employment and financial policy'.
26. Modern Record Centre University of Warwick (hereafter MRC), TUC Archives: TUC Economic Committee 11/1, 'The public ownership and control of industry', 9/4.1944.
27. Brooke, 'Revisionists. . .', *op. cit.*, 169–74.
28. The official structure of reconstruction committees is slightly confusing. Many departments of state had reconstruction committees but the most important bodies were the Committee on Reconstruction Problems within the Offices of the War Cabinet, established in 1940; the Office of the Minister without Portfolio and Paymaster General, again within the War Cabinet Offices, established in 1942; and the Board of Trade itself, which dealt with industrial reconstruction continually from 1940. There was also the Reconstruction Joint Advisory Committee, a tripartite body, established in 1943 under the aegis of the Board of Trade. Lord Woolton became Minister of Reconstruction in 1944, but as Churchill was wont to remark, this was because it was felt that Woolton would prevent anything very radical getting as far as the Cabinet. Until 1944 almost all industrial reconstruction matters were dealt with below Cabinet level.
29. H. Mercer, 'The evolution of British government policy towards competition in private industry, 1940–1956', unpublished Ph.D. thesis, University of London, 1989, pp. 96–108.
30. CAB 117/199: memo by A.S.J. Baster, 'FBI reconstruction report', 9 June 1942.
31. BT 64/3088: unsigned 'Note on the Report of the Special Committee of the Association of British Chambers of Commerce on post-war industrial reconstruction' January 1943.

32. CAB 87/15: unsigned note 'Organisation of Industry', 20 November 1942.
33. Ibid.
34. CAB 117/203: unsigned note 'Suggested re-draft of section on industrial questions', 28 January 1943; CAB 87/57: letter 'Approach to industries on reconstruction', 30 January 1943; and BT 28/1089: 'Ministry of Production Committee on Reconstruction', 11 March 1943.
35. BT 64/3067: unsigned memo 'Internal reconstruction Board of Trade approach to internal problems' 19 January 1943.
36. BT 106/17: unsigned note 'Post-war reconstruction', 10 February 1942.
37. BT 106/17: Report by Regional Controller for the Midlands, 'Midland region', February 1943.
38. BT 106/17: Reports of Regional Controllers for Wales, Scotland, northern, north-west and south-east, February 1943. The only regions where the Controllers envisaged little or no unemployment problems were London, eastern and those areas of the south-east which were not dominated by government contracts. See CAB 124/224: Office of the Minister of Reconstruction, letter from C.U. Peat (Parliamentary Secretary, Raw Materials, Ministry of Supply) to Sir William Jowitt (Minister without Portfolio), 18 December 1943: 'All classes in the North-East coast and especially the working classes are obsessed with the fear that the Government are not making effective plans to avoid the North-East Coast becoming a depressed area when the war and its immediate aftermath of productive activity is over. Duncan Sandys, who has been visiting Ordnance Factories in South Wales, told me that the same thing was true in that area.' See also 'Report by the Parliamentary Secretary, Raw Materials, Ministry of Supply on a tour of private contractors factories in Tyneside and Teeside', 9–12 October 1943.
39. BT 64/3155: unsigned memo 'Post-war redundancy in the war expanded industries', April 1943.
40. BT 64/3155: unsigned memo 'Redundancy schemes', 8 April 1943.
41. Quoted in P.M. Williams, *Hugh Gaitskell*, paperback edn, Oxford, 1982, p. 107.
42. CAB 87/15: unsigned memo 'Management efficiency', February 1944.
43. BT 64/3452: unsigned memo 'Industrial organisation. Re-organisation—general policy', 17 March 1944.
44. CAB 87/14: memo by the Board of Trade, 'Long term prospects of British industry', June 1944.
45. BT 106/25: unsigned memo 'Suggested functions of factory control in regard to the dispersal of government factories and storage premises', March 1944. See also, letter from R. Walters, Controller of Factory and Storage Premises (Midland Region) to R.J.W. Stacy, Board of Trade: 'I am very perturbed that no industrialist appears to be making contact with us with a view to our assessing what requisitioned premises, and I am wondering whether this state of affairs exists only in my region or whether it is general.'
46. CAB 87/14: memo by the Board of Trade 'Long term prospects of British industry', June 1944.
47. CAB 87/14: memo by the President of the Board of Trade (H. Dalton) 'Ministerial Sub-Committee on Industrial Problems—post war exports', 23 June 1944.
48. MRC CBI Predecessor Archive, MSS 200/F/1/1/156: 'Meeting of members of trade associations', 26 July 1940.
49. Federation of British Industries, *Reconstruction*, 1942; and Association of British Chambers of Commerce, *Reconstruction*, 1942. The reports of the National Union of Manufacturers and the London Chamber of Commerce are

in BT 64/3088.

50. FBI: *Reconstruction*, 1942.
51. Ibid., 25–6.
52. CAB 117/72: letter from S. Courtauld to Jowitt and copy of speech made to the Engineers' Club, Manchester, June 1942. This speech was the text of an article on industrial reconstruction which Courtauld published as 'An industrialist's reflections on the future relations of government and industry', *Economic Journal*, vol. 51, no. 205 (April 1942) 1–17. This piece had begun life as a private report on reconstruction for Conservative MPs and had been seen by J.M. Keynes who had recommended publication.
53. Ibid.
54. Ibid.
55. *A National Policy for Industry*, 1942.
56. C. Madge, *Industry After the War: Who is going to run it?*, 1943, pp. 33–4.
57. MRC, MSS 200/F/3/D2/3/1: unsigned memo 'Liaison with other associations' (undated).
58. MRC, MSS 200/F/3/52/14/8 and 9: letter Sir G. Locock (Director FBI) to district secretaries 13 November 1942.
59. MRC, MSS 200/F/3/D2/3/1: letter Locock to Lord Herbert Scott 23 November 1942. For a complete analysis of the NPI signatories, their industrial directorships, links with industrial associations, government and politics, see Mercer *op. cit.*, appendix 4, 361–5.
60. MRC, MSS 200/F/1/1/166: meeting of the 'Organisation of Industry Committee' of the FBI, 20 April 1943.
61. MCR, MSS 200/F/1/1/166: memo by Sir C. Bruce-Gardner 'Working of export groups', 11 May 1943.
62. MCR, MSS 200/F/1/1/166: meeting 1 June 1943, comment by L. Worthing of the Electrical and Mechanical Engineers.
63. MRC, MSS 200/F/1/1/166: meeting 1 June 1943, comment by Sir Raymond Streat.
64. MRC, MSS 200/F/1/1/166: meeting 25 June 1943, comment by Bruce-Gardner.
65. CAB 87/19: Reconstruction Joint Advisory Committee meetings, 3 February 1943 and 31 March 1943.
66. CAB 117/204: correspondence Locock and Jowitt, 7 April 1943 and 5 May 1943.
67. Ibid.
68. CAB 117/204: report of speech by Lord Dudley Gordon, May 1943.
69. CAB 117/202: report of speech by Lord McGowan to the Institution of Chemical Engineers and London Section of the SCI, April 1943, and correspondence between Lords McGowan and Melchett. See also an article in *The Sunday Times*, 25 July 1943 'Combines and Cartels' by Lord McGowan.
70. BT 64/3359: letters from Capt. Lindsay (Morgan Crucible) and H.L. Bostock (Lotus) to G.L. Watkinson, 10 December 1943 and 29 September 1943.
71. CAB 117/205: note by T. Daish 'Reconstruction Joint Advisory Committee, 18 May 1943. Just to prove that all was not well, the Ministry of Production Reconstruction Committee reported at its second meeting that they had seen representatives of the Engineering and Allied Industries but that 'their contribution had been disappointing as they had tended either to ask for firm indications of Government post-war commercial and fiscal policy before going any further, or to take a hopeless view of the future generally. Similar tendencies had been encountered by the Board of Trade in their approach to other industries'. See also BT28/1088: letter from Lord Riverdale and Moir McKenzie

to Jowitt 9 September 1943: 'The fact of the matter is that nobody is standing up for British export trade at the present time at all and unless some more general hope is infused into the export trade of this country nothing can prevent vast unemployment or a vast fall in our standard of living.'

72. MRC, MSS 200/F/4/58/3: speech by Sir G. Nelson 'Industry and the future: post-war prospects; the place of private enterprise', 29 October 1943.
73. Federation of British Industries, *The Organisation of British Industry*, 1944, pp. 4–5 and 12–14. See also BT64/3072: memorandum initialled J.K. to Miss MacInnes 4 December 1944: 'The Journal [of the National Union of Manufacturers] has been carrying out a questionnaire about the future of controls, without coming to any useful conclusions. All associations agree that no control should be continued merely for the sake of control, but the controls should be relaxed and finally abandoned as soon as the necessity for them ceased to exist. Beyond this, there is a wide divergence of opinion, some Associations object strongly to all controls and want them removed as soon as possible, others consider them necessary and even beneficial.'
74. Sir Stafford Cripps in *The Statist*, 10 February 1945.
75. MRC, MSS 200/F/3/D3/4/13: meeting of Presidents' Advisory Committee (Kipping-Walker) to discuss 'Private enterprise', 7 February 1945.
76. MRC, MSS 200/F/3/52/14/64: 'The Economic League. Summary of activities for four monthly period ending April 30, 1945'.
77. MRC, MSS 200/F/3/52/14/64: letters to Nelson 20 February 1945 and 7 March 1945. See also 'The Economic League (Central Council)'; and 'Notes and comments on private enterprise at war', 27 April 1945.
78. MRC, MSS 200/F/4/60/1: speech by Sir Clive Baillieu, Chamber of Commerce lunch, 1 June 1945.
79. MRC, MSS 200/F/3/51/14/16: memo by Locock 'Industry: private enterprise', 22 October 1945.
80. MRC, MSS 200/F/D3/9/4: Federation of British Industries, *Statement of Policy*, February 1946.
81. MRC, MSS 200/F/D3/9/4: report of Proceedings of the Conference of Employers, 'National Situation', 7 March 1946.
82. BT64/3599: unsigned, undated memos 'Industrial reconstruction.
83. BT64/3599: memo by W.B. Reddaway 'The export problem', 2 May 1944.
84. CAB87/14: memo by the Board of Trade 'Long term prospects of British industry', June 1944.
85. BT64/3497: memos by N.E. Welch, E.W. Reardon, H.I. Tout and H.A. Shannon on 'The export problem', 12, 15 and 16 May 1944.
86. BT64/3497: memo initialled H.A.S. 'IR draft on long term prospects of British industry', 12 May 1945.
87. Ibid.
88. BT64/3555: unsigned draft memo 'Proposals on industrial and export policy. Suggestions for the President's paper', 28 June 1944.
89. BT64/3599: unsigned 'Draft note on export policy in the transition period' (undated).
90. Cmd. 6527, *Employment Policy*, HMSO, 1944, paragraph 18A.
91. CAB 87/14: memo by Lord Woolton, 'Export trade prospects', 30 June 1944.
92. CAB 87/14: memo by Dalton, 'Measures to promote exports and industrial efficiency', 8 July 1944; and note by Dalton, 'Export policy in the transition period', 12 September 1944.
93. Labour Party Archives, RDR 265 April 1944: 'Full employment and financial policy'.

94. Brooke, 'The Labour party during the Second World War', *op. cit.*, 18–19.
95. Barnett, *op. cit.*, 237.
96. Ibid., 268.

4 'Reflections on a revolution'? The political mood in wartime Britain

Tony Mason and Peter Thompson

On 3 August 1945 the headline in *Tribune* had a triumphalist ring. 'Reflections on a revolution' it proclaimed. It was referring to that most dramatic of twentieth century electoral turn-ups: the victory of the Labour Party in the first post-war election. In the euphoria of the moment it was easy to exaggerate the scale of Labour's success. The peculiarities of the British electoral system meant that only 48 per cent of the vote was enough to give Labour its first parliamentary majority of 149 over all other parties.[1] The significance of this victory has been regularly debated ever since. At the time, *Tribune*'s editor was 'convinced' that Labour's win reflected 'a situation which [had] . . . existed . . . for a number of years'.[2] A substantial majority of the British people had been moving steadily to the left and the Labour Party was the beneficiary.[3]

The purpose of this chapter is to re-examine the evidence for the idea of a 'Labour revolution' in 1945. Why did some contemporaries think so, how far have some historians agreed and what does an exploration of the political mood of the population in one industrial city, Coventry, at the end of the war, contribute to the arguments?

In general historians are agreed that the popular political mood swung to the Left between 1940 and 1945. The historial debate has largely concerned itself with the meaning of that swing: its strength, timing and the degree to which Labour genuinely reflected this new mood. Such questions are not always the product of disinterested scholarship. What historians think of Labour's victory in 1945 often reflects their own positions on the political spectrum.

The most recent work has come from those on the political Right and can be seen as part of that general critique of the post-war settlement which gathered momentum during the 1980s. For Correlli Barnett, the leftward shift in the popular political mood after 1940 can be largely explained by the propaganda successes of a centre-left consensus of intellectuals and planners, or New Jerusalemists as he calls them. This kind of explanation is in part little more than a repetition of that advanced by a number of leading Tory figures in the immediate aftermath of Labour's victory in 1945.[4] Labour's post-war vision of a New Jerusalem was not, according to Barnett, 'the spontaneous effusion of the Nation at large', but was instead a high-minded gift, which the New Jerusalemists 'proceeded to press on the British people between 1940 and 1945'.[5]

A more influential interpretation can be found in the work of historians like Paul Addison, Arthur Marwick and Kenneth Morgan.[6] For them the relationship between Labour and the popular political mood is largely unproblematic. According to Morgan, 'Labour was uniquely identified with a sweeping change of mood during the war years, and with the new social agenda that emerged.'[7] To vote for Labour was to endorse consciously that new agenda. Indeed Marwick has argued that 'at the end of the war the majority had a clearer idea than ever before of what it was they expected of a modern civilised industrial society.'[8]

Those expectations are widely held to have their origins in the conduct of the British war effort. The war, or so it is argued, most powerfully by Marwick,[9] led to a levelling of standards and fostered an increased sense of egalitarianism. Wartime full employment bolstered this feeling still further. The almost total mobilization of labour stood in stark contrast to the unemployment of the 1930s, and as a consequence state intervention seemed both credible and desirable.

Some Marxist scholars have been even more impressed by this point about the war's impact, arguing that unprecedented levels of participation gave the British people 'a new consciousness of their collective strength'.[10] That new consciousness was first identified by Ralph Miliband in the early 1960s, and has remained a vigorous feature of some interpretations to the present.[11] The popular political mood was, according to this analysis, considerably in advance of Labour thinking. It was strongly ideological. Its hatred of Fascism was matched by its admiration for the Soviet Union. Miliband has conceded that this popular radicalism was not revolutionary, nor even consciously socialist. Nevertheless, it did offer the *potential* for sharp political change. In Hinton's view, during 1944–5 'the opportunities for Socialists were brighter than at any time since the end of the First World War.'[12]

In recent years the notion that the war brought social change has come under increasing attack—most notably in a collection of essays edited by Harold Smith.[13] This process of historical revision is by no means complete. The Smith volume contains nothing on popular politics (and indeed this chapter might profitably be seen as an attempt to redress the balance). Nevertheless, it seems clear that for good or ill, historians are convinced that in 1945 people knew what they wanted—and what they wanted was contained between the covers of *Let Us Face the Future*. In a moment we shall examine the mood of Coventry in this period. First, however, we need to remind ourselves of the national evidence on which historians have based their judgements.

It is the politically radical whose voice has been loudest in the existing historical accounts of wartime public opinion. This is perhaps unsurprising, as it was those contemporaries on the Left who most strongly believed that the popular political mood was radically transformed during the Second World War. This is evident in a number of studies written after the 1945 election. The Fabian socialist, Margaret Cole, spoke for many when she said that Labour's success represented a 'real revolution in feeling'. This was an electorate who had 'consciously voted for a change'.[14] Others on the Left had identified this radical shift in the popular political mood some years earlier. Its origins and arguably its highpoint, according to notable commentators like George Orwell and J.B. Priestley, lay in the crisis of 1940 and 1941.[15] Nevertheless, even in 1943 and 1944 a plethora of radical commentators were still noting with some enthusiasm that the popular political mood remained largely leftwards.[16] Few, however, were prepared to predict a Labour election victory. One exception was Tom Harrisson, the director of Mass-Observation. Writing in 1944, he noted 'an incontestable unanimity of evidence towards a much reduced Conservative prestige, plus a big, if not immense, shift to the left'.[17]

It is important to note that Harrisson—like many of the other commentators we have cited—was not simply a disinterested observer. He was actively involved in promoting the new participatory democracy that he and others claimed to detect in wartime Britain.[18] That said, it would be extremely foolish to ignore such an astute commentator as Harrisson. After all, he was one of the very few who predicted Labour's electoral triumph. However, despite a failure of most analysts and activists to predict a Labour victory, all were convinced of the radical transformation of public opinion.[19]

Nevertheless, evidence of political radicalism is not confined to the opinions of progressive and socialist commentators. All the political parties of the Left enjoyed substantial increases in membership during the war years. Membership of the Labour Party increased significantly from 2,663,000 in 1939 to 3,039,000 in 1945,[20] and at a time when it had lost many members through population movements and conscription to the armed forces. Furthermore, the party was effectively barred by the wartime electoral truce from almost all political activity outside Parliament. The flag of left opposition was upheld from 1941 by the newly formed Commonwealth Party, committed to socialism with a high moral Christian tone. By 1944 it had between 300 and 400 branches, some 15,000 members and two seats in Parliament.[21] Unrestrained by the electoral truce, Commonwealth and a number of often radical independents fought by-elections and inflicted several humiliating defeats on Conservative candidates.[22] Even further to the Left, the British Communist Party—for once benefiting from its close ties with the Soviet Union—expanded rapidly, to a membership of between 50,000 and 60,000, three times its pre-war peak.[23]

There was also something of a growth industry in propaganda advocating the necessity of post-war planning and reconstruction. Subscriptions to PEP's journal *Planning*, for instance, increased fourfold between 1942 and 1944.[24] Who might have subscribed to PEP or joined one of the radical political parties? Some evidence is available from a Ministry of Information survey on public reaction to reconstruction plans, made in November 1942.[25] The survey identified a 'thinking minority' and estimated its size to be between 5 and 20 per cent of the population. It was pan-class: numerically largest in the working class, proportionally largest in the 'professional classes'. The views of this 'thinking minority' generally encompassed the major features of Labour's post-war programme, including a belief in full employment, social security, decent homes and education for all.[26]

It seems probable, then, that in 1942 at least, those who thought about the political future at all could only have been little more than a vocal but significant minority—this moreover during a period when, according to Addison, 'opinion may have been further to the left . . . than it was to be in 1945'.[27] On the other hand, it could be argued that such a conclusion is somewhat misleading, because the analysis upon which it is based ignores developments that were occurring in the armed forces. Tom Harrisson was certainly not alone in thinking that 'service personnel have been *more* affected by radical trends than civilians'.[28] Were soldiers, sailors and airmen at the heart of the new radicalism?

It is important to remember at the outset that the armed forces made up barely one-sixth of the electorate, so that even if radicalism was widespread in the ranks, this would not be enough to substantiate the picture of a Left majority in the nation as a whole, which Miliband and others have identified. Having said this, however, it must quickly be conceded that evidence of a growing radical politics in the forces is not difficult to find.[29] It was apparent, for example, in the widespread enthusiasm for the Soviet Union.[30] It could be detected, too, in the workings of the Army Bureau of Current Affairs (ABCA) and the Forces 'Parliaments',[31] organizations which some politicians, at least, later saw as having decisively shaped the outcome of the 1945 election.[32]

Nevertheless even here the evidence is perhaps less straighforward than it appears at first sight. ABCA's influence with the troops was disputed by contemporaries,[33] and it has remained a matter of controversy ever since.[34] A fair conclusion seems to be that the Bureau's reputation has been inflated: ABCA was responsible for the growth of more critical attitudes amongst the ranks, but this did not mean an automatic tendency for the Army to vote Labour.

The situation of the Forces 'Parliaments' can be summarized with greater certainty.[35] The most famous of these 'Parliaments' was in Cairo, and a brief outline of its history is instructive. The 'Parliament' involved a 'government' and an 'opposition', and since Labour supporters predominated amongst those who had been responsible for the idea in the first place, it was Labour which proposed the first two debates, on bills to nationalize the retail trade and restrict inheritances, both of which were passed. A few weeks later, in early 1944, the 'Parliament' held a mock general election, at which Labour gained a comfortable victory, with 119 votes to Commonwealth's 55, the Liberals' 38 and the Conservatives' 17. This was apparently too much for the military authorities, who then closed the 'Parliament' down, thus ensuring it widespread notoriety.

Some have argued that this whole episode is highly significant: the 'Parliament' shows opinion in the ranks was moving leftward, a trend confirmed by the panicky reactions of the authorities. Again, however, close attention to the evidence reveals a rather different picture. For example, it seems likely that the majority of those involved at Cairo (as at Deolali in India a year later) were not infantry but rather technical and administrative troops, who often had had prior trade union or university experience. The 'Parliaments' can hardly be seen, then, as simple proof of radicalization amongst the ranks. On the contrary, they were the creation of those who were most likely *already* to have acquired left-wing sympathies.

All of this seems to point to the conclusion that the self-consciously radical—in the Army and in civvy street—were perhaps smaller in number than might be imagined, and concentrated quite noticeably amongst the skilled working class and the young (often professional) middle classes.[36] But what of the population in general? Labour's standing with the electorate during the war was certainly quite high. Indeed, Gallup regularly predicted that Labour would win the first peacetime general election from the summer of 1943 onwards (in answer to the question, 'If there was a general election tomorrow, how would you vote?', on average, 39 per cent said Labour, 28 per cent Conservative and 10 per cent Liberal).[37] At the same time, enthusiasm on reconstruction matters continued to be very evident, with, for example, the Beveridge Report selling well over half a million copies.[38]

Yet, against this, there is good reason to believe that public opinion often remained rather unfocused, or agnostic about anything other than 'bread and butter' measures of amelioration. In a Gallup poll of April 1943, 57 per cent of those questioned agreed that they would like to see 'great changes' in their way of life after the war. Of these, 35 per cent had 'no comment' on what changes they had in mind, 16 per cent wanted 'better working conditions' and full employment, 15 per cent desired a 'better standard of living' including old age pensions, and 8 per cent chose 'better homes', but only 3 per cent mentioned 'socialism' or a 'changed economic system'.[39]

Moreover, enthusiasm for change did not necessarily imply a belief in class-wide aspirations or, indeed, even in collective solutions. A civilian lecturer touring RAF camps in October 1945 remarked that airmen were 'genuinely interested in education so far as it concerns their own children'.[40] Post-war employment was viewed—not surprisingly, given the fiasco which followed the 1914–18 war—in similar personal terms. Large-scale surveys of troop opinion in both the army and the RAF reveal little evidence of increased aspirations. Some 86 per cent of those questioned in the army wished to return to their pre-war occupation—and quickly too![41] E.S. Conway concluded from his survey of army attitudes to post-war employment that

> as yet, the war has not stimulated an interest in post-war personal problems. The men might have retained their pre-enlistment convictions and ambitions. . . . To most soldiers, the end of the war means no more than the continuation of a life which had been suddenly and unpleasantly disturbed.[42]

Housing was just as narrowly conceived. Popular interest in housing was not in doubt. Gallup polls demonstrated clearly that it was by far the most important issue in the 1945 election. Yet interest in housing should not be taken to infer interest in wider issues about the urban environment. Indeed, as the journalist Hugh Pilcher put it, ideas on popular planning invariably ended 'at the garden gate'.[43] Evidence from a variety of sources suggests that the majority of the public disliked the trend to shared living arrangements that had inevitably been encouraged by the war, and longed for more privacy. People wanted their own homes and gardens when the hostilities ended, with no hint of sharing.[44] A report for Mass-Observation later concluded: 'It is clear that the war gave an unnatural spurt to neighbourly relations; and equally clear that peace has to some extent allowed them to revert to a level which is presumably the more natural one.'[45] Very often, to summarize, the desire for change was most about recovering the familiarities of the pre-war world, albeit a pre-war world cleansed of mass unemployment and slums. Reporting on his country for a European audience in 1944, the socialist intellectual G.D.H. Cole could thus write:

> The old political parties remain intact: the old ways of social and political thinking have not, so far, been greatly changed. It is still possible for many Englishmen to think of the return to peace as in the main a return to the *status quo anti bellum*.[46]

So far the discussion has concerned the politically committed or at least aware. Yet it is worth remembering that apathy, cynicism and lack of interest about politics had not simply disappeared with the war. Certainly, for many radical politicians and progressive commentators, the major problem seemed to be how few people cared at all. In 1945 Charles Madge, one-time co-director of Mass-Observation, even compiled a guide to the forthcoming election in an effort to persuade people of their democratic duty.[47] Similar anxieties were expressed about the low registration of service personnel. The War Office cited practical difficulties and inadequate administration as part explanations, but apathy and isolation were understood to be more potent ones. Mass-Observation concurred, adding in a famous article in *Picture Post* that it was not that many soldiers did not want to vote but that they had no one they wanted to vote *for*.[48] In the event, only about 66 per cent of those eligible to vote actually registered.[49]

Civilians were perhaps somewhat less cynical than service personnel, although it should be remembered that we are talking about degrees of cynicism, not its absence. It is well known that early popular enthusiasn for reconstruction was somewhat blunted by government prevarication. However, by 1943 Mass-Observation had detected a wider malaise. Increasingly people were viewing the post-war period in terms of a distinction between what they desired and what they expected. The memories of the First World War were still vivid. For many, 'homes fit for heroes' and full employment seemed particularly laughable.[50] The Ministry of Information's weekly Home Intelligence reports are yet another indicator of the public's widespread cynicism. This comment from October 1943 is typical: 'the "brave new world" is thought unlikely to materialise.'[51] A 40-year-old working man questioned by Mass-Observation shortly before VE

Day would have agreed. When asked what he thought we were fighting for, he replied: 'For what we shan't get.'[52]

A range of general evidence indicates, it has been suggested, that the mood of wartime Britain was not as clear-cut as some have argued. Nevertheless, a degree of caution has to be exercised here. It might be that the broad trends referred to are themselves deceptive because they obscure important regional or local differences. Labour did not win the whole country in 1945. Might there not have been islands of radical fervour—quite significant islands at that—the length and breadth of the lukewarm sea?

To answer this particular question, we turn now to a study of Coventry during the war years. This city was an important armaments and engineering centre, which had been badly bombed in 1940–1. It boasted a strong trade union movement, and had elected a Labour majority to be its local council in 1937.[53] Surely here, more than anywhere else, it should be possible to identify an uncomplicated popular radicalism growing during the war?

For ease of exposition, it will be convenient to divide the survey of Coventry into three parts. First, we need to look at the conventional political radicals and try to assess how much their numbers increased during the war. What happened to the Labour and Communist Parties in Coventry between 1939 and 1945? Second, we must see how far the war had stimulated local politics away from the two main radical groups, and indeed, outside the normal area of party politics altogether. Finally, we must look for evidence that might help us not only to identify the views and hopes of the politically less active, but attempt to monitor those areas of social life which did seem important in that last year of war, 1944–5.

If we look at the Labour Party first, it was, of course, subject to both the electoral truce and the stresses and strains of life in wartime Britain in general and Coventry in particular, to which we have already alluded.[54] There had been just over one thousand individual members of the Party in 1939. This had already declined to 450 by 1940. The November bombing of the city did not help, damaging premises and destroying records. By 1942, according to that year's Labour Party *Annual Report*, only 247 members had paid their subscriptions. This was probably the low point for the Coventry Labour Party as it was for the fortunes of Britain in the war. Things began to improve after that, partly because Labour took a leaf from the Communist Party's book and established several factory groups. By September 1944, three munitions factories had functioning groups with a combined total of 160 members. Not only did this help to keep the Party in Coventry ticking over: these groups also probably assisted in the rebuilding of some ward organizations towards the end of the war. They do not appear to have long survived the outbreak of peace. By the end of the war individual membership had risen to 3,017—a modest number but a sign of progress and some reflection on the shift of political opinion.

The ups and downs of the Coventry Communists have been skilfully documented by James Hinton.[55] He shows that like the Party nationally, membership rose significantly once Germany had invaded Russia in June

1941. From about 70 active members in 1939, the Coventry Branch grew to 320 by December 1941, to 600 by February 1942, at which time Bill Alexander was appointed the first local full-time organizer, and to 1,500 by September of that year (making the Communist Party roughly six times the size of Labour). The Communists were particularly keen to establish factory branches and there may have been as many as forty by 1942. There are no published membership figures after 1942–3 but that was probably the peak for the Coventry Communists. After this period it was downhill all the way. By the summer of 1943 the low level of actual attendance at branch meetings was causing King Street some anxiety. By 1944, it was clear that the party as a whole and the Coventry branch in particular were characterized by a low level of activity, high turnover, and slow recruitment. Membership fell sharply in 1944 and by April 1945 was down to 520 in Coventry. In 1946, after a lost deposit in Coventry East at the previous year's election, it had fallen to 260, of which a third, according to Hinton, were of the 'transient variety'. Early in 1945 the party decided to reorganize on residential instead of workplace lines, which may not have helped its cause much.

So the evidence from membership figures does suggest that more people were turning Left, but the numbers were not spectacularly large. What the bulk of the Coventry population thought about politics is less easy to discover. As we noted above, public opinion polls certainly suggest that housing and employment were seen as key issues in Britain as a whole and there is some evidence that Coventry reflected the national mood. So far as employment was concerned, anxieties about redundancy and the transition from war to peacetime production were major concerns in the city. The local branch of the Citizens Advice Bureau had over a thousand queries about employment during 1944.[56] In October of that year the Transport and General Workers Union ran a Sunday conference of shop stewards, collectors and branch officers—all the activists—who demanded to meet representatives of the City Council, the Ministries of Labour, Production and the Board of Trade, the local Chamber of Commerce and the Engineering Employers' Association to thrash out the post-war industrial future of the city.[57] The conference concluded that the aim should be to provide work for all those who had moved into the city's booming wartime industries and wanted to stay. What was needed was the same co-operation and consultation between government, management and unions which had been such a feature of wartime. It was also agreed that non-union labour in the engineering industry had no claims for retention. Wartime entrants into engineering from other industries should be helped to find a transfer to suitable work. Long service and 'immobile labour' should receive special consideration for the retention of their present jobs. Women with domestic responsibilities should be allowed to leave industry if they wished. Overtime should be reduced wherever possible. The meeting also requested that further war contracts should be awarded to Coventry. In general, the move to civilian production should be accelerated, and in particular the building industry should be allowed to go full speed ahead on house-building.

This last comment reflected the other major popular contemporary concern—housing. Local newspapers regularly reminded their readers that it was the admittedly expensive duty of the community to tackle the housing shortage with a vigour and earnestness which had been lacking after the First World War. Decent housing was widely recognized as a right. Families with children should have priority. By the spring of 1944 the Council's housing committee had estimated the post-war demand for three-bedroom houses at 10,599 units.[58] Prefabs were already being assembled in local factories for erection on sites in the city,[59] and local voluntary organizations like the Soroptimists were taking an energetic interest in this key question, in their case going so far as setting up a committee on the subject themselves and trying—but failing—to persuade the Council that there ought to be a Women's Advisory Committee on housing.[60] Other not notably radical organizations were also outspoken about housing. The Warwickshire Council of the British Legion condemned the 'sharks who were profiteering by charging excessive rents for furnished rooms'. The Coventry branch decided to send a deputation to the Council about it.[61] The interest of young servicemen in this issue suggests that it was sometimes seen as a generational problem. This impression emerges too from a report of a meeting involving young freemen of the city, which deplored the lack of interest in housing displayed by their older colleagues.[62] The young freemen had their own solution. They did not want priority over servicemen, but they did demand it over 'outsiders'—people who had migrated to Coventry in order to work, but might easily still be in possession, the freemen claimed, of houses elsewhere. This, perhaps as well as anything, illustrates the extent—and the fragility—of wartime community.

There were other signs that the experience of war had stimulated Coventry people to think about the future of both city and country and to establish or join a variety of voluntary organizations pledged to do something about both. The city branch of the National Council of Women, for example, almost doubled its membership in 1944–5 and twenty-eight other local organizations were affiliated to it.[63] There was also a branch of the Social Security League, whose aim was to persuade the government to put the Beveridge scheme into operation as soon as possible, but nothing is known either about its strength or its activities. A more interesting political development, however, was the setting up of the Coventry Guild of Citizens towards the end of 1943.

The Guild of Citizens soon had between twenty-five and thirty local branches claiming over 600 members.[64] The chairman was the city's Director of Education, and as he said on the occasion of the formation of the Lower Stoke branch in the city, it was an organization whose aim was to build on the active citizenship which the war had so clearly promoted. The experience of war had taught a 'neighbourly and co-operative spirit' and 'if we were to continue democratic government it was essential that every member of the community should do his bit'.[65] The purpose of the Guild was to arouse a sense of responsibility and to persuade people to take an intelligent interest in matters affecting the life and government of the community. Its aim was not simply to be another discussion group. It should be involved in all kinds of voluntary work and community service.

The time might also come when some of its members might be elected to the City Council. All kinds of citizens were claimed as members but the only named ones appear to have been from Coventry's professional middle class. One of them, the Reverend E.L. Cooke, emphasized at a later meeting why such a group of activists was necessary. Misgivings had been aroused, he claimed, by the persistent apathy of the people towards their governing institutions. Even the recent reforms of education and social insurance had received an apathetic response. If the City Council and the London Parliament knew that their deliberations were being followed by a responsible, thinking electorate, then the result would be better government.[66]

So the experience of war did certainly make some citizens in Coventry think more about existing and future political possibilities. Yet it is also clear that for the majority of the city's population, abstract ruminations were simply irrelevant. In fact, in the final phase of the war, they were preparing for the peace in a very different way, by attempting to return to those things which they considered to be the essence of normal life.

There were no air raids on Coventry after August 1942 and this must have been the most powerful single factor in encouraging a sense that the worst was over. Air raid shelters were no longer used for business but for best-kept shelter competitions, with the winning underground facility open to the public.[67] Transport restrictions were eased during holiday periods. In the face of some local opposition the City Council ran late buses—after 9.00 p.m.—in the July holiday week in 1944, and ten special trains were put on to take transferred workers back home on the September holiday weekend in the same year.[68] The first softening of the blackout restrictions was a particularly symbolic moment. Poor transport and the blackout were two of the features of life in wartime Coventry about which workers most frequently complained. Another sign that normality was not far off was the government's encouragement to women workers to leave munitions and to take up less essential work for which there were shortages of labour: to go on the buses or take up domestic work in hospitals and hostels for directed workers.[69]

Nowhere was the common urge for the familiar more pronounced than in relation to recreation. Thus, when in March 1944 one local paper called for the revival of leisure activities suspended when war broke out, it was only recognizing a head of pressure that had already gained significant proportions.[70] The Coventry Amateur Operatic Society, for example, had not met since 1939. In early 1944 officials decided that they could not yet mount a full-scale production, but they could arrange regular sing-songs and begin auditions for future productions.[71] Most organized cricket and football had been played on Sundays for over three years. However, the Coventry Sports and Social Association, boasting well over one thousand active members, discontinued Sunday play because the vast majority of players could now obtain release from work to play on Saturday afternoons. The 1944 cricket season was expected to be the best and most competitive seen during the war.[72] Spectator sports and commercial entertainments flourished almost to the extent they had done in the prosperous 1930s. Coventry City Football Club had not even played in the season 1941–2. In

1943–4, it made profits of over £3,500. Gates were continually on the increase and it was expecting to run a reserve team in 1944–5.[73] The cinema and theatre were boasting record attendances. Yet another sign of a return to normal was the selection of Coventry as the venue for the fortieth annual general meeting of the National Federation of Anglers. Coventry still had almost 7,000 members of the NFA, a figure surpassed by only Birmingham and Sheffield.[74] Gardeners were beginning to return to growing flowers and shrubs, provoking some anxiety amongst local civic leaders, who warned not only that the war was not yet won, but also that even when it was, post-war food shortages would still require a horticultural emphasis on vegetables.[75] There were even letters in the local press looking forward to what cars would be like after the war,[76] and newspaper advertising began to take on a very peacetime tone with the Midland Bank, for example, under the heading 'Business enterprise after the war', proclaiming its willingness to consider enquiries from existing and potential entrepreneurs.[77] The space devoted to personal and situations vacant columns began to expand.[78] Life was beginning to have the flavour of peacetime with all its possibilities and plethora of distractions. On the eve of the 1945 general election the political activists were mostly under no illusion that it was going to be difficult to keep the mind of the electorate on the political job.

In Coventry both major parties were anxious about the outcome. The Conservative Party claimed to have taken the political truce especially seriously. As soon as war broke out it had stopped meeting and it did not meet again until 16 April 1945. On this occasion, there was only a small attendance to hear that there was no secretary, no agent and no money.[79] Richard Crossman, Labour's candidate in the new division of Coventry East, thought Labour had suffered from the political truce, too, and that the only fully organized party was the Communists.[80] Both he and the sitting Conservative in Coventry West, Captain Strickland, were anxious that 30,000 Coventry workers would be disenfranchized because the date of the election fell in Coventry's holiday week. Both tried, but failed, to have the election date changed.[81] Crossman in general would have preferred October with an up-to-date electoral register and a better chance of maximizing the forces' vote. There is little sign here of confidence in the outcome of the poll.

The campaign itself in Coventry seems to have been relatively low key. Big name speakers could always draw a full house but it was a house largely filled by their own activist supporters, as during the visits of Cripps on 7 June and Attlee on 21 June.[82] There was some feeling both nationally and locally that the Conservatives were putting all their eggs in the Churchill basket, but it was Churchill who drew the one really big crowd of the election on 25 June. An estimated 20,000 waited during a Monday lunch-time even though Churchill arrived almost two hours later than advertised. It is clear that he received a great ovation and that many of those who were there wanted to be able to tell their grandchildren that they had seen the man who had won the war. There were some interruptions during a speech in which Churchill urged those present not to 'run away with the idea they can vote [against the two Conservatives] without voting against me!' There was also some opposition which manifested itself in boos and heckling;

eventually a man 'assisted by some of his fellows' climbed up one of the slender tripods holding the loudspeakers and dragged them down into the crowd. Captain Strickland was later able to characterize such behaviour as left-wing hooliganism.[83] The dangers of relying on Churchill prompted the *New Statesman* to satirical verse:

> 'One Empire; One Leader; One Folk!'
> Is the Tory campaign master-stroke
> As a National jest,
> It is one of the best
> But it's not an original joke.[84]

In contrast to the huge turnout for Churchill only a very small crowd assembled to hear the declaration of Labour's two resounding victories outside the Council House. One question begged by all this is how far Labour's victory in Coventry owed much to wartime experience at all. Labour had first won what was then the city's only parliamentary constituency in 1929, but lost it in the panic-stricken débâcle over the economic crisis and the National government in 1931. Four years later Philip Noel-Baker had reduced the 1931 Conservative majority of over 15,000 to 2,472 in a straight fight.[85] A further sign of the way things were going was Labour's first majority on the Coventry City Council in 1937. There was a widespread feeling that Labour would regain Coventry in the election scheduled for 1940. By 1945, of course, the electorate was much larger, swollen by wartime population movements and now divided into two constituencies, Coventry East and West. Clearly these changes added a further dimension of unpredictability to the occasion. However, surely in Coventry it would have been a surprise if Labour had lost in 1945. In the event, the turnout was slightly below the national average in Coventry West, 67 per cent, and at about the national average, 71 per cent, in Coventry East. Labour's majorities, at 15,013 and 18,749, also suggest that the service vote played no decisive part in the result. In Coventry East only 5,166 voters were on the service register, with 5,318 in Coventry West.[86]

In the end, therefore, Coventry seems to confirm rather than qualify the picture that has been presented of national trends. The war did stimulate discussion of politics in the city, but those involved in the debate remained relatively few, and often self-consciously aware that they were somewhat isolated. Against this, it is evident that the majority of Coventrians were most concerned with returning to some kind of normalcy. The popular aspiration was for a reversion to much of the familiarity of the pre-war world, but this time with its blemishes—unemployment, slums and insecurity—removed.

It is not surprising that some contemporaries, especially those on the Left, were astonished and delighted by the Labour victory in 1945. For one thing hardly any of them expected it, even though many had striven hard to bring it about in both the factories and in the forces. And as is well known, in terms of seats it did appear a landslide. In terms of votes though, the result was much closer, reflecting very clearly not only the divisions within the electorate, but also the inescapable fact that most people's political ideas and commitment had probably not been dramatically transformed by the war. In any event voting in an election was one thing: taking on more permanent political responsibilities was entirely another. Who was in favour of that when there was normal life to be getting on with? Activists could still hope of course. Mass-Observation noted that although there had been a change in viewpoint at the end of the war, it was not so much a swing to the Left as a swing away from the established institutions of a bitter past. The future could still go either way:

> At present, many are in a mental limbo with nothing on which to pin their hopes, and it is not surprising they feel that there is nothing much they personally can do about things. But the hopes and energies are there. They may well unfold themselves before long.[87]

This was activist hope and optimism of a fairly high if vague order. There were intelligent radical contemporaries who sang a very different tune—G.D.H. Cole, for example. Reflecting on the outcome of the 1945 election in *The Intelligent Man's Guide to the Post-War World*, published in 1947, he was

> quite unable to recognise the many millions of voters who voted—and from my point of view voted sensibly—at the election as constituting a democracy. [They were more victims] of a system which was still denying them the means to become a democracy. Their political knowledge, on the average, was disastrously inadequate; and the scales were weighted against their human common sense . . . by the concentration of many of the most effective forms of propaganda in the hands of persons who wished, not to enlighten them, but to bemuse.[88]

Presumably the only hope was for them to read his book.

Most people do not seem to have wanted to do the joining, meeting and organizing that they would have had to do if the neighbourly collectivities of the war years were to be translated into active citizenship in the post-war world. Yet enough of those too young to vote in 1935 but who had seen the Conservatives preside over unemployment and the drift to war were prepared to give Labour its chance. And enough of their elders remembered the broken promises of 1918 to join them in voting against 'the same old gang'. As R.H. Tawney wrote in October 1945: 'whatever it [the British people] wanted, it knew that what it did not want was a repetition of that nightmare.' Their thoughts were of 'houses, full employment and social security', and they preferred a party 'which spoke to them as men to one whose fluency in clap-trap would have shocked an infant school'.[89] However, it was a closer-run thing than some contemporaries—and some historians—have allowed. It would, of course, be absurd to deny that the political mood of the British did not shift to the Left between 1940 and 1945. Yet it is the limit of that shift rather than its extent which seems so remarkable. All this suggests Labour's mandate was probably as much a constraint as a support.

Notes

1. M. Cole, *The General Election 1945 and After*, 1945, p. 3.
2. *Tribune*, 3 August 1945.
3. The best contemporary study of the 1945 election remains R.B. McCallum and A. Readman, *The British General Election of 1945*, 1947. But see also, M. Abrams, 'The Labour vote in the general election', *Pilot Papers*, vol. 1, no. 1 (January 1946); F.V. Cantwell, 'The meaning of the British election', *Public Opinion Quarterly* (Summer 1945); Cole, op. cit.; J.H. Humphreys, 'The general election: an analysis', *Contemporary Review* (September 1945); and P.G. Richards, 'The Labour victory', *The Political Quarterly*, vol. 26, no. 4 (October–December 1945).
4. The party chairman, Ralph Assheton, wrote: 'Throughout the war the Socialists have never ceased to preach their materialist gospel . . . in their popular Press, in yellow-backed books and pamphlets, on platforms and at street corners, and above all, by ardent disciples in guard rooms and wardens' posts, on fire watches and at factory benches. The flow of propaganda never ceased' (*The Onlooker* (August 1945) 3).
5. C. Barnett, *The Audit of War*, 1986, p. 19.
6. P. Addison, *The Road to 1945* (1945); A. Marwick, *Britain in the Century of Total War*, 1968, and his 'People's war and top people's peace? British society and the Second World War', in A. Sked and C. Cook (eds) *Crisis and Controversy*, 1976; and K.O. Morgan, *Labour in Power 1945–1951*, 1985.
7. Morgan, op. cit., 44.
8. Marwick, *Britain in the Century*, op. cit., 322.
9. The original statement of this thesis, at least in the context of British historiography, is R. Titmuss, *Problems of Social Policy*, 1950.
10. R. Miliband, *Parliamentary Socialism*, 2nd eds, 1973, p. 273.
11. It has recently been restated by E.P. Thompson in 'Mr. Attlee and the Gardarene Swine', *The Guardian*, 3 March 1984; J. Saville, *The Labour Movement in Britain*, 1988, esp. pp. 3–6 and 82–6; and J. Schneer, *Labour's Conscience, The Labour Left 1945–51*, 1988, which speaks 'of a popular radicalism which found expression in unprecedented support for the Left' (p. 2).
12. J. Hinton, 'Coventry communism: a study of factory politics in the Second World War', *History Workshop*, 10 (Autumn 1980) 110.
13. H.L. Smith (ed.) *War and Social Change*, Manchester, 1986.
14. Cole, op. cit., 23, 25. See also Herbert Morrison, *An Autobiography*, 1960, pp. 232–44; and John Parker, Labour Marches On, Harmondsworth, 1947, pp. 27–8.
15. This view found its most famous expression in J.B. Priestley's BBC radio 'Postscripts' and in the 'Searchlight' books edited by T.R. Fyvel and George Orwell—most notably Orwell's *The Lion and the Unicorn*, published in 1941.
16. A classic example is H. Laski, *Reflections on the Revolution of our Time*, 1943. Laski compares the radicalizing effects of the war with 1789.
17. T. Harrisson, 'Who'll Win?', *The Political Quarterly*, vol. 15, no. 1 (January–March 1944), 27.
18. Mass-Observation was employed by the Ministry of Information from the

spring of 1940 to monitor public opinion. According to Penny Summerfield, Harrisson saw this job 'as a means to the end of changing the government's orientation—one of the objectives, after all, of Mass-Observation as a social movement'. P. Summerfield, 'Mass-Observation: social research or social movement?', *Journal of Contemporary History*, vol. 20, no. 3 (July 1985), 446.
19. For instance, in early 1945 the political commentator Peter Richards concluded that on the basis of by-election results, 'the swing to the Left is a great political reality'. P.G. Richards, 'The political temper', *The Political Quarterly*, vol. 16, no. 1 (January–March 1945), 65.
20. Morgan, op. cit., 32.
21. A. Calder, *The People's War*, 1971 edn, pp. 631–5; and D.L. Prynn, 'Common Wealth—a British "Third Party" of the 1940s', *Journal of Contemporary History*, vol. 7, nos 1–2 (1972) 169.
22. P. Addison, 'By-Elections in the Second World War', in C. Cook and J. Ramsden (eds) *By-Elections in British Politics*, 1973.
23. Hinton, op. cit., 90–1.
24. From just under 500 to 2,057; see M. Young, 'The Second World War', in J. Pinder (ed.) *Fifty Years of Pep*, 1981, p. 94.
25. CAB117/209: 'Ministry of Information survey on public reaction to reconstruction plans', November 1942.
26. See also T. Harrisson, 'Notes on class consciousness and class unconsciousness', *The Sociological Review*, vol. 34, nos 3 and 4 (July–October 1942), 149–50.
27. Addison, *Road to 1945*, op. cit., 15.
28. Harrisson, 'Who'll Win?', op. cit., 26.
29. The following sections are largely drawn from T. Mason, 'Politics in the Army, 1918 and 1945', unpublished paper, n.d.
30. WO32/15772: Morale Report Army at Home, May–July 1943.
31. See Penny Summerfield, 'Education and politics in the British armed forces in the Second World War', *International Review of Social History*, vol. 26, part 2, 1981; and Neil Grant, 'Citizen soldiers: army education in World War II', in *Formations of Nation and People*, 1984.
32. See e.g. R.A. Butler, *The Art of the Possible*, 1973, pp. 126–7; and L. Manning, *A Life for Education*, 1970, pp. 163–4.
33. E.g. *The Conservative Agents' Journal*, July 1944, 40–1; and October 1944, 55–6.
34. See e.g. Summerfield, 'Education', op. cit.; and Grant, op. cit.
35. Mason, op. cit., 10–15.
36. T. Harrisson, 'The British soldier: changing attitudes and ideas', *British Journal of Psychology*, vol. 35, no. 2 (1945), 36; Denis Bell, 'The young electors', *Socialist Commentory* (June 1945); and Abrams, op. cit., 25.
37. Richard Sibley, 'The swing to Labour during the Second World War: when and why?', *Labour History Review*, vol. 55, no. 1 (Spring 1990) 30.
38. Barnett, op. cit., 28. On reconstruction enthusiasms in general, see W. Harrington and P. Young, *The 1945 Revolution*, 1978, passim.
39. G.H. Gallup, *The Gallup International Public Opinion Polls. Great Britain 1937–1975*, New York, 1976, p. 75.
40. ED143/15: 'Lecture tour in Italy. Report by S.H. Wood.' (n.d.)
41. WO32/9430: 'Report on the educational preferences of a sample of the Army', 12 September 1944; WO165/85: 'RAF Educational and Vocational Training Scheme . . .', 11 November 1944.
42. E.S. Conway, *Post-War Employment*, 1943, p. 112.
43. H. Pilcher, 'Planning propaganda', *Town and Country Planning*, vol. 11, no. 42

(Summer 1943) 76.
44. A survey of 15,634 service personnel and war workers revealed that at least 95 per cent wanted a private garden. On popular aspirations in relation to housing, see e.g. The Scottish Housing Advisory Committee, *Planning Our New Homes*, Edinburgh, 1944, p. xxix; S. Pollak, 'Living in hostels and living in cities', *Adult Education*, vol. 16, no. 1 (September 1943); and Mass-Observation, *People's Homes*, 1943, esp. pp. 171–5.
45. Mass-Observation, *Bulletin*, no. 15 (New Series) (February 1948) 1.
46. G.D.H. Cole, Papers, Nuffield College Oxford, B3/3/E Box 2/27.
47. C. Madge (ed.) *Pilot Guide to the General Election*, 1945.
48. *Picture Post*, 19 August 1944.
49. Mason, op. cit., 19.
50. Mass-Observation, *The Journey Home*, 1944, chs 1, 2, 4 and 12.
51. INFI/282: Weekly Report no. 158, 14 October 1943.
52. Mass-Observation, File Report 2234, June 1945.
53. N. Tiratsoo, *Reconstruction, Affluence and Labour Politics: Coventry 1945–60*, 1990, pp. 7–10.
54. This paragraph is based on Tiratsoo, ibid., 48 and 149.
55. Hinton, op. cit., 117.
56. *The Coventry Standard* (hereafter *Standard*), 28 April 1945.
57. *Standard* 28 October 1944.
58. Tiratsoo, op. cit., 12; *Standard*, 11 March 1944.
59. *Standard*, 27 April 1944.
60. *Standard*, 8 July 1944.
61. *Standard*, 15 July 1944.
62. *Standard*, 16 September 1944.
63. *Standard*, 5 May 1945.
64. *Standard*, 16 September 1944, 21 October 1944.
65. *Standard*, 29 January 1944.
66. *Standard*, 21 September 1944.
67. *Standard*, 5 February 1944.
68. *Standard*, 8 and 21 July 1944, 23 September 1944; H. Ichihashi, 'Leisure policies for war workers 1939–1945, with special reference to Coventry', unpublished M.A. thesis, University of Warwick, 1990.
69. *Standard*, 8 July 1944, 5 August 1944.
70. *Standard*, 18 March 1944.
71. *Standard*, 26 August 1944.
72. *Standard*, 22 April 1944, 6 May 1944, 1 July 1944.
73. *Standard*, 11 March 1944.
74. *Standard*, 28 April 1945.
75. *Standard*, 26 February 1944, 8 July 1944, 23 June 1945, 21 July 1945.
76. *Standard*, 4 March 1944, 15 April 1944, 20 May 1945.
77. *Standard*, 29 April 1944.
78. *Standard*, 25 March 1944, 29 April 1944, 7 October 1944.
79. *Standard*, 21 April 1945.
80. *New Statesman*, 30 June 1945.
81. *Standard*, 16 June 1945.
82. *Standard*, 9 and 23 June 1945.
83. *Standard*, 30 June 1945.
84. *New Statesman*, 30 June 1945.
85. *Standard*, 28 July 1945.
86. *Standard*, 23 June 1945.

87. Mass-Observation, File Report 2234, April/May 1945.
88. G.D.H. Cole, *The Intelligent Man's Guide to the Post-War World*, 1947, p. 639.
89. R.H. Tawney, 'Some thoughts on the election' *The Highway* (October 1945) 2.

5 The Labour Governments of 1945–51 and private industry

Helen Mercer

It is well established that the Labour governments of 1945 to 1951 had little in the way of clear policy guidelines for the conduct and role of private industry within the 'mixed economy', and lacked the theoretical basis to formulate one.[1] In 1945 a Labour Party researcher noted with surprise: 'There appears to be a gap in Party policy with regard to industries other than those scheduled for nationalisation.'[2] By 1950 little had changed, and Harold Wilson, President of the Board of Trade since 1947, stated that 'this problem of the relationship between Government and private industry is almost a vacuum in Socialist thought.'[3]

It has recently been argued that to the extent that any body of doctrine did inform the actions of the post-war Labour governments towards private industry, it was that of 'reformist economic management' associated with the 'embryonic Gaitskellites', Douglas Jay, Hugh Gaitskell, Evan Durbin and Hugh Dalton.[4] Partly as a result of this ideology and partly through having to respond to a series of economic crises the Labour governments sought co-operation and compromise with business interests.[5]

The broad outlines of policies for the private sector were documented by writers closer to the events, either during or soon after Labour's period in office.[6] The question became a major element in the rethinking of party policies in the 1950s, for instance in Anthony Crosland's essay 'The transition from capitalism'.[7] However, since then, interest has focused either on nationalization or on the development of economic management and the 'Keynesian revolution'.[8] While this focus is natural, there was little in these policies that was distinctively Labourite. Even the party's 1945 manifesto argued for specific nationalizations on empirical grounds almost identical to those outlined in Harold Macmillan's *The Middle Way*.[9]

This chapter therefore moves away from a concern with macro-economic 'planning', nationalization and problems of the short-term transition. It looks, instead, at the overall context of government–industry relations: the general attitude each side adopted towards the other. It then examines one strategy of the Labour government to 'modernize' British manufacturing industry—the Development Councils—as a key illustration of the Labour government's relationship with the private sector. Development Councils have been described as 'Labour's one distinctive policy for the private sector'.[10] The policy was spectacularly unsuccessful, running into 'extraordinary opposition' from private industry and so 'led to one of the few major open confrontations between industry and the Labour Government'.[11]

The broad lines of argument are that private industry viewed the Labour government with hostility and disdain from the beginning. Having few coherent policies themselves, either for an overall industrial policy, or for the future of individual industries, businessmen simply defended the status quo in industry against the 'big black cloud of nationalization' and against any other policies which, in their eyes, were half-way houses to nationalization, or challenged industrial self-government. The Labour government had both a wealth of ideas available through a quite vibrant Research Department, headed by Michael Young, an awareness of potential opposition to their plans and ideas on how to counteract it. The Labour Party lacked coherent policies for the private sector, just as it lacked unity on the issue of nationalization,[12] but came to power with a strong commitment, if not to 'socialism', at least to modernization within the confines of the 'mixed economy', a commitment which was shared in full by its immediate allies, the trade unions and the Co-operative Societies. Party and government reiteration of the need for efficiency and competitiveness, and the emphasis in 1940s publications on industrial restructuring, science, industrial design and improved management add up to a living refutation of alleged 'anti-industrial spirit', or of a willingness to sacrifice industrial progress to 'New Jerusalems'.[13] It was an outlook which continued to be central and strongly held in the Labour Party, appearing in the 1960s in the plans for the 'white heat of the technological revolution'.

Modernization is a shorthand term for industrial policies which might have reversed 'a long-term decline in our relative economic performance'.[14] In the context of the problems facing the post-war Labour government it involved

> not merely getting back to the peace-time economy but also . . . creating a structure of the economy which was viable on the basis of such exports as we might be able to make, not only in the short term, with Germany and Japan out of the world markets, but also when they were back in them.[15]

It has recently been argued that Britain peculiarly lacks strong modernizing forces, and that direct industrial intervention by the state has been weak and inconsistent.[16] Labour's policy for Development Councils represented a modernizing strategy to be applied at first to certain consumer industries, but eventually to much of British industry. Yet Labour was unable to implement even this mildest of 'modernization' strategies because it relied on co-operation from industry which was not forthcoming, and the main peak representative of British businessmen at the time, the Federation of British Industries (FBI), adhered rigidly to its hostility to state intervention.

The great majority of British industrialists were appalled at the prospect of a Labour government. An extraordinary page from Norman Kipping's account of his time as Director-General of the FBI describes an 'atmosphere of near panic that had for a short time prevailed'.[17] Industrial recovery, he argued, was jeopardized by two issues, the fuel and transport crisis, and the election of the Labour government and the consequent threat of nationalization:

> Many people were just plain frightened for they could not see where nationalisation would end. The concept of a mixed economy that has since become reality was not at that time within the imagination of industrial people; they thought there would turn out to be no half-way house between complete socialism and complete private enterprise . . . Angry men shout the loudest and there were plenty of intemperate demands that we should 'man the barricades'—whatever that meant—and defend out beliefs and our businesses by all means we could devise.[18]

Sir Clive Baillieu, a director of Dunlop and the President of the FBI, therefore felt constrained to caution industry to 'temper the spirit of faction with wise restraint'.[19] In August 1945 a meeting of the President's Advisory Committee saw agreement 'in deprecating an attack on the likely policies of the government'.[20] Baillieu reported to the Grand Council his meeting with new Labour MPs. He had, he said, assured them that 'industry as a whole recognized that His Majesty's Government had to be carried on, and would not be in any way obstructive'.[21]

Instead of outright opposition, the FBI early formulated a two-pronged response. On the one hand it proposed to use the 'first-class opposition', that is, the Conservative Party, 'to try to influence Government circles with reasoned statements of the industrial case where it appeared that Government policy was on the wrong lines'.[22] On the other hand the FBI began to look at methods of propaganda 'indicating the virtues which private enterprise possessed', especially 'the great achievements of private enterprise in some of those industries which might be subject to public ownership'.[23] In this it was to be approached also by Conservative Party members, concerned to counter left-wing attacks on private industry.[24]

All of this indicates that Stephen Blank's judgement on the FBI's reaction is wide of the mark. He argues that 'the keystone of the Federation's strategy for dealing with the government was to avoid any ideological conflict. It sought to keep industrial questions out of politics and propaganda was studiously avoided, as were any 'party political' attachments'.[25] On the contrary the FBI saw the Conservative Party as fundamental to its cause, and it was precisely on the ideological front that it first prepared to challenge Labour's attacks on the private sector. To this end it began again to search for closer links with the British Employers' Confederation (BEC). and by August 1945 a small committee of representatives from the two organizations existed to pool ideas and ensure they acted in harmony.[26] It was, however, the case that the FBI represented the moderate, more politically mature wing of British industrialists. In early 1946 the President of the FBI met the newly formed Aims of Industry. The FBI was criticized at the meeting for its alleged passivity in defence of private enterprise.[27]

Private industrialists pursued a successful policy of damage limitation in the period of the Attlee governments. Profits in the post-war years were high.[28] Successful campaigns were waged against the proposed nationalization of cement and sugar, and the opposition on steel nationalization had its effect. Tidy levels of compensation were paid to those industrialists who were dispossessed,[29] and 'huge sums' released for investment, much of it speculative in the private sector, often in related industries.[30] The period was one when industries like cotton received government subsidies for amalgamation and re-equipment but with limited controls on the use of the money.[31] Downgrading trade associations and the increased participation of the unions in the sphere of management threatened in the Development Councils were resisted and this policy lay in ruins by 1950–1. Businessmen administered their own controls while controls persisted, while also campaigning for their removal. The period is remarkable for the peacetime presence of businessmen in Whitehall.[32]

Indeed, as early as 1947 the FBI was congratulating itself on its congenial relations with the government, and felt that the crisis of that year, along with the continuing balance of payments problems had brought Labour to heel.[33] Nevertheless, to talk of Labour's period of 'honeymoon with management'[34] until 1949 is highly misleading. It was probably the case that with iron and steel nationalization and stronger moves to establish Development Councils relations became very strained. Yet industrial opposition was implicit throughout. And it was precisely at those points where Labour most sought change—issues of ownership, industrial restructuring and state supervision—that the FBI waged its most spirited defence from the very beginning. If there was a honeymoon period it was based on the Labour government's eagerness to compromise.

There was, moreover, a deafening silence from industrialists when it came to positive policies for their industries. The FBI and other 'peak associations', in so far as they had any plans for reconstruction, had no intention of radical changes. Labour ministers and Labour economists had frequently expressed their frustration, during wartime discussions, with industrialists' limited outlook.[35] Even discreet and cautious civil servants were moved to remark that businessmen had lost hope of competing successfully in the post-war world and 'forecast a Britain brooding like a miser over a dwindling treasure'.[36] Lord Woolton, himself a businessman, remarked testily that if businessmen were not prepared to take a more risk-bearing approach to the post-war world, 'there was no real argument left against wholesale socialisation'.[37] This critical approach was echoed by members of the Tory Reform Group, and found some expression in the Conservative Party's Industrial Charter of 1947.[38]

There are few studies of businessmen's own plans for reconstruction, but recent writers are aware of the highly restrictionist outlook of most industrialists as they turned to the post-war world.[39] British millowners, for instance, 'knew that cotton was finished. . . . They were aware that nothing could save them except a regime of government-backed price supports combined with a strengthened system of imperial preference'.[40] The Conservative manifesto reflected this malaise among British businessmen. In contrast, Labour's 1945 manifesto was dynamic, with an emphasis on modernizing the British industrial scene.

However, Labour came to power with no coherent ideas about how it was going to handle the private sector.[41] The 1945 manifesto *Let Us Face the Future* had diatribes against the 'hard-faced' profiteers of the post-First World War period, and attacks on monopolists and big business. The commitment to promote full employment and to plan investment was prominent, but outside those scheduled for nationalization the only concrete policy for private industry was for the public supervision of monopolies and cartels and the prohibition of 'anti-social restrictive practices'. Other promises were for state help for export industries, economic and price controls in the transition from war to peace, the gearing of government departments to 'spur industry forward', and some indication of a policy for science, strengthening links between research and industry.[42]

This 'Keynesianism Liberalism . . . a limited sphere of public enterprise . . . and therewith a retention of the profit motive as the main driving force in industry' was essentially to continue unchanged and it was roundly criticized by G.D.H. Cole as 'bastard socialism'.[43] However, within this general framework policies for the private sector grew both more prominent and more detailed in Labour publications and Research Department discussions, in the same measure as the extension of public ownership became more curtailed.[44] In 1948 when the party's Policy Committee set up subcommittees to discuss policies for the next election manifesto, that on privately-owned industry was an important one, chaired by Aneurin Bevan.[45]

It was through these discussions and subsequent publications that the concept of the mixed economy, always implicit in Labour's outlook, became explicit. As early as August 1945 Cripps, President of the Board of Trade from 1945 to 1947, deciding that nationalization would not affect Board of Trade industries, told his staff: 'The object of the Government will be to create orderly conditions by which private enterprise can make the most effective contribution to the country's economic welfare.' To this end it was essential that the Board of Trade 'obtain the confidence of industry'.[46]

'Consolidationism' triumphed in 1948 on the subcommittee on privately owned industry. A 1947 research paper on the relationship between Labour and private industry, 'Socialism and private enterprise', threw doubt on the likelihood of a co-operative attitude from industrialists, given, for instance, 'the short-sighted pursuit of quick and easy personal gains by greedy shareholders or businesses'.[47] Most members of the Policy committee roundly criticized the document for failing to highlight the *benefits* of private capitalism.[48] The remit of the subcommittee went to more moderate hands,[49] and the final report of the subcommittee is a monument to consolidationism, both in its policies for the private sector and in the role which it saw for publicly owned industry. The function of the public sector, it said, was 'to emancipate industry from the bonds imposed by capitalism in decline—from the control of financiers . . . and from the stranglehold of restrictive monopolists'. In the private sector:

> Labour's aim is to give a fair chance to become fully efficient to all those engaged in industry, including the small man who has been the most ruthlessly exploited by monopoly capital. . . . The aim of Government policy should be to stimulate enterprise on the part of managements.[50]

The intention outlined here is the strengthening of private enterprise through a mixed economy.

However, as the border between public and private enterprise became clearer, and as the 'honeymoon' turned into an estrangement, a certain hardening of attitudes towards the private sector developed. This came out clearly in the case of Development Councils, and Wilson's reflective 1950 paper was defiantly 'aggressive' in its tone, repeating earlier warnings that 'there is no guarantee that industry in general will be prepared to subordinate private profit to the national interest'.[51]

Within these overall developments three issues dominated the formulation of long-term policies for the private sector: efficiency, monopoly and the evolution of a permanent relationship between state and industry. A fourth theme was that of industrial democracy. This was a cause dearer to the 'Keep Lefters' than to the parliamentary party, but gradually gained in significance in publications.[52] The first two concerns were strongly linked; as one pamphlet put it: 'Labour intends to help private industry to become more efficient; to encourage it to get rid of restrictive practices, price rings and rigged markets.'[53] One each of these questions Labour was faced with a choice of methods of approach to the private sector: compulsion or persuasion.

Policy on monopoly was an issue which came early to the attention of party policy-makers.[54] However, the limited policy enacted, the 1948 Monopolies and Restrictive Practices Act, failed even remotely to approach the hopes of a joint Labour Party/TUC committee, which wanted the Monopolies tribunal to be part of Labour's planning mechanism.[55] On restrictive practices, as on many other issues, the approach was instead *ad hoc*—a series of unrelated inquiries into specific industries, only given some coherence when the Monopolies Commission started functioning in 1949. A White Paper promised the prohibition of resale price maintenance but floundered in the face of industrial opposition before the Conservatives came to power.[56]

Although introduced to promote efficiency, the monopolies legislation had few coercive powers and was designed to educate industrialists, not discipline them. A similar lack of coercion limited the use of controls to induce efficiency as party researchers suggested. A paper written by G.D.N. Worswick declared: 'a policy for private industry is a policy of price control', and hoped to use this method to control monopoly profits.[57] But only one report on restrictive practices was conducted by the Central Price Regulation Committee, to little practical effect.[58] In addition, the paper outlined the way that permanent price control could be used to stimulate efficiency and redistribute income. However, here again the use of government powers was surrendered, for reasons which are still obscure, although a Bill to introduce permanent controls was under discussion in 1950, and Wilson's 1950 paper also took up the use of control as an efficiency policy.[59]

Thus, on the whole, policy to promote efficiency was mainly of the persuasive variety, described in party documents under the heading of 'equipping industry'. Labour publications gave prominence to science policy[60] (indicating a need to revise the orthodoxy that science policy only emerged as a central policy issue in 1959[61]). Increased funds were made available through the Department of Scientific and Industrial Research. The application of science to industry was emphasized through the National Research Development Corporation under the Development of Inventions Act, 1948, and a number of advisory committees, such as the Advisory Council on Scientific Policy, and the Defence Research Policy Committee. However, these attempts at the co-ordination of research had only temporary success, and the whole experiment was soon dominated by issues of defence and nuclear energy.[62]

A second set of policies in this area was an emphasis on standards of management and design. The Council of Industrial Design had been set up in December 1944, and the British Institute of Management in March 1946. The government increased grants to the British Standards Institution, but failed to reform it along lines proposed in party discussion documents, which described the body as largely controlled by big business and failing actively to promote standardization.[63]

Policy on efficiency also took the form of making industry 'put its own house in order'. Here two institutional initiatives were made. One was in the range of bodies established to promote improved productivity, especially the Productivity Efficiency Service (which grew out of a wartime Ministry of Aircraft Production Board), and the Anglo-American Council on Productivity.[64] The second initiative was policy on Development Councils, which involved a major institutional departure, and embodied some coercive measures.

The other major concern of Labour researchers was the establishment of a permanent relationship between private enterprise and a Labour government.[65] The issue was linked with the question of industrial democracy and a belief that efficiency could be improved, both in the public and private sectors by the active involvement of the work-force. The latter aim was not achieved. The advisory councils in cars and shipbuilding seem to have been little more than talking-shops.[66] Attempts were made to revive Joint Production Committees but success was limited, partly because of government anticipation of employer opposition.[67] The one permanent system with both private industry and unions was expressed in policy for Development Councils, which was also unsuccessful.

Only the system of government–industry relations embodied in the wartime controls persisted. Most controls relied on trade associations for the day-to-day allocations of raw materials, for instance, and they were also used as the representatives of a trade in the regulation of prices. Originally, however, trade associations had been formed to operate cartel agreements, and their extension into an arm of the wartime state represented a powerful combination of economic and avowedly political functions.[68] Although serving an immediate function in reconversion, it is still curious that the system of controls should have been taken over without any changes to the business personnel.[69] Indeed, the enhanced position of trade associations locked the government into a set of economic institutions which were to scupper any attempt to change the nature of government–industry relations, for instance through the Development Councils.

A final area where proposals were made to change the government's relationship with private industry was via the use of government wholesale agencies. G.D.N. Worswick, following suggestions made by E.F. Schumacher, proposed that the state monopolize the wholesale of key consumer items, such as foodstuffs and building materials, and so gain certain far-reaching powers, including the ability to promote standardization and break price rings. The idea was explicitly modelled on the existing practices of large private buyers like Marks and Spencers. In addition this power would allow the government to control retail outlets, an area of concern to the Labour government as a rich jungle of restrictive practices and resulting inefficiencies in the use of manpower.[70] This idea seems to have died, and actual policy on distribution was confined to yet another inquiry and a subsequent policy statement banning resale price maintenance.[71]

To conclude this review of Labour policies, the researchers and Labour writers of the 1945–51 period took the question of relations with private enterprise increasingly seriously. The debate on it became an issue at stake between the consolidators and the Labour Left.[72] The search for co-operation and the willingness to concede a large area for private enterprise meant that persuasion had to be the main method adopted.

Development Councils are an important illustration of these points. They embodied a faith in industrial democracy, and therefore carried the support of the Labour Left and the TUC, they embodied the commitment to co-operation, not conflict with private enterprise, the commitment to efficiency, science and research and better management, and they were often also seen as a way of achieving certain planning objectives. In the original TUC proposals they had also been seen as a way of dealing with the monopoly problem. Finally, they were the government's desired way of solving the question of how a permanent relationship was to be established with the private sector.[73]

The basic history of the Development Councils has been told elsewhere.[74] The following section uses the experience with Development Councils to illustrate the failure of Labour's hopes to co-operate with industry and thus achieve modernization and industrial restructuring.

A series of tripartite working parties between 1945 and 1947 investigated ways of improving efficiency in the consumer industries. Many recommended the establishment of permanent central bodies in the various industries to carry out working party recommendations and to provide a range of common services, such as R&D, standardization, marketing, recruitment and training of the work-force. The subsequent Industrial Organization and Development Act enabled Ministers to establish Development Councils. These were to be tripartite voluntaristic bodies, to be set up only where 'substantial' numbers in an industry wanted them. They were to provide the services described above, which Cripps, introducing the Bill in the House of Commons, said were 'essential to modern industrial development and progress' but which 'are sometimes available to large organizations but not to smaller organisations'.[75]

Cripps further described the Bill as one 'designed to provide methods for enabling private enterprise industries to bring themselves up-to-date and to make themselves as efficient in the production and in the distribution of their products as possible'.[76] He emphasized not only the broad aims but also the methods of co-operation with industry and of bringing employers and employees together to discuss the organization and development of the industry. The Act thus embodied a modernization strategy, introducing joint services and work-force involvement. It did not directly broach the issue of rationalization, preferring a certain flexibility in forms of industrial organization. It was thus a course which has been advocated since, albeit on a local and regional level, by some modern analysts of British economic decline.[77]

There were distinguishable trade union and business inputs into the legislation. The TUC's wartime proposals for 'industrial boards' prefigured the Development Councils, in seeing work-force involvement in management as crucial to the scheme.[78] Development Councils have also been seen as an extension of demands made by some business organizations since the 1930s, like the Industrial Reorganization League,[79] for statutory legally enforceable trade associations.[80] Indeed, Labour Party researchers were quite critical of the TUC's 'industrial boards', pointing out that they might do little more than add trade union representation to existing restrictionist trade associations.[81] In similar vein later commentators have expressed surprise at Labour's adoption of this policy.[82]

In fact, although the Development Councils have been described as 'distinctively Labourite', the government was clearly influenced in its choice of instruments by institutional innovations proposed by civil servants at the Board of Trade under the Coalition government. G.L. Watkinson, Under-Secretary at the Board of Trade, and his colleagues there were preoccupied with which 'industrial organization' would be best after the war. They submitted a memorandum entitled 'General support of trade', to the Steering Committee on Employment at the end of 1943. It proposed financial schemes to promote amalgamations in some industries, with legislation to set up tripartite industrial boards in industries that wished for them, to pursue such tasks as research, marketing, the improvement of design and standards, and recruitment and training of the work-force. An Industrial Commission was to oversee all these plans for industrial efficiency, and check any moves towards restrictive practices.[83]

The scheme was created after repeated frustration at industry's unwillingness to consider industrial restructuring, combined with fears about British productivity if industry was to remain small-scale, especially in motor cars, iron and steel and textiles. Watkinson was trying to overcome the weaknesses of the small firm without challenging its continuance, indeed seeing a fairly dynamic role for it:

> The object is to combine, as far as possible, the virtues of private initiative, and the flexibility and resilience resulting from numbers of independent firms, with co-operation among them in connection with various services, which, if undue waste and inefficiency are to be avoided, should be pooled for particular industries.[84]

His measures were intended to calm industrial hostility while encouraging industry to overcome expected post-war difficulties.[85]

The Coalition government had approved in principle the preparation of an Enabling Bill, which would allow industries to set up Boards for co-operative research and development 'on the lines of the Cotton Board', but preliminary soundings of the business community to the idea had yielded an ambiguous response. Cripps' interest in industrial efficiency, especially in improving design and management, prompted the resurrection of these schemes by Alix Kilroy and G.L. Watkinson at the Board of Trade, but incorporating Cripps' stress on 'the need to bring the workers fully into the picture'. The speedy establishment of the working parties is testament to Cripps' energy on the issue and his commitment to worker involvement, but this was brought to bear on schemes previously developed by civil servants.[86]

As a way of encouraging, let alone enforcing industrial reorganization and development, the Act allowing the creation of Development Councils was vague and weak and the results were minimal. Four Development Councils were established: the Cotton Board was reconstituted as a Development Council in April 1948, the Furniture Development Council and the Jewellery and Silver Development Council were established in April 1949 and the Clothing Industry Development Council in January 1950. The last two were dissolved on January 1953. In addition four industrial groups made use of Section 9 of the Act to raise levies for specific purposes. Levies for research were raised by the Wool Textile Research Council and by the Lace Research Association, and levies to promote exports were raised by the Wool Textile Export Corporation and the British Lace Furnishings (Overseas) Ltd. The Board of Trade also had extensive negotiations with wool, pottery, hosiery, cutlery, footwear, china clay and jute manufacturers.

The root cause of the failure of the Act was FBI opposition, which dated from the very moment of the introduction of the working parties and was not suddenly withdrawn after the Industrial Organization and Development Act came into force, as most writers have suggested.[87] Kipping makes this clear in his account of the working parties:

> I am sure this move was made with a constructive—one might say reconstructive—motive; but coming as it did on top of a campaign of denigration, it was taken as having a derogatory intention. Also it was interventionist and seemed to foreshadow compulsory legislation and government interference.[88]

After the first two working parties had reported in June 1946, both recommending some form of permanent tripartite body, Baillieu called a meeting of the employer members of all the working parties to consider the 'serious implications for industry as presently organized'.[89] In boots and shoes and heavy clothing employers dissented from the working parties' recommendations.[90] In October 1946 the joint FBI/BEC committee on trade organization made clear its commitment to the current system of trade associations and total opposition to an Enabling Act to establish industrial supervisory boards. These 'should never be forced upon an unwilling industry'.[91]

In spite of Conservative opposition, the Bill was enacted, but within a year, in June 1948, Wilson told the Cabinet Production Committee that 'progress had been hampered by the continued opposition of the employers and that, in his view, the time had come, if the Act was not to become a dead letter, to take some more drastic action.'[92] He therefore proposed to impose an Order establishing a Development Council in hosiery.

From this time on, the FBI sustained and organized direct opposition to Labour plans. The Grand Council of the FBI agreed the same month that 'the time had come to challenge the government on the issue.'[93] A month later a special meeting of the FBI's trade organization committee called together representatives of trade associations affected by the Development Councils policy to co-ordinate their response.[94] In June 1949, when the Cabinet was again preparing to press the issue, the FBI tacitly agreed to sabotage industrial policy. The imposition of Development Councils

> would jeopardise the constructive work which had been proceeding in the industries concerned, as well as prejudicing the attitude of industry to wider issues such as that of exports to hard currency areas, in which the Government were seeking the co-operation of free enterprise.[95]

The previous September Wilson had already been told that controversy over the issue could seriously impair production, so this was no idle threat.[96]

In November 1949 Parliament approved the Clothing Industry Development Council Order, which effectively allowed the government to establish a Council without industry's consent. The employers challenged the legality of the Order in the High Court, on the basis that the Act required that a 'substantial majority' of the industry should desire such a Council, and that this did not exist. In December 1949 Wilson laid a similar draft Order for a Development Council in the woollen industry before Parliament. Immediately the Wool Textile Delegation informed Wilson that they too would be taking proceedings in the courts. After some debate, and with obvious reluctance, the Cabinet agreed that the Wool Order should not be put before Parliament until the courts had given a ruling on the Clothing Industry Development Council Order.[97] The courts upheld the validity of the Order, but the Attorney-General told Wilson that the basis of the judgement was such that, in future, it would be dangerous to act in a case where there was no evidence of any support from the employers' side.[98]

The final admission of defeat came in July 1950 when Wilson recommended to the Production Committee, and it agreed, that the government should think about amending legislation to make clearer that the 'substantial number' referred to in Section 1(4) of the Act might consist of employers or employees or both, and that the Government must be free in the last resort to impose a Development Council against the wishes of one side of an industry.[99]

Meanwhile, given the absence of significant employer support for Councils in the remaining industries, except cutlery, he proposed to take no further steps towards establishing Development Councils until the next election, and only afterwards if Labour had 'a workable majority'.

This whole episode represented a complete defeat for the government at the hands of private industry. The scale of the defeat is apparent given the place of Development Councils in Labour's plans for the private sector.

What was the basis of business opposition?[100] First, some saw Development Councils as a half-way house to nationalization,[101] although the Board of Trade strove to disabuse them of the idea.[102] However, some businessmen were originally willing to tolerate Development Councils in order to avoid nationalization.[103] Thus fear of nationalization was a factor but does not explain opposition, which became more focused *after* the threat of nationalization had receded from 1948.

The most important factor was the threat, not to ownership, but to management. Employer hostility took two forms, described by Wilson as

> a feeling that Development Councils will diminish the influence and importance of trade associations, and a reluctance to accept anything which would give workers a statutory right to be brought into the consideration of matters which are regarded as largely the prorogative of management.[104]

Some businessmen were willing to accept that 'the time had arrived for trade union collaboration to be given some more permanent form'. However, the majority of employer members of the working parties present at the FBI's discussion of their value had grave misgivings about bringing trade unions permanently into 'financial and other questions in which they had not been concerned in the past'. Even the union presence on the working parties could be dismissed somewhat patronizingly, and many employers were opposed to any permanent body giving trade unions equal representation.[105]

Similarly, there were divisions among employers about the impact of Development Councils on the trade association system. Industries with weak and incomplete trade organization and a multiplicity of small manufacturers, like jewellery, found the notion of a comprehensive representative body useful. Other industries, like furniture, glassware and pottery, said they had found their working parties very useful, and welcomed the opportunity for co-operation in areas such as design and training.[106] However, strong opposition to the idea of Development Councils came from industries like linoleum, boots and shoes and heavy clothing, all with strong trade associations and each jealous of that association's rights.

Nevertheless, many industries were at first not unfavourable to considering the idea of permanent bodies, and it was the FBI which took the initiative in sounding an alarm. Civil servants and Wilson in fact believed that 'the common factor behind the uniformly unco-operative attitude of employers in different industries . . . was to be found in the policy of the FBI.'[107] In its traditional adherence to industrial self-government, the FBI emphasised that trade associations should be strengthened and extended but should have complete freedom from government intervention.[108] Indeed, the FBI saw one wartime corporatist plan, the National Policy for Industry, as a threat to its own position as the peak representative of industry.[109] Thus the FBI's fight to preserve the existing trade associations, was also a fight for its own position.

Central to FBI opposition was the statutory nature of the Development Councils. This would not only grant government and trade unions a power which 'would tend to weaken the right of management to manage', but would also put business members of the Councils in a position of divided loyalty.[110] Thus the FBI leadership had taken a hostile stance from the beginning. The delaying tactics it co-ordinated pushed the Labour government to compulsory methods. The subsequent history of successful opposition to the scheme illustrates the dangers faced by the Labour government when it departed from the framework of co-operation with private industry.

Changing economic circumstances also explain the absence of interest in schemes for industrial reorganization in the ranks of businessmen. The Labour government had introduced policies deriving from a combination of the rationalization movement and the use of 'industrial diplomacy' during the 1930s. However, under the conditions of a sellers' market much of the basis for industrial co-operation in rationalization was removed.[111]

The Labour government nevertheless retained a dogged commitment to the idea of Development Councils, because these embodied all its hopes for co-operation with industry. Recognition that the whole basis of the legislation rested on employer co-operation and that this vital ingredient was lacking forced the abandonment of the policy.[112] Reaction to the failure of the policy was bitter, however, and prompted a reconsideration of policy towards private enterprise. Wilson's paper showed deep disillusionment with the Development Councils. Their main limitation, he argued, was their consensual nature, and they lacked powers to 'force new capital expenditure, or even up-to-date methods of production . . . on the individual firm'. In particular 'they are not effective at the crucial point, the board room, where the decisions are taken.' The response of Wilson was to advocate stronger powers for the Councils, but also to proceed with other, more draconian powers elsewhere, including the establishment of price control on a permanent basis.[113] The Labour government was also to raise the idea of a further Development Council in a potentially controversial area—shipbuilding.[114] The scheme did not end in 1950, therefore, and saw a revival in the National Economic Development Councils of the 1960s.

Although successful in terms of reconversion to a peacetime economy, the period of the 1945–51 Labour government must represent something of a lost opportunity to reverse long-standing symptoms of industrial malaise. The study of Labour research papers and publications allows easy dismissal of claims that an 'anti- industrial spirit', and the sacrifice of industrial policy to the welfare state and New Jerusalem, were evident in the Labour Party's overall outlook. The actual industrial policies adopted were weak and only tinkered with 'the gigantic scale and depth of the problem',[115] but this situation was the result not of any failure to recognize the problem or emphasis on welfare before industry, being due rather to a perceived need to compromise with industrialists.

Of the many prescriptions that have been made for the historical solutions to Britain's industrial problems, two opposing views may be briefly discussed. This study shows that if enforced rationalization was the answer to British industrial decline, as Peter Hall maintains, it is on industrial organization and industrialists' attitudes that analysis should focus, and thus Hall emphasizes too much the inhibitiveness of trade unions.[116] In understanding the 'post-war conjuncture' as a moment in British industrial decline, the political and economic power wielded by industrial trade associations is most important.

On the other hand, Hirst's and Zeitlin's claims, based on a rejection of greater concentration as a solution to Britain's competitiveness, that governments have never considered the possibility of an 'industrial "public sphere"', is contradicted by the attempt to establish Development Councils. The experiment bears an uncanny resemblance to many, though not all, of their proposals, but floundered in the face of British industry's aversion to any interference with self-government in industry, either by the work-force or the state.

The other major area of debate is how to understand the parameters imposed on government policy by private industry. The Blank/Streat/Finer thesis that industry did not 'bitterly resist' or 'subvert' Labour government policies, that there was an absence of 'obstructiveness', and that relations were 'friendly',[117] cannot survive the opening of government and FBI records to public inspection. The experience with Development Councils shows that industry could be very obstructive when it felt that issues of ownership, control and the right to manage were at stake. It is crucial to Blank's outlook to prove that the cosy relationship between government and industry broke down later rather than sooner. A study of FBI documents indicates an immense fear of Labour from the very start and the beginnings of organizations geared to opposing Labour ideologically, and, through the trade organization committee of the FBI, politically. That 1949 brought a crisis in relations in indicative not of a change of heart in industry, but of a change of tactics.

In fact, perhaps the major parameter imposed on the Labour government by private industry was Labour's own commitment to the private enterprise system.[118] This prompted an inevitable reliance on voluntary and co-operative methods of control, an inability to compel, and the necessity for retreat in the face of opposition, and failure to sustain, therefore, 'modernizing' programmes. Certainly in the private sector, developments were not forced along new paths.[119] In this regard the period of the Labour government may be placed on a continuum stretching from the 1930s and the emergence of the 'managed economy.[120] That this was so, at least in relation to the Development Councils, is a tribute to the continuity provided by the Civil Service, operating in a vacuum of real alternative policies.

Notes

1. D. Coates, *The Labour Party and the Struggle for Socialism*, Cambridge, 1975, pp. 54–5, 62; J. Leruez, *Economic Planning and Politics in Britain*, Bath, 1975, pp. 61–2; K. Morgan, *Labour in Power*, Oxford, 1984, p. 130; A.A. Rogow and P. Shore, *The Labour Government and British Industry, 1945–1951*, Oxford, 1955, p. 7.
2. Labour Party Archives (hereafter LPA), R.D.R. 285/April 1945: 'Labour policy for privately owned industry'.
3. CAB124/1200: memo by H. Wilson, 'The state and private industry', 4 May 1950.
4. B. Pimlott, *Labour and the Left in the 1930's*, Cambridge, 1977, p. 201.
5. R. Eatwell, *The 1945–51 Labour Governments*, 1979, p. 100.
6. Rogow and Shore, *op. cit.*; R. Brady, *Crisis in Britain*, 1950.
7. C.A.R. Crosland, 'The transition from capitalism', in R.H.S. Crossman (ed.) *New Fabian Essays*, 3rd edn, 1970, pp. 33–68.
8. For an archetypal example of this focus, see A. Cairncross, *Years of Recovery*, 1985. A criticism of it is A. Robinson, 'The economic problems of the transition from war to peace: 1945–49', *Journal of Economics*, vol. 10 (June 1986) 165–85.
9. H. Macmillan, *The Middle Way*, 1938, pp. 237–8; and H. Macmillan, *Tides of Fortune, 1945–1955*, 1969, p. 74; Labour Party, 'Let us face the future', in F.W.S. Craig (ed.) *British Election Manifestos 1900–1974*, 2nd. edn, 1975.
10. Rogow and Shore, *op. cit.*, 76; Morgan, *op. cit.*, 129.
11. S. Blank, *Industry and Government in Britain: the F.B.I. in Politics, 1945–65*, Farnborough, 1973, p. 85.
12. S. Brooke, 'Revisionists and fundamentalists: the Labour Party and economic policy during the Second World War', *Historical Journal*, vol. 32, no. 1 (1989) 157–75.
13. C. Barnett, *The Audit of War*, 1986.
14. S. Newton and D. Porter, *Modernisation Frustrated*, 1988, p. x.
15 Robinson, *op. cit.*, 169.
16. B. Fine and L. Harris, *The Peculiarities of the British Economy*, 1985; S. Wilks, *Industrial Policy and the Motor Industry*, Manchester, 1984.
17. N. Kipping, *Summing Up*, 1972, p. 16.
18. Ibid.
19. Ibid.
20. Modern Records Centre University of Warwick (hereafter MRC), CBI Predecessor Archive MSS200/F/1/1/215: Minutes of the President's Advisory Committee, 8 August 1945.
21. MRC, MSS200/F/1/1/188: Minutes of the Grand Council, 22 August 1945.
22. Ibid. and MRC, MSS200/F/1/1/215: Minutes of the President's Advisory Committee 8 August 1945.
23. Ibid.
24. MRC, MSS200/F/3/D3/5/26: letter R. Maudling (Conservative Party researcher) – Sir N. Kipping, 25 May 1946.
25. Blank, *op. cit.*, 77.
26. MRC, MSS200/F/1/1/215: Minutes of the President's Advisory Committee, 26 March 1946 and 29 April 1946.
27. MRC, MSS200/F/1/1/215: Minutes of the President's Advisory Committee, 29 April 1946.

28. T. Barna, 'Those "frightfully high" profits', *Oxford University Bulletin of Statistics*, vol. 11, no. 2 (July 1949), 213–26.
29. Cairncross, *op. cit.*, 466.
30. J.W. Grove, *Government and Industry in Britain*, 1962, p. 250.
31. Ibid., 257; Brady, *op. cit.*, 549–51.
32. Rogow and Shore, *op. cit.*, pp. 49–71.
33. MRC, MSS200/F/3/D3/5/26: memo by Kipping on the post-war world (n.d. but c. 1947).
34. K. Middlemas, *Power, Competition and the State. Volume 1: Britain in search of balance 1940–61*, Basingstoke, 1986, p. 205; Blank, *op. cit.*, 97–8.
35. H. Mercer, 'The evolution of British government policy towards competition in private industry, 1940–1956', unpublished Ph.D. thesis, University of London, 1989, pp. 134–6.
36 CAB117/199: note A.S.J. Baster – Sir Alfred Hurst, 9 June 1942; A.S.J. Baster, *The Little Less*, 1947.
37. L.S.E. Dalton Papers, Diaries I, Box 30, 27 June 1944.
38. N. Harris, *Competition and the Corporate Society*, 1972, pp. 59–60; J. Hoffman, *The Conservative Party in Opposition, 1945–51*, 1964, p. 133.
39. Harris, *op. cit.*, 46; L. Johnman in this volume; Mercer, *op. cit.*, 123–34.
40. J. Singleton, 'Planning for cotton, 1945–1951' *Economic History Review*, vol. 43, no. 1 (February 1990) 71. A different emphasis is given in M.W. Dupree, 'Struggling with destiny: the cotton industry, overseas trade policy and the Cotton Board, 1940–1959', *Business History*, vol. 32, no. 4 (October 1990) 106–28.
41. I. Taylor, 'War and the development of Labour's domestic programme', unpublished Ph.D. thesis, University of London, 1977.
42. 'Let us face the future', in Craig, *op. cit.*
43. G.D.H. Cole, *Labour's Second Term*, Fabian Tract No. 273, May 1949, pp. 7–8.
44. M. Young, *Labour's Plan for Plenty*, 1947; LPA R.D.1/September 1945: 'A Labour policy for privately-owned industry'; R.D.32/October 1946: 'Research programme 1946–47'; Labour Party, *Speakers' Handbook 1949–1950*, 1949, pp. 120–62; Labour Party, *Labour Believes in Britain*, April 1949; CAB124/1200: memo by H. Wilson, 'The state and private industry', 4 May 1950.
45. LPA, R.D.69/October 1947: G. Miller, 'Socialism and private enterprise', and Home Policy Committee Minutes 25 November 1947; LPA, R.D.128/July 1948: 'Proposed membership of election programme sub-committees'.
46. BT13/220A M/M/24: memo by S. Cripps, 'Draft directive to the Board of Trade', 28 August 1945.
47. LPA, R.D.69/October 1947: G. Miller, 'Socialism and private enterprise'.
48. LPA, Home Policy Committee Minutes, 25 November 1947; Morgan *op. cit.*, 121.
49. LPA, R.D.147/September 1948: M. Young, 'Policy for private ownership'.
50. LPA, R.D.236/December 1948: 'Report to Policy Committee of subcommittee on privately-owned industry'.
51. Ibid.; LPA, R.D.69/October 1947: G. Miller, 'Socialism and private enterprise'.
52. R. Miliband, *Parliamentary Socialism*, 2nd edn, 1973, p. 289; J. Schneer, *Labour's Conscience: the Labour Left 1945–51*, Boston, 1988, pp. 143–51.
53. Labour Party, *Speakers' Handbook*, op. cit., 122.
54. LPA, Policy Committee Minutes, 25 July 1944.
55. LPA, R.D.60/July 1947: 'The public control of monopolies', revised memoran-

dum for the Trusts and Cartels Committee.
56. Cmd. 8274, *A Statement on Resale Price Maintenance* (P.P. 1950–1, vol. 27); Mercer, op. cit., 190–2, 226–7.
57. LPA, R.D.1/September 1945: 'A Labour policy for privately-owned industry'.
58. BT64/279: report by the Central Price Regulation Committee, 'Prices of radio valves', 1946.
59. N. Rollings, '"The Reichstag System of Government"—the Labour government and controls', in H. Mercer, N. Rollings and J. Tomlinson, *The Attlee Governments and Private Industry*, Edinburgh, forthcoming; CAB124/1200: op. cit.
60. For instance, Young, *op. cit.*, 90–2.
61. J.B. Poole and K. Andrews (eds) *The Government of Science in Britain*, 1972.
62. N. Vig, 'Policies for science and technology in Great Britain: post-war developments and reassessment', in T.D. Long and C. Wright (eds) *Science Policies of Industrial Nations*, New York, 1975, p. 65; D. Edgerton, 'Science and technology in British business history', *Business History*, vol. 29, no. 4 (December 1987) 84–99.
63. LPA, R.D.199/November 1948: J. Stewart Cook, 'Memorandum on standardisation'; Young, *op. cit.*, 92–3.
64. J. Tomlinson, 'Productivity policy', in Mercer et. al., *op. cit.*
65. BT13/220A M/M/24: S. Cripps, 'Draft directive to the Board of Trade', 28 August 1945; Young, *op. cit.* 86–9.
66. L. Johnman, 'The shipbuilding industry', and N. Tiratsoo, 'The motor vehicle industry' in Mercer et. al., *op. cit.*
67 J. Tomlinson, 'Labour's management of the national economy 1945–51', *Economy and Society*, vol. 18, no. 1 (February 1989) 17.
68. PEP *Government and Industry*, 1952, pp. 155–60.
69. Rogow and Shore, *op. cit.*, 60.
70. LPA, R.D.1/September 1945: 'Labour policy for privately-owned industry'; E.F. Schumacher, 'An essay on state control of business', *Agenda*, vol. 3 (February 1944) 42–60.
71. Cmd. 8274, *Resale Price Maintenance*, op. cit.
72. Schneer, *op. cit.*, 94–6.
73. Young, *op. cit.*, 86–89.
74. Brady, *op. cit.* 531–68; R.S. Edwards and H. Townsend, *Business Enterprise*, 1961, pp. 386–91; P.D. Henderson, 'Development Councils: an industrial experiment', in G.D.N. Worswick and P.H. Ady (eds) *The British Economy 1945–1950*, Oxford 1952, pp. 452–62; Rogow and Shire, *op. cit.*, 76–80.
75. *Hansard*, vol. 433, cols 547–9, 13 February 1947.
76. Ibid.
77. P. Hirst and J. Zeitlin, 'Flexible specialisation and the competitive failure of UK manufacturing', *Political Quarterly*, vol. 60, no. 2 (1989) 172.
78. TUC, *Interim Report on Post-War Reconstruction*, 1944, paras 63–81.
79. T. Smith, *The Politics of the Corporate Economy*, Oxford, 1979, p. 37.
80. PEP, 'Development Councils', *Planning*, vol. 17, no. 326 (March 1951) 210–13; Rogow and Shore, op. cit., 79; Brady, *op. cit.*, 555–8.
81. LPA, R.D.1/September 1945: 'Labour policy for privately-owned industry'.
82. Brady, *op. cit.*, 557; Rogow and Shore, *op. cit.*, 79.
83. CAB87/63 E.C. (43) 4: memo by the Board of Trade, 'General support of trade', 15 October 1943; Barnett, *op. cit.*, 268–74; and Middlemas, *op. cit.*, 80.

84. CAB87/63: E.C. (43) 4, memo by the Board of Trade, 'General support of trade', 15 October 1943.
85. BT64/3346: note G.L. Watkinson – H. Dalton with draft memorandum on general support of trade, 1 September 1943.
86. BT64/2180: note A. Kilroy to G.L. Watkinson, 6 August 1945, minute by A. Kilroy, 21 August 1945, and comment by Cripps on this, 23 August 1945; BT64/3607: memo by A. Kilroy, 'Industrial Development Boards', 27 September 1945; BT13/220A: minutes of the President's morning meetings, 9 August 1945 and 20 August 1945; BT13/220A M/M-19: memo by S. Cripps, 'Reorganisation of industry', 21 August 1945. Watkinson's denial of Civil Service involvement in policy-making seems disingenuous, see M. Dupree (ed.) *Lancashire and Whitehall: The Diary of Sir Raymond Streat. Volume* 2, Manchester, 1987, entry for 3 September 1945, p. 281.
87. Blank, *op. cit.*, 87; P.D. Henderson op. cit., 458–9; Rogow and Shore, *op. cit.*, 65.
88. Kipping, *op. cit.*, 17.
89. MRC, MSS200/F/1/1/188: Grand Council Minutes, 10 July 1946.
90. BT13/220A: M.M. (46) 48, note for President's morning meeting, 'Boot and shoe working party'; CAB132/5: L.P. (46) 252, memo by S. Cripps for Lord President's Committee 'Industrial Organisation Bill', 14 October 1946; TUC archives, Modern Records Centre, of Warwick University MSS292/560.1/5 Economic Committee 1/1: 'The formation of Development Councils', 8 October 1947.
91. MRC, MSS200/F/1/1/188: Grand Council Minutes 9 October 1946, and FBI/BEC, *Trade Organisation—Relationship with the government*, October 1946.
92. CAB134/636: P.C. (48), 13th meeting, 2 July 1948.
93. MRC MSS200/F/1/1/188: Grand Council Minutes, 9 June 1948.
94. MRC MSS200/F/1/1/215: Minutes of the Trade Organization Committee, July 1948.
95. MRC MSS200/F/1/1/190: Minutes of the Grand Council, 15 June 1949.
96. BT64/2357: Brief for the President of the Board of Trade, 2 September 1948.
97. CAB128/16: CM (49), 70th meeting, 8 December 1949.
98. CAB134/647 P.C. (50) 72: memo by H. Wilson for the Production Committee, 'Development Councils under the Industrial Organisation and Development Act', 5 July 1950.
99. Ibid.
100. Various reasons have been given, see 'Development Councils', *Planning*, vol. 27, no. 326 (March 1951); Blank, *op. cit.*, 86; Henderson, *op. cit.*, 459; Rogow and Shore, *op. cit.*, 82–3.
101. MRC MSS200/F/1/1/215: meeting of employer members of the working parties, 24 September 1946.
102. BT64/2357: Minutes of the National Production Advisory Council for Industry, 23 July 1948; *Hansard*, vol. 433, col. 550, 13 February 1947.
103. MRC MSS200/F/1/1/215: Meeting of employer members of working parties, 14 June 1946.
104. BT64/2357: P.C. (48) 41, Memo by H. Wilson to the Cabinet Production Committee, 'Development Councils under the Industrial Organisation and Development Act 1947', 19 March 1948.
105. MRC, MSS200/F/1/1/215: Meeting of employer members, 14 June 1946.
106. Ibid.
107. BT64/2357: 'Proposals for further action on the establishment of Development Councils', 2 January 1948.

108. FBI *Reconstruction: A Report by the Federation of British Industries*, 1942.
109. Mercer, op. cit., 133.
110. MRC MSS200/F/1/1/215: Meeting of employer members, 14 June 1946.
111. P.D. Henderson, op. cit.
112. CAB134/647: P.C. (50) 72, memo by H. Wilson, 'Development Councils under the Industrial Organisation and Development Act', 5 July 1950.
113. CAB124/1200: memo by H. Wilson, 'The state and private industry', 4 May 1950.
114. Johnman in this volume.
115. Barnett, *op. cit.*, 270–1.
116. P. Hall, 'The state and economic decline', in B. Elbaum and W. Lazonick (eds) *The Decline of the British Economy*, Oxford, 1986, pp. 274–6.
117. Blank, *op. cit.*, 75. He is citing R. Streat, 'Government consultation with industry', *Public Administration*, vol. 34 (Spring 1959), and S.E. Finer, 'The political power of private capital', *Sociological Review*, vol. 4, no. 1 (1956).
118. R. Miliband, *The State in Capitalist Society*, 1969, p. 77.
119. Morgan, *op. cit.*, vii for a contrary view.
120. P. Addison, *The Road to 1945*, 1975; A. Booth, 'Britain in the 1930's: a managed economy?', *Economic History Review*, vol. 40, no. 4 (November 1987), 499–522.

6 The Labour government and the trade unions, 1945–51

Jim Tomlinson

If 1945 was the apogee of the Labour Party's electoral fortunes, it was also in the late 1940s that trade unions in Britain reached the peak of their influence.[1] This by no means simply reflected the election of a Labour government, but fundamentally rested on the transformation in the labour market during the Second World War and the political consequences of that transformation. Essentially during the war labour as a factor of production became *the* constraining factor in the war economy, the ultimate resource by which the war effort was planned.[2] This economically vital role was transformed into major political gains by the general recognition that labour's new-found strength must be conciliated and adjusted to, and more specifically by the use of labour's bargaining power by the wartime Ministry of Labour and National Service, headed by Ernest Bevin, to advance the position of labour and the trade unions.[3] All this amounted to a fundamental shift of influence towards labour and its organizations by the end of the war.[4]

By the Labour Party's coming to power in 1945, trade union membership had risen to almost 8 million from a low of 4.5 million in 1931, and the figure continued to rise until 1948. The TUC, as undisputed mouthpiece of the unions, was represented on one government committee in 1932, on twelve in 1939 and on sixty by 1948.[5] However, trade unions were not, of course, just an 'outsider' pressure group on the Labour government but an integral part of the 'Labour movement' of which the government was, in ambiguous degree, the ultimate expression. This intimate relationship is most obviously illustrated by the 120 trade union sponsored members out of 393 newly elected Labour MPs, six of whom became Cabinet ministers. By far the most important of these was Ernest Bevin, who played a key role not only directly in foreign affairs but on a variety of domestic issues.[6]

What was the relationship between the Labour government and these newly powerful trade unions? The existing historiography generally paints a picture of a compliant trade union movement, almost always anxious, in some eyes over-anxious, to support 'its' government through thick and thin. Morgan talks of an 'intimate symbiosis between unions and the Labour Party', for which he sees the main causal factor as the 'community of outlook between the ideas and instincts of the Labour Party and the TUC at every stage, from 1945 onwards'.[7] Allen's detailed study of trade union–government relations suggested that

> the main advantages from a trade union and Labour government relationship have gone to the government. Trade unions from 1945 to 1951 were loath to exert pressure on the government because they did not want to embarrass it and they made concessions to enable the Government to implement its policy.[8]

Panitch concurs in this argument, seeing a triumph for the Labour government's attempts to assert the national interest over the potential claims for working-class power represented by trade union militancy.[9]

Dissent from this view of a largely compliant trade unionism has been voiced. The main originator of this argument seems to be Roberts, who argued that 'of all the pressure groups to which the Labour Government might be vulnerable the trade unions were the most powerful and the most awkward to deal with', and that the unions were unappreciative of the dilemmas of economic policy, wanting 'absolute full employment, cheap money, massive government expenditure, stable prices and freedom to bargain for higher wages as and when they liked, without limitation'.[10] This very general condemnation of the unions' role is mainly based on one specific policy area—that of wage relativities and their relation to trying to attract labour to the undermanned industries of the late 1940s. Roberts argues that the crucial barrier to such a planned allocation of labour was the unions' attachment to free collective bargaining, and their unwillingness to be turned by manpower planning into administrative agencies of the state.[11] Beer, largely basing himself on Roberts, argues for a general picture of 'trade unions versus planned economy' under the Attlee government,[12] and Pelling echoes this approach.[13]

To assess how far in fact the trade unions did act as a constraint on the Labour government requires first of all a clear idea of the objectives that the government was pursuing. In this chapter the focus is on economic policy, thus ignoring, for example, the significant contribution the unions made to social welfare policy in this period. What were the main economic policy objectives of the Attlee government?

The pre-eminent objective was undoubtedly to correct the balance of payments, which, especially in relation to the dollar area, was in chronic disequilibrium almost throughout 1945–51. This objective in turn led to an emphasis on constraining consumption, diverting resources into exports and investment, and above all encouraging the growth of production and productivity.[14] Policy was also concerned to control inflation, partly for balance of payments reasons. However, this policy objective, and the incomes policy of 1948–50 which flowed from it, has played an excessive part in the historiography of the Labour government and its relations with the unions, based no doubt on the post-war obsession with wage costs as the (implausible) central problem of British economic policy.[15]

The central issue addressed in this chapter is then, how far did the trade unions constrain the Labour government in achieving its policy objectives of raising production and productivity, without a parallel increase in personal consumption, in order to overcome its balance of payments inheritance? These objectives may helpfully be subdivided into three policy areas: the 'manning up' of undermanned industry, the attempt to raise industrial production and productivity, and the attempt to maintain exports by holding wages in check. Each of these will be addressed in turn.

'Undermanning' arose from the failure of demobilized workers to return to certain industries in numbers sufficient to supply the output which was strongly demanded at this time. This problem arose especially in coal, textiles and agriculture.[16] In the war period labour allocation had been central to the planning of the war, and many people on the Left at the war's end saw some kind of manpower budgeting as the way to ensure both full employment and an appropriate allocation of labour. In fact, whilst the wartime state had acquired unprecedented and ferocious powers of labour control, these had been used very sparingly and most labour distribution relied on traditional methods of market-based recruitment and allocation.[17]

For the Labour government the problem may be seen in general terms as a clash between a strong if underspecified commitment to economic planning, which logically implied the planning of wages and labour, and a very strong commitment to the traditional voluntary pattern of collective bargaining. As noted above, some commentators have seen this as essentially a clash between a desire by the government to plan, and a successful resistance by the trade unions to accept the upsetting of traditional differentials in order to attract labour into the undermanned industries by higher wages. However, as an account of the issue this story plainly will not do.

The Attlee government never decided in favour of 'wage planning' as a response to the problem of undermanned industries. Certainly such a response was widely discussed throughout the years of Labour government. In late 1945 a working Party was set up on wages policy, which reported in early 1946.[18] In the discussion of this at the Lord President's Committee (a crucial home policy committee), Morrison, the Lord President, suggested that 'much of the agitation for a national wages policy was meaningless', and endorsed the Working Party's rejection of anything more than a body to educate trade union and employer opinion on national economic needs to be considered in pay bargaining.[19]

However, there were dissenting voices. Emanuel Shinwell (Minister of Fuel and Power) argued for a wages policy based on three elements: a minimum wage, higher wages in unattractive industries, and in other circumstances wage increases to be based on increased productivity. Shinwell pursued this matter, and produced a written proposal for such a policy, which was responded to by George Isaacs, the Minister of Labour.[20] In his paper Shinwell argued that a wages policy was needed to deal both with the potential inflationary effects of full employment and the difficulty of adjusting wages to cope with the undermanning problem. His proposed solution was a tripartite National Wages Authority to, amongst other things, set wages to attract sufficient recruits to the undermanned industries. Isaacs' opposition was centrally based on the belief that such an authority would turn every wage negotiation into a political issue, and in addition undermine the whole basis of wage determination by consent, at present secured via the trade unions' ability to negotiate freely.

In the debate on these two memoranda, Shinwell argued that without some wage planning such as his, 'it would be idle for the government to claim that they were pursuing a policy of economic planning'.[21] Whilst Morrison and Isaacs strongly opposed such a policy, Shinwell was by no means alone in advocating it, and the issue was referred to another committee, the Steering Committee on Economic Development, and from there to the Ministerial Committee on Economic Planning. Here much the same arguments were produced, and the opposition of the key ministers, Morrison and Isaacs, seems to have prevented the policy from going further.[22] The one result of all this was the revival of the National Joint Advisory Council (NJAC) as a tripartite (TUC/British Employers Confederation/Government) body to consult on wage issues, and in the government's eyes, educate the other parties in economic realities.[23]

This debate over the scale of governmental intervention in wage bargaining continued throughout the lifetime of the Labour government albeit in different guises. In 1947 for example, discussion focused on the proposal for a 'central arbitration tribunal', and later, on TUC fears that the government's anti-inflationary stance would lead to radical change in wage-setting.[24] These debates tended to be highly repetitive, and at most led to proposals for new advisory bodies.[25] The government's view throughout was aptly summarized by Attlee: 'We have always taken the line that wages must be fixed by the two sides in industry; but in considering these wages we wanted both sides to take into account the particular economic position of the country'.[26] Whilst of course the 1948–50 period saw the government intervene significantly in *overall* wage bargaining, it never went beyond exhortation as far as relative wages were concerned.

As the above account of the debate shows, despite pressure from some ministers the government never emerged with a wages policy for the undermanned industries. Equally there was no monolithic trade union opposition to such a policy. For example, at the 1945 TUC Conference, L.J. Gregory of the ETU urged the unions to develop a 'wage strategy that corresponds to a planned economy of a Labour government', a proposal strongly opposed by the General Council.[27] As Panitch rightly points out, there was a significant minority of trade unionists who in the early post-war years followed through the logic of their belief in economic planning by urging a wage plan.[28]

There was a division in the Labour movement at this time over the degree of state intervention in wage bargaining, but this was by no means a division between government and unions. Rather it was (in 1945–7) a broadly Left/Right ideological split, with the Left's enthusiasm for economic planning fighting the Right's emergent pragmatism on planning. There may also have been some tendency for those ministers most clearly affected by labour shortages (Shinwell with coal, Ben Smith for food) to see the urgency of doing something about labour supply, in contrast to those more remote from the issue. Within the trade union movement the issue was curiously recast by the government's lurch into incomes policy from 1948. Now it was the Right generally who urged acceptance of the policy in the name of loyalty to the government, whilst the Left, who could see the new policy had little to do with planning as they understood it, recovered their faith in free collective bargaining.[29]

The failure of the Attlee government to adopt wage planning was not a consequence of trade union opposition. This is not by any means to deny the commitment of most trade unionists to voluntarism in industrial relations, to the idea of free collective bargaining. However, this was by no means a purely trade union view, for it permeated not just the Labour Party but many other political forces as well. In that sense the *laissez-faire* tradition of industrial relations remained strikingly unchallenged by wartime and post-war reform. As Morgan notes, this was one area where reform was never mooted: 'The government and the TUC made no effort to alter the adversarial character of relations between labour and management—even while, ironically enough, Britain was encouraging moves towards *Mitbestimmung* in Western Germany at precisely this period.'[30] The government's reform of industrial relations was largely limited to the straightforward reversal of the 1927 Trade Union and Trade Disputes Act, discussion of which seems to have generated no issues about the general pattern of British industrial relations.[31] In a curious way, as Middlemas notes, 'the Second World War experience encouraged a somewhat complacent and very insular belief in the value of British institutions and traditions, especially when these were compared with those of other European nations.'[32] This would apply to nothing more strongly than the institution of free collective bargaining.

The strength of the commitment to free collective bargaining in a paradoxical manner eased one potential trade union constraint on the government's economic policies. Many people in the 1940s saw the direction of labour as a superior alternative to wage planning. This would seem in part to account for the TUC's acceptance of the direction of labour under the reintroduced Control of Engagement Order in 1947. Indeed, the TUC showed notably more enthusiasm for such direction than its wage bargaining counterpart, the British Employers' Confederation (BEC).[33] In the event little was done with the government's new powers, largely as a result of the feeling that freedom of labour movement was a basic freedom, which only the direst emergency could justify restricting.

Recent historiography has emphasized the extent to which the Attlee government's economic policy agenda was dominated by attempts to raise production and productivity. This followed rapidly from the recognition that the pre-eminent goal of full employment was threatened, not by a lack of demand but by the incapacity to finance a full employment level of imports. The desire to raise production quickly led to a focus on productivity (mainly labour productivity), for it was quickly realized that with full employment and a capital stock unable to expand quickly in the short run, enhanced productivity in combination with labour reallocation to the undermanned industries was the only way to raise production.[34]

This campaign to raise production and productivity had no single policy instrument—indeed, the whole area might be seen as characterized by rather unclear diagnoses and prescriptions for the problem. But undoubtedly many initiatives were taken.[35] As with policy in most areas, in pursuing higher production and productivity the government put a lot of emphasis on gaining the consent and, if possible, support of unions and employers. At the highest level this meant most initiatives in this area were brought before the National Production Advisory Council for Industry (NPACI), or where the issue impacted on wage bargaining, the NJAC.[36] A reading of the minutes of these two bodies show a clear pattern of positive response by the unions to governmental initiatives on production and productivity issues. Only right at the beginning of NPACI was union opposition voiced, when Citrine objected to the Production Efficiency Service, basically a government-sponsored management consultancy, on the grounds that this meant government help to raise private profits and would threaten increased unemployment. Such objections were quickly withdrawn on a promise of full consultation with the unions.[37]

The picture that emerges from the minutes of these bodies is of a trade union movement fully backing government initiatives as long as proper procedures are followed and consultation takes place. On a number of issues the unions were critical of the employers for not fully backing government initiatives to raise production and productivity. This point and others can best be discussed by looking in more detail at some of the government's policy initiatives.

Best known of these initiatives is undoubtedly the Anglo-American Council on Productivity (AACP).[38] The initiative for the AACP came from the American head of the European Co-operation Administration, the body set up to administer Marshall Aid in 1948. The Chancellor of the Exchequer, Stafford Cripps, enthusiastically responded to the idea of a non-governmental, employer/union body as a way of involving the Federation of British Industries (FBI), BEC and the TUC in the productivity drive—and also as a way of evading governmental responsibility if the drive failed.[39]

Both unions and employers seem to have welcomed the AACP as a way of getting the government 'off their backs'. The employers in particular used the existence of the AACP as a reason for trying to resist other government productivity initiatives.[40]

The TUC support from the AACP evoked significant hostility from within the trade union movement. In particular there was a quite common belief that the AACP threatened the importation of the worst of US industrial relations. As one Trades Council put it, 'The introduction of American methods, such as the Taft-Hartley anti-union bill, the use of tear gas against strikers, lynching and the Ku-Klux-Klan, will not increase productivity.'[41]

However, the TUC saw definite advantages in both responding positively to the government's initiative and in simultaneously gaining as much as possible of the productivity drive under its own control. It was also believed that the AACP would provide a means of reducing 'unfair' criticism of

British industry. Jack Tanner of the AEU argued that 'criticism has been levelled by certain Americans as semi-official visits to this country not against the British workers but against managements and he thought it would not be harmful for American industrialists to realise the difficulties which British industry was facing.'[42] Such arguments led to unanimous support amongst the General Council for TUC participation in the AACP.[43]

Once the principle of participation was accepted, the main area of activity quickly proved to be the sending of 'teams' from British industry to the United States and the production and dissemination of 'Teams Reports' on their findings. Some sixty-six reports were produced, forty-nine on specific industrial sectors and the rest on specific functions, for example, management accounting. It was a condition of TUC involvement in the AACP that all the sector teams included workers, almost all of whom were also union members. Apart from a few problems of communists being excluded by the Americans,[44] more difficult for the TUC was the role of Trade Associations in putting up some of the money for the team visits and therefore acquiring a veto on union members. This led to difficulties, most notably in the Steel-Founding Report, where the union, piqued by the team selection process and the handling of the final report, issued their own highly critical 'Observations on the steel-founding productivity team's report'. For this the union executive was hauled over the coals by the TUC General Council, who denounced the 'Observations' as full of distortion and omission and calculated to 'influence shop stewards to take an antagonistic view of the Report'.[45]

This incident reflected the strength of the TUC's public commitment to the AACP. This did not mean they had a passive role on the Production Council. For example, they were highly critical of both an early internal assessment of the AACP team visits and a later consultant's report which after much amendment became a book which rather glibly and one-sidely tried to summarize the work of the AACP.[46]

This hostility from the TUC was aroused by the tendency in these reports, following many of the individual team reports, to give space to highly tendentious disquisitions on the alleged characteristics of the 'American way of life'. These the TUC thought ill-informed, opinionated and unhelpful.[47]

The TUC also resisted the employers' tendency to use the AACP as a place for expressing their opposition to certain aspects of the Attlee government's economic policies, especially high taxation with its alleged effects on investment levels. Tewson, the TUC General Secretary, was particularly keen to emphasize that the AACP should work within the existing constraints on investment, and focus attention on improving productivity with existing equipment.[48]

This approach could, of course, be highly problematic for the trade unions: was higher productivity to be bought at the price of harder work, longer hours and the erosion of traditional union practices? This was the not ungrounded fear of some on the Left who saw the AACP as a way of attacking labour standards in the United Kingdom.

This view was, not surprisingly, resisted by the TUC. In concert with the employers they resisted attempts by the US members of the Council to place restrictive practices (both employers' and unions') at the centre of the AACP agenda.[49] Second, the TUC seems to have been quite successful in making industrial relations issues appear as not the key to Britain's productivity problems. Whilst it is very difficult to summarize the contents of sixty-six reports, I do not see the AACP as having by and large ended as a propaganda victory for employers' views of where British industry's difficulties lay.[50]

From the point of view of the overall theme of this chapter, the success of the TUC in stopping the AACP from focusing on worker effort and related issues may be seen as problematic. Does it mean that the unions were able to prevent the AACP from exposing the 'real' problems of British industry, and hence constraining the necessary changes in industry? On balance the answer seems to be that the team reports were largely the unconstrained products of the teams themselves, dominated as they were by managerial personnel, so that they therefore cannot be seen as ignoring the 'real truth' about British industry. The TUC's main concern was to stop the reports from degenerating into vague generalities on the 'competitive spirit' or 'spirit of enterprise' in the United States, which they probably rightly thought would do most to undermine worker and union support for the AACP.[51]

In sum the TUC played a positive role in the AACP and indeed, was keener in its reports than the employers, who were rather negative about the exercise, especially wnen it became apparent that the teams' pronouncements were not going to be a means of reinforcing employers' prejudices either on broad political issues like taxation or on the fault of the worker for Britain's poor productivity performance.[52]

Another, if lesser-known, part of the productivity drive was the attempt to revive Joint Production Committees (JPCs), bipartite factory level bodies which had flourished in many sectors of industry in the war period. This was one area where the trade unions seem to have taken the initiative, the TUC pressing for the revival of JPCs before this issue was taken up by the government.[53]

Employers were less than enthusiastic at the idea of a revival of JPCs, which they saw as a potential source of challenge to managerial prerogatives, but eventually it was agreed at the NJAC that unions and employers should be encouraged to set them up 'for the regular exchange of views between employers and workers on production questions'. This was subject to three qualifications: that the machinery would be purely voluntary and advisory in character, would not deal with terms and conditions of employment, and would be only in the form that each industry individually decided.[54]

JPCs undoubtedly expanded in numbers from 1947 onwards, but to an unquantifiable extent.[55] Expansion seems to have been largely limited by employer resistance.[56] Resistance seems to have stiffened as employer–government relations generally worsened from mid-1948, as the government made clear its intention of pressing on with steel nationalization and compulsorily imposing Development Councils in some industries (see p. 98 below).

This slow pace of expansion was resented by many trade unions, who, along with the Labour Party Conference, pressed for their adoption to be made compulsory. However, the TUC was divided on this issue, fearing that compulsion would mean JPCs in non-unionized firms and that this would cut across them as *union*/employer bodies.[57] The government resisted compulsion, partly because of the fears of employer opposition, partly because of the strong Ministry of Labour desire not to disrupt existing good industrial relations.[58] In addition, Cripps, the main government enthusiast for JPCs, was very keen on the psychological approach to JPCs, which emphasized the beneficial effects on productivity of worker involvement. This emphasis on the consensual and co-operative basis of such bodies obviously contradicted the idea of making them compulsory.[59]

The government saw JPCs very much in the context of production and productivity, certainly not as part of a drive for industrial democracy or workers' control. Indeed, ministers tended to stress the dangers of JPCs 'overreaching' themselves in a manner parallel to the fears of employers.[60] Undoubtedly there were trade unionists who saw JPCs in a more radical light, and wanted to use them to challenge managerial prerogatives,[61] but they were in a small minority. There was a substantial convergence between the official trade union and the Ministry of Labour views of JPCs. They were to be encouraged as a limited expansion of consultation, fully compatible with the traditional pattern of good industrial relations, and not in any way an attempt to usurp managers' right to executive powers in the enterprise.[62]

Another significant initiative which may be seen under the rubric of the productivity drive was the policy on Development Councils.[63] These Councils were tripartite (employer/union/independents) bodies which had been suggested by the Board of Trade in the war period for industries in need of rationalization and concentration. The idea drew on the rationalization movement of the inter-war period, and was supported by the various Working Parties which reported in the early post-war years. Especially after the 'honeymoon' in government–employer relations up to 1947, they were generally resisted by employers as a form of 'backdoor nationalization'. Eventually the government took powers to impose Councils, but actually did so only in jewellery and silverware, lace, furniture and cotton. Of these, only the Council in cotton could be considered of any great importance.[64]

The trade union role in this controversy was marginal, though the unions were keen supporters of the idea of Development Councils, and supported the idea of compulsion in face of employer resistance. The most that can be said of the impact of the unions is that they formed one part of a pressure on the government to do something to maintain political credibility in the face of employer opposition—seemingly the main motive for the government's rather reluctant recourse to compulsion.[65]

So far an account has been given of a generally enthusiastic union response to government initiatives on production and productivity, and an active initiation of the idea of reviving JPCs. Beyond this, the trade union leadership acted to spread the gospel of production and productivity amongst the membership, and win their support for such policies. Soon after the beginning of the Production Campaign in 1946, the TUC called a conference of union executives to gain support for its *Statement of Policy on Problems of Production*. This statement emphasized the links between increasing output and securing full employment, and gained almost unanimous support.[66] At the TUC Congress of that year a motion was passed calling on the General Council to organize further support for a policy of increasing productivity, and set up its own machinery to examine and promote new methods to this end.[67] The General Council's response involved creating a special Committee on the Fuel Crisis and the Economic Situation; taking a full part in the newly established Economic Planning Board; and holding a series of industrial group conferences 'in order to discuss ways and means of removing present difficulties in the way of full production'.[68]

At the 1948 Congress the General Council was called on to encourage further the expansion of productivity, and in reply produced a paper on the subject, discussed by a conference of union executives in November 1948.[69] There was little articulated dissent from the General Council's view that the unions should do everything in their power to increase productivity in order to provide

> goods in such quantities and at such prices as will enable us to trade on a scale which will ensure that we pay for the essential food and raw materials which we must import and also to have adequate supplies of home produced goods available to provide the needs of the growing population of the country.[70]

The same policy stance was continued through the remaining years of the Labour government's period in office, and was symbolized by the TUC establishing its own Production Department in 1950.[71] However, it is obviously questionable how far this enthusiasm at the level of trade union leaderships translated itself into action on the factory floor. First, it is worth observing that for all the growth in membership of trade unions and their apparent strength, widespread grass roots apathy was diagnosed in a major study of Britain's biggest union, the Transport and General Workers.[72] So we should not in a sense see this period as a 'golden age' of mass trade unionism.

Opposition to the 'productionist' line of the leadership could be due to such apathy, or it could be due to direct opposition to what was undoubtedly a major switch in emphasis for the trade unions. Whilst the role of the Communist Party in these years should not be exaggerated, it clearly had substantial support when it changed its line to one of opposition to productionism.[73] To assess the extent of such resistance to the trade union leadership is very difficult, but the issue may be illustrated by one, important, example, that of the cotton industry.

As already noted, the cotton industry was deemed a major export earner, constrained by undermanning and low productivity.[74] From the productivity aspect, the campaigns unleased by the government called for both changes in work practices and longer hours. As regards work practices, later assessments of the union response to such calls are divided, but quite strikingly the government did persuade the Weavers Amalgamation to accept more looms per worker—a change previously resisted. The spinning unions seem to have been more hostile to any such changes. In cotton the question of job redesign seems to have been particularly sensitive because what was proposed gave skilled *women* workers the help of unskilled *male* labourers.[75]

As regards hours of work, the picture is complicated by the intermixing of two issues. Staggered hours of working were imposed on the industry as a response to the fuel crisis in 1947, and partly because of resentment at this, a referendum of the industry's workers had gone against an extension of hours, though it was argued the result also reflected the slowing down of the pace of re-equipment in the industry. On the whole the unions seem to have officially supported the extension of hours, subject to conditions.[76]

In general the cotton unions appear to have gone along with the government's policies to raise productivity, whilst being sensitive to maintaining consent at the workplace. They also urged the need to be sparing with general exhortations to work harder: such exhortations, unsurprisingly, usually fell on deaf ears, as for example in the famous 'Nelson Campaign' to raise output and productivity.[77]

Tensions between the union leaderships and their members were by no means confined to the cotton industry. This is one of the important points which emerges from discussion of the unions' role in the third government policy objective—reducing inflation.

As already indicated, a central aspect of anti-inflation measures, the incomes policy of 1948–50, has been well covered in the literature.[78] Here, only the briefest of sketches needs to be given prior to making a few points about the significance of this episode for government–union relations.

Between 1945 and 1948 the government issued periodic exhortations for moderation in wage bargaining, and the NJAC was established primarily to educate bargainers on the economic realities and the implications of full employment. A *Statement on the Economic Considerations Affecting Relations Between Employers and Workers* was issued in January 1947, a rather timid affair, rendered non-controversial in its passage through the NJAC.

Activity moved into higher gear with the convertibility crisis of 1947, and whilst joint discussions continued, in February 1948 the government suddenly produced a unilateral *Statement on Personal Incomes, Costs and Prices*. This called for a voluntary freeze of wages and other incomes, except where increases could be justified by undermanning or increased productivity. After being initially upset at the lack of consultation, the TUC fell in behind the policy. This support was maintained, though under increasing pressure, down to the summer of 1950, and seems to have had a significant impact on moderating wage increases.[79]

This incomes policy, it should be stressed, was concerned with aggregate incomes—it was not an attempt to regulate relative wages, or to introduce wage planning as discussed above. As Panitch puts it, 'This was not a wages policy which set out to establish wage differentials as part of a programme of manpower planning. It was expressly a policy of wage restraint.'[80] This characteristic facilitated trade union support for the policy, and also underlay the switch of the Left from support of wages policy to opposition. Hence the incomes policy was most strongly supported by the trade union Right, above all in the name of loyalty to the government, and opposed by the Left, who eventually were able to mobilize enough discontent to end the policy.[81]

One of the points which emerges from the incomes policy episode is the extent to which unions focused as much on being consulted about policy as on the actual content of policy itself. Much union anger was aroused by not being treated as a full partner in policy-making;[82] equally, there were seemingly few things the unions could not be persuaded to do if approached in the right manner.

Second, what is apparent from the incomes policy period is the extent to which a split between the trade union leaders and members grew under Labour, and was increasingly perceived as a threat by those leaders. This supports Tolliday's view that in the motor industry in these years a too compliant trade union leadership in the TGWU and AEU facilitated the growth of a combination of unofficial action and the growth of small competing unions.[83]

More strongly, the general pattern of 'good' industrial relations in the Attlee years[84] was obviously not prevalent in the docks.[85] The dock case is particularly important because here the unions had taken on a managerial role in the National Dock Labour Board, established in 1947 to run the decasualized industry. On the one hand, this enabled the government to stress the union's role in setting the rules in the industry; on the other, it undoubtedly led to substantial tensions in the unions involved when the leadership was seen to act as an agent of official policy.[86]

Such tensions between the leaders and the led may be inevitable, but they were undoubtedly sharpened in this period by the unprecedentedly cosy relation between the Labour movement hierarchies. This relationship was based partly on a sharing of objectives: the broad thrust of the Labour government's policy of full employment, the welfare state and nationalization was very similar to the kinds of policies evolved by the TUC from the 1930s while the unions had obviously played a significant role in formulating Labour's own policies.[87] Union leaders generally felt that a great deal of support for the government was justified by the administration's delivery of this reform programme. This is not to say that a picture of a totally compliant union leadership should be painted: there was, for example, notable resistance to the use of foreign workers in certain industries.[88] However, there can be little doubt that the unions were willing on most issues to go as far as the membership would allow in support of the government, producing especially remarkable results in production and productivity. The major dissenting view from this conclusion, which alleges that the unions stopped a policy of wage-planning, seems almost entirely ill-founded.

Were the unions too compliant? The answer to such a question depends on views of what the alternatives to actual policies might have been. Certainly, as regards the key issue of production and productivity, there is a contrast to be drawn between the government *negotiating* with employers whilst largely being able to take union support for granted.[89] Yet it is far from clear that a more reluctant trade union movement could have improved policy, because it must be noted that the unions had few positive policies to suggest. They were largely reactive to government initiatives. They lacked a research and intelligence capacity to provide alternative answers, let alone to set a different policy agenda. If that agenda was conservative—in its support for 'free collective bargaining', and its limited concern with effective industrial democracy, for example—this was a conservatism which cannot be traced back to union constraints on government, but rather has to be seen as one of the peculiarities of the development of the British Labour movement in general.[90]

Notes

1. I am grateful to Nick Tiratsoo for helpful comments on this chapter.
2. M. Gowing, 'The organisation of manpower in Britain during the Second World War', *Journal of Contemporary History*, vol. 7, no. 2 (June 1972) 147–67.
3. A. Bullock, *The Life and Times of Ernest Bevin, vol 2, Minister of Labour 1940–45*, 1967.
4. S. Beer, *Modern British Politics*, 1982, pp. 214–6; K. Middlemas, *Power, Competition and the State, vol. 1, Britain in Search of Balance 1940–61*, 1986, p. 7, exaggerates, however, when he talks of 'an unprecedented extension in the power of organized labour, almost to the point of equivalence with management'.
5. V.L. Allen, *Trade Unions and the Government*, 1960, pp. 260, 32–4; K. Coates, 'The vagaries of participation 1945–60', in B. Pimlott (ed.) *Trade Unions in British Politics*, 1982.
6. Allen op. cit. (Allen notes that the role of trade unionists in the government tended to decline over the lifetime of the Labour government, reflecting basically a shortage of competent trade unionists (p. 265); and A. Bullock, *Ernest Bevin, Foreign Secretary*, 1985, for example, ch. 11.
7. K.O. Morgan, *Labour in Power 1945–1951*, Oxford, 1984, p. 79.
8. Allen op. cit., 312.
9. L. Panitch, *Social Democracy and Industrial Militancy*, Cambridge, 1976, ch. 1. Whilst containing a great deal of interesting material, Panitch's general approach seems undermined by the key unargued assumption that industrial militancy represents the 'true' interests of the working class. See J. Tomlinson, 'Corporatism: a further sociologisation of Marxism', *Politics and Power*, 4 (1981) 237–48.
10. B.C. Roberts, *National Wages Policy in War and Peace*, 1958, pp. 62, 64.
11. Ibid., 63.
12. Beer, op. cit., 200–8.
13. H. Pelling, *The Labour Governments of 1945–51*, 1984, p. 265.
14. A. Cairncross, *Years of Recovery, British Economic Policy 1945–51*, 1985, ch. 2.
15. Some brief further discussion of this incomes policy is given below. For an excellent summary of this episode, see R. Jones, *Wages and Employment Policy 1936–1985*, 1987, ch. 4. Much more detail is in J. Corina, 'The British experiment in wage restraint with special reference to 1948–50', unpublished D.Phil. thesis, University of Oxford, 1961.
16. Cairncross, op. cit., 393–9.

17. Gowing, op. cit.
18. CAB 132/3: LP (46)71, *Report of Official Working Party on Wages Policy*, 26 June 1946.
19. CAB 132/1: Minutes of Lord Presidents Committee, 19/3/1946.
20. CAB 132/5: LP (46)255, 'A proposed national wages policy', 22 October 1946; LP (46)259, 'National wages policy' 29 October 1946.
21. CAB 132/1: minutes of Lord President's Committee, 2 August 1946.
22. The Steering Committee's support for the Ministry of Labour's position is argued in CAB 134/189: E.D. (46)52, memo by E. Shinwell 'Wages and prices policy and means of carrying out planning decisions', 21 December 1946. The ministerial discussion is at CAB 134/503: minutes 7 January 1947.
23. A 'National Industrial Conference' had been proposed by the original Working Party on Wages Policy, and this led to the idea that the NJAC, which had been largely superseded by the Joint Committee in 1941, could be revived to do the job.
24. CAB 132/6: minutes of Lord President's Committee, 6 June 1947; T172/2033: 'Discussion with TUC representatives on wages and wages policy 1947–51'; Deputation at Downing Street, 1 October 1947.
25. CAB 134/224: minutes of Economic Policy Committee EPC(50) 31st, 10 August 1950.
26. T172/2033: 'Discussion with TUC representatives on wages and wages policy 1947–51'; Deputation at Downing Street, 1 October 1947.
27. TUC, *Annual Congress Report 1945*, pp. 342–3; TUC, *Annual Congress Report 1946*, p. 230.
28. Panitch, op. cit., 170–8.
29. Ibid., 29–40.
30. Morgan op. cit., 136. More generally, see R. Currie, *Industrial Politics*, 1979.
31. LAB 10/74.
32. Middlemas, op. cit., 114.
33. LAB 10/652: minutes of National Joint Advisory Council, 6 August 1947, 10 October 1947, 22 October 1947.
34. Cairncross, op. cit., ch. 2, Conclusion; J. Tomlinson, 'Labour's management of the national economy 1945–51: survey and speculations', *Economy and Society*, vol. 18, no. 1 (February 1989) 1–24.
35. For a survey, see J. Tomlinson, 'A missed opportunity? Labour and the productivity problem', in G. Jones and M. Kirby (eds) *Competitiveness and the State in Twentieth Century Britain*, Manchester, 1991; and J. Tomlinson, 'Productivity policy', in H. Mercer, N. Rollings and J. Tomlinson (eds) *The Attlee Governments and Private Industry*, Edinburgh, forthcoming. On the propaganda aspect of the policies, see W. Crofts, *Coercion or Persuasion: Propaganda in Britain after 1945*, 1989.
36. BT 190/2: NPACI agendas and minutes 1945–54 (The papers of this Committee are at BT190/4–190/6); LAB 10/652: NJAC minutes and agenda 1939–53. Also relevant is LAB 10/653: Joint Consultative Committee agenda and minutes 1940–48. The JCC effectively replaced the NAJC between 1941 and 1946, and then became its executive committee. (The JCC minutes for 1949/60 remain closed.) From 1947 trade unions also participated in the Economic Planning Board: T229/28–42, CAB 134/210–214.
37. BT 190/2: NPACI meetings 7 December 1945 and 15 February 1946. Modern Records Centre, University of Warwick (hereafter MRC), TUC Archives MSS 292/20/30: minutes of TUC General Council, 19 December 1945; and MSS 292/557.1/1: minutes of NPACI (General Council Side), 15 February 1946 and 8 August 1946.

38. A. Carew, *Labour Under the Marshall Plan*, Manchester, 1987, ch. 9; J. Tomlinson, 'The failure of the Anglo/American Council on Productivity', *Business History*, vol. 33, no. 1 (January 1991); G. Hutton, *We Too Can Prosper*, 1953.
39. CAB 134/592: minutes of Productivity (Official) Committee, 30 September 1949.
40. BT 195/66.
41. MRC, MSS 292/522.3/5: letter Sec. Hornsey Trades Council – TUC, 19 January 1949.
42. MRC, MSS 292/20/30: minutes TUC General Council, 28 July 1948.
43. Ibid.
44. Carew, op. cit. 139.
45. MRC MSS 292/557.1/2: NPACI (General Council Side) 'Report of meeting between G.C. members of NPACI and Executive of Amalgamated Union of Foundry Workers', 13 January 1950.
46. MRC MSS 292/552.31/1: minutes of General Council Side of AACP, 10 December 1950; Hutton, op. cit.
47. MRC MSS 200/F/3/S1/36/28: CBI Predecessor Archive TUC 'Note on Fleming–Waddell Report', 10 October 1950.
48. MRC MSS 292/552.312/1: 'Verbatim account of A.A.C.P. meetings', e.g. 25 October 1948.
49. MRC, MSS 292/552.31/2: 'Summary of discussion of A.A.C.P. U.K. Section', 26 October 1948.
50. Tomlinson, 'Failure', op. cit.; compare Carew op. cit., 139–47.
51. This view was strongly expressed by J. Cotes, 'The politics of free enterprise. Whose productivity?', *New Statesman*, 29 December 1951.
52. Tomlinson, 'Failure', op. cit.
53. LAB 10/655: JCC Paper 183, TUC, 'Production under full employment', 5 November 1946.
54. LAB 10/652: minutes of NJAC, 23 April 1947.
55. LAB 10/722.
56. LAB 10/725: Ministry of Labour Joint Consultation 'North West Region'; LAB 10/724: 'Midlands region'.
57. TUC, *Annual Congress Report 1947*, pp. 433–7.
58. LAB 10/721: 'JPCs: Report to NJAC', 25 May 1949.
59. LAB 10/811: 'National Union of Bank Employees proposal for Joint Efficiency Committees in banks', 2 March 1948.
60. E.g. LAB 10/655: JCC Papers No. 200, 'Meeting between the P.M. and the special committee of the TUC', 7 May 1947.
61. Ibid., remarks by H. Morrison.
62. Ibid., remarks by J. Tanner, AEU.
63. P.D. Henderson, 'Development Councils', in G.D.N. Worswick and P.H. Ady (eds) *The British Economy 1945–50*, Oxford, 1952, pp. 452–62.
64. Ibid.
65. MRC, MSS 292/560.1/5: 'TUC Economic Committee and note of meeting with Harold Wilson', 8 October 1947; CAB 134/637.
66. TUC, *Annual Congress Report 1946*, p. 229.
67. Ibid., 325–8.
68. TUC, *Annual Congress Report 1947*, p. 240.
69. TUC, *Annual Congress Report 1948*, pp. 365–6; TUC *Productivity: Report of the General Council to Special Conference of TU Executive Commitees*, 18 November 1948.

70. TUC *Productivity*, op. cit., 3.
71. TUC, *Annual Congress Report 1949*, p. 366; TUC, *Annual Congress Report*, 1950, p. 296. MRC, MSS 292/557.1/3–4: minutes of Production Committee, 1950/1 and 1951/2.
72. J. Goldstein, *The Government of British Trade Unions: A study of apathy and the democratic process of the T and GWU*, London, 1952.
73. In the war period the Communist Party was a major supporter of the productionism embodied in JPCs.
74. J. Singleton, 'Planning for cotton, 1945–1951', *Economic History Review*, vol. 43, no. 1 (February 1990) 62–78; Crofts, op. cit., chs 8–10; LAB 10/656: Ministry of Labour, 'Undermanned industries: the cotton industry', 10 June 1947.
75. H.A. Turner, *Trade Union Growth, Structure and Policy: A comparative study of cotton unions*, 1962, pp. 305–6, 332; BT 195/4: 'Notes from PM's meeting with cotton industry 22/3/1948'; LAB 10/656: Ministry of Labour, 'Undermanned industries: the cotton industry', 10 June 1947.
76. T229/39: minutes of Economic Planning Board, 22 January 1948.
77. F. Zweig, *Productivity and Trade Unions*, Oxford, 1951, p. 157; Crofts, op. cit., 150–2 is more optimistic on the effects of this campaign.
78. Jones, op. cit., 35.
79. Ibid., 36–40. Cairncross, op. cit., 404–8.
80. Panitch, op. cit., 22.
81. Ibid., 20–40.
82 Where the unions believed themselves to have a legitimate role. The TUC, for example, might send suggestions on the Budget to the Treasury, but they were not consulted, and did little to protest when their suggestions were not heeded.
83. S. Tolliday, 'British motor industry', in S. Tolliday and J. Zeitlin (eds) *Shop Floor Bargaining and the State*, Cambridge, 1985, pp. 117–21.
84. The number of days lost through strikes in the first post-war years was one-tenth of the level of the post-First World War period.
85. N. Whiteside, 'Public policy and port labour reform', in S. Tolliday and J. Zeitlin (eds) op. cit., 91–107.
86. For example, in the April 1949 strike (PREM 8/1085).
87. On the TUC's policies, see TUC, *Annual Congress Report 1944*, Appendix D, 'Interim report on post-war reconstruction'.
88. J. Tanner saw 'no prospect of Polish workers being accepted in engineering': T229/28: minutes of Economic Planning Board, 21 July 1947.
89. Middlemas, op. cit., 148.
90. A contrast may be drawn here between the role of the TUC and the *initiating* role in policy-making of the Swedish equivalent, the L.O., for which see A. Martin, 'Trade unions in Sweden: strategic responses to change and crisis', in P. Gourevitch (ed) *Unions and Economic Crisis: Britain, Germany and Sweden* (1984).

7 'Don't know and don't care': popular political attitudes in Labour's Britain, 1945–51

Steve Fielding

'No, we're fighting for a real democracy, which is something more than having an occasional vote.'

(Sergeant Ben Joseph in J.B. Priestley, *Desert Highway*)

'Vote? What's the good of a vote? All I want to vote for is my ticket, I'd vote for that all right.'

(British soldier, July 1944)[1]

In 1945 the Labour Party won a majority in the House of Commons for the first time and began to implement one of the most far-reaching programmes of reform Britain has ever known.[2] Many overenthusiastic contemporaries conflated the Labour vote with a supposed mass zeal for a radical transformation of society. To such progressives there appeared the possibility of establishing a new type of democracy, in which ordinary people would take a more active role. Furthermore, a number of subsequent commentators have suggested that the level of popular political interest reached previously unknown heights during Labour's time in office. Raphael Samuel has stated that during the late 1940s political parties were 'monolithic, exclusive in the loyalties they demanded, fervent in the support they were able to muster, unquestioned—at least by their followers—in moral authority and organisational imperatives.' Moreover,

The polarization of opinion between Left and Right, already overwhelming in 1945, grew even more dominant in the subsequent years . . . Two great parties, with huge memberships rising to an all-time peak in the early 1950s, confronted each other in two class blocs.[3]

In the eyes of many sociologists and historians innate class feeling determined such deeply-held political loyalties. Working-class affiliation to Labour, in particular, has been conceived as the almost automatic consequence of an overlapping set of relationships based on work, residence, leisure and family.[4] It was only when these social bonds began to attenuate during the later 1950s that Labour's vote suffered a decline.[5] The pronounced attachment of the middle class to the Conservatives has also been conceived as the direct consequence of social conditioning.[6]

The extent to which class influenced voting patterns has been discussed at length.[7] Notwithstanding this debate, it is clear that class feeling did not in itself guarantee interest in politics. Moreover, during the 1940s the public was not overly concerned to enhance its voice in the democratic system. This is not to imply that the electorate was for the most part stupid: the popular pastime of filling in football pools coupons required a level of intelligence that could easily have been applied to politics.[8] The answer lies more in the reluctance of the parties to engage directly with popular opinion rather than the failure of the voters to be absorbed in political issues. Feminists have denied that women's apparent ignorance of party politics has anything to do with their being more apathetic than men. Instead, they have suggested that those issues conventionally identified as 'political' have much less relevance to the female experience.[9] So, it may be said, of the population at large: the public was disengaged from a system preoccupied with issues felt to be all too remote from their everyday concerns.

It is the purpose of this chapter to suggest that Samuel's two seemingly monolithic voting blocs each contained a substantial number of press-ganged supporters. Non-voting was simply the most extreme symptom of a prevalent popular confusion, apathy and cynicism about the political system that survived the war. That the parties cajoled a majority of electors into polling booths says more about their power of organization than argument. Such apathy did not constrain the implementation of Labour's reform programme, for this was predicated on the continued existence of popular passivity. Except as a general and vague principle, the party leadership had no wish to encourage the public to take a more active role. Nevertheless, during the economic crises that followed 1946, the government's indifference was temporarily overcome, although its attempt failed miserably to challenge popular antipathy for politics.

To many historians 1945 was the *annus mirabilis* of popular radical feeling, which, if it did not quite take on a socialist hue, at least demanded more than Labour was able to offer.[10] Progressive contemporaries also thought the war had caused a fundamental break with old attitudes to politics. During the early days of the conflict, the author and broadcaster J.B. Priestley hoped that it would allow for the reconstruction of a lost 'real democracy' in which 'the people' would actively participate.[11] According to the academic John Hawgood, the war had created the 'active citizen' so that 'it is the person *not* interested in politics, *not* watching what the Government is doing, *not* concerned about giving full weight to his vote, who is the exception.'[12] Even parish council elections apparently enjoyed an unprecedented interest.[13]

Although Labour increased its share of the vote from 37.9 per cent in 1935 to 47.8 per cent in 1945, some doubt must be raised in regard to this optimistic view. Mass-Observation described the 1945 campaign as being observed by a 'dispirited electorate', which considered its options under a 'cloak of apathy'.[14] Even amongst first-time voters—probably the group most responsible for Labour's victory—these feelings were not uncommon. When asked if they were following the election, two such electors replied, 'I'm not interested in it, but if I do vote at all I'll vote Labour,' and, 'I don't feel all that interested, but I'm going to vote all the same, for Labour of course.'[15] As Mass-Observation's Tom Harrisson pointed out, the party's victory was more the product of a widespread disillusion with the Conservatives rather than the result of any hopes generated by Labour.[16]

Superficially, electoral turn-out for the three general elections held between 1945 and 1951 appeared to support the progressive case. Despite the disruption of a just-completed European war and a Pacific conflict still in progress, 73.5 per cent of the electorate voted in 1945. More impressive still, the contests of 1950 and 1951 respectively mobilized 84 per cent and 82.5 per cent of all voters: these stand as the two highest participation rates under universal suffrage.[17] Even so, such outstanding rates of popular participation still meant that an average of 20.3 per cent of the electorate failed to cast its vote at a general election. It should be borne in mind that all those who appeared on the electoral register need not have been able to vote. Some might have died, others perhaps were ill, whilst a number could have moved out of the constituency. The further from the time a new register was implemented, in February of each year, the greater the number of such people. A large proportion of those who failed to vote in 1945 probably belonged to this category, although it has been estimated that only 6 per cent of the electorate was prevented from voting by wartime conditions.[18] Jean Blondel has suggested that in most national contests about 8 per cent of the electorate would be physically unable to vote.[19] Thus, at least one in ten of electors willingly abstained at each of the three general elections held during this period.

As Table 7.1 indicates, non-voting was much more pronounced in other types of contests, especially those for local office where the proportion of abstainers sometimes rose to nearly 70 per cent.[20] In parts of working-class London lassitude was especially acute: during 1945, the supposed apogee of mass zeal, 77.4 per cent of electors in Dagenham and 71.5 per cent of those in West Ham failed to vote. As a former Labour Mayor of Dagenham declared, 'The apathy of the non-voter is dangerous.'[21] Two years later a match between Newcastle and Doncaster apparently took precedence over voting in the minds of a number of local football fans.[22]

That politics in a directly party—or indeed any—sense rarely intruded into everyday life can be seen in the type of films most people watched during Labour's time in office. The 1940s saw cinema-going at the peak of

Table 7.1 Non-voting at national and local elections, 1945–51 (all figures are per cent)

	1945	1946	1947	1948	1949	1950	1951
General elections	26.5					16.0	17.5
By-elections (average)	44.6	41.1	35.1	32.4	28.8	28.7	34.1
County boroughs	54.4	57.5	47.4	47.8		54.5	55.6
Admin. counties	69.9			57.5			
Rural districts	52.1	63.9	45.5	48.4		53.7	54.8
Municipal boroughs and urban districts	53.6	59.2	50.2	53.0		52.1	54.1

Source: Registrar-General, *Statistical Review of England and Wales*, 1945–51; F.W.S. Craig, *British Parliamentary Election Results 1918–1949*, Glasgow, 1969, *British Parliamentary Election Results 1950–73*, Chichester, 1983.

its popularity: in 1946 one-third of the population watched at least one film a week; 13 per cent saw two.[23] The fare provided mainly consisted of light, diversionary entertainment: between 1939 and 1949 one-quarter of all films produced in Britain were comedies. Moreover, before 1939 the British Board of Film Censors' imposed an embargo on all 'controversial' issues, a ban which embraced anything remotely critical of government. As these restraints were eased there was an unprecedented opportunity for film-makers to insert political points into their work. Furthermore, an increasing number of prominent post-war producers supported Labour, including the Boulting brothers, Michael Powell and Sydney Box. They were, however, partly held in check by the extensive influence of mogul J. Arthur Rank, well known for his Conservative sympathies. More crucially, they were also hampered by the absence of any widespread desire to watch films dealing with explicitly political topics: the few brave enough to tackle such subjects invariably faced financial disaster.[24]

The most explicitly political film of the period, the Boulting brothers' *Fame is the Spur* (1947), traced the career of a character very much in the mould of Ramsay MacDonald. Members of the Cabinet watched the film and Stafford Cripps was particularly impressed by the production. Despite such high-level praise the film was 'political but not popular'.[25] In fact, the film's political content was blamed by distributors for its very lack of success.[26] Another worthy failure was *Chance of a Lifetime* (1950), which took up the Labourist message that workers and management should co-operate on the basis of mutual respect in order to arrive at the common good. The film became a *cause célèbre* when the three major circuits denied it distribution, claiming that it was an uncommercial proposition. The suspicion was that they actually disapproved of its political content. Even after an eventual Rank release and the priceless publicity caused by the dispute, the film did not make much of an impact.[27] A Mass-Observation survey of one audience's response to the film revealed that only just over one-third had deliberately chosen to watch *Chance of a Lifetime*, whereas nearly half went to the cinema either out of habit or because they had nothing better to do. As a consequence, just under two-thirds were completely oblivious to the film's political message.[28]

Apathy and lack of interest were no less evident in the very foundations of the Labour movement, where, it might be supposed, political enthusiasm would have been at its greatest. Even in Labour strongholds like Derby and industrial Lancashire, the Co-operative movement had ceased to hold any political significance for the majority of members.[29] Despite trade union membership increasing from 7.87 million in 1945 to 9.48 million in 1951, there was little apparent rise in political interest among workers. In 1952 *Socialist Commentary* wearily noted that 'At every educational gathering of trade unionists the problem of apathy is invariably brought up.'[30] In 1948 Political and Economic Planning (hereafter PEP) estimated that about 80 per cent of trade union members were inactive, to the extent that they did not even vote in branch elections, let alone turn up for meetings.[31] This was more than confirmed by Joseph Goldstein's investigation of a Transport and General Workers' Union branch in the Labour heartland of Battersea during the late 1940s. Despite the Transport Union having one of the highest participation rates for elections, Goldstein discovered that between 1942 and 1949 attendance at meetings averaged no more than 7 per cent of the total membership. In fact, with the increase in numbers after the war the proportion fell to 3 per cent by 1949.[32] During the later 1940s the prevalence of apathy within some trade unions was blamed for the disproportionate influence of the Communist Party. As Communist renegade Bob Darke grimly noted, the British worker's 'tendency to let those he regards as his leaders within his own sphere do his own thinking for him is the Party's greatest opportunity'.[33] This was, however, an attitude many Labour-inclined union leaders also exploited in order to maintain their position.

Despite the factious nature of debate between the front benches in Westminster, a substantial proportion of the public refused to take partisan positions on many of the seemingly vital issues of the day. As *Picture Post* noted, 'What will flummox the party directors will be the strange cross-currents of feeling inside the opposing camps.'[34] This was especially true with regard to the role of the state in the economy, despite the increasingly significant place of this issue in party rhetoric during the months immediately prior to the general elections of 1950 and 1951.[35] Even on this well-rehearsed matter, attitudes were not easily reducible to particular partisan loyalties. In 1949 the magazine *Future* commissioned a survey of popular feeling about private enterprise.[36] In the face of over four years of Labour rule it was revealed that whilst 33 per cent of those polled disapproved of big business, 49 per cent approved; only 38 per cent of working-class respondents and 55 per cent of Labour voters were hostile.

Mistrust of further nationalization, evident by the late 1940s, contrasted with the popular mood during 1944 and 1945. Gallup polls indicated widespread support for Labour's plans to extend public ownership as the end of war approached.[37] The first signs of discontent with further inroads into the private sector were exposed in a poll taken in October 1946:

although 37 per cent supported the nationalization of road transport, 46 per cent opposed it. After this date majorities against additional nationalization were universal and most pronounced in the case of iron and steel. In five polls taken between January 1949 and January 1951, never fewer than half were against the industry's nationalization, whereas a maximum of 32 per cent favoured the measure. Moreover, an October 1950 poll revealed that between 49 and 59 per cent opposed the nationalization of the cement, insurance, chemical, sugar and meat industries. In contrast, those who supported these proposals failed to amount to more than 31 per cent. A 1949 *Picture Post* survey suggested that these doubts were also felt by Labour supporters, 19 per cent of whom actually opposed such measures, whilst 20 per cent were undecided.[38]

The most striking feature of public opinion with regard to the future of iron and steel was its stability, despite the increased propaganda issued by both sides. Three *Picture Post* polls taken between July 1948 and January 1949 showed that those favouring nationalization ranged from only 28 to 30 per cent, whilst those who opposed it extended merely from 42 to 44 per cent. Respondents unable to express an opinion varied between 27 and 29 per cent—rather high for such an apparently vital topic. The July 1948 poll again indicated indecision amongst the Labour ranks: 27 per cent of supporters were unable to come to a conclusion on this notionally high profile issue.[39] Five Gallup polls taken between April 1948 and October 1950, in relation to controls in trade and industry, demonstrated that attitudes towards state intervention were also highly provisional. Between 16 and 21 per cent agreed that controls were 'necessary but badly carried out'; between 33 and 37 per cent felt that 'some but not all are necessary'; whilst no less than 21 and never more than 29 per cent thought that they were 'necessary at the present time'. No more than 12 per cent ever felt they were 'wholly bad'.

The *Future* poll also indicated that a declining number of workers sought employment in the state sector: this might have been the key to changing attitudes towards nationalization. Between 1947 and 1949 this figure had fallen from 37 to 31 per cent, whilst those who preferred work in the private sector over state employment rose from 45 to 48 per cent. Only 49 per cent of Labour voters looked on working for the state with favour. The reasons for this lack of enthusiasm appear to have been pragmatic rather than principled. First, in a period when shortage of labour rather than unemployment was the rule, the security offered by the state sector was less important. By the late 1940s employees looked forward to improving their position at work rather than grimly holding on to an existing job. It was no accident that although only 34 per cent of workers as a whole favoured state employment, this proportion increased amongst the very poor for whom job security was least assured. The second factor was related to the failure of nationalized industries to inaugurate a new deal for employees. There was a widespread desire for trade unions to have a say in formulating business policy: 46 per cent of all respondents advocated this, 53 per cent of workers and 64 per cent of Labour supporters. This was, of course, something equally opposed by both the nationalized and private sectors. However, such an approach might have improved attitudes amongst state employees at least, if only in the mining industry. By 1948 many coal-miners were disillusioned with the way nationalization had been applied by the government. Although referred to as partners in an industry nominally 'managed on behalf of the People', in reality industrial relations had hardly changed. Miners had expected more of a voice; instead, managers employed under private ownership remained in place, exerting an almost undiminished authority.[40] Therefore, despite enjoying a greater sense of security and benefiting from better pensions than their counterparts in private firms, state employees were nevertheless not so content. This is indicated by the desire of 31 per cent of miners, 40 per cent of railway, gas and electricity workers and 43 per cent of those employed in road transport to see their industry returned to private hands.

Despite the time devoted to the issue by leading politicians, changing attitudes towards state intervention appear to have only slightly effected Labour's fortunes. In October 1950 only 10 per cent of respondents told Gallup that the government's proposed nationalization of steel had influenced their party choice. This was not unprecedented, as the public had not blindly supported state intervention for its own sake even in 1945: it was always seen as means towards an end, rather than the end itself. The question was: would nationalization hasten or impede greater social justice?[41] In the early stages of Labour rule the answer appeared to be the former, near the end increasingly the latter—or, more likely, the whole question had become irrelevant. As Richard Williams-Thompson, chief information officer at the Ministry of Supply between 1946 and 1949, noted of Labour's attempt to nationalize steel, despite the great fuss made about the issue, 'the general public could not have been less interested.'[42]

It now can be no surprise, despite the high turn-out, that the elections of 1950 and 1951 failed to furnish much evidence of a more 'politicized' electorate than might have been found in earlier or later periods. Apart from voting, the majority of the public continued to play a minor part in the democratic process. In Bristol North-East only 10 per cent of electors attended a political meeting during the 1951 campaign, most of this number being party stalwarts.[43] As in Glasgow during the 1950 contest, those who went to meetings in order to come to a decision formed a minority of a minority.[44] In London, although there were 'few signs of complete apathy', only 16 per cent of voters bothered to attend even a minimum of one meeting.[45] Some 20 per cent of the Bristol electorate chose not to read any local or national newspapers; only half consulted election material delivered to their homes.[46] This latter figure echoes a confession, made by 51 per cent of those surveyed in Greenwich during 1950 that they were 'uninterested' in politics.[47] When asked if they could recall discussing politics in the previous four weeks, 27 per cent of men and 51 per cent of women were unable to do so.[48]

The Greenwich study also made the astonishing revelation that about one-fifth of Conservative and Labour Party members thought they had 'little interest' in politics[49] At the very least this suggests that even during a general election campaign, amongst the supposed shock troops of party conflict, politics was a long way from dominating personal horizons. Labour's leaders were sadly aware of the limited political commitment amongst its own rank and file. As one member of Glasgow's Govan Hill party complained, the organization was run by the 'faithful few'—the majority being almost wholly apathetic.[50] It was a common complaint that most members were especially unenthusiastic about helping out during municipal contests.[51] In 1951, an admittedly demoralizing time for Labour, it was stated that some members in the northern region preferred gardening to canvassing.[52] Concern with this lack of animation caused the National Executive to discuss raising the level of both political and general knowledge within the party.[53] However, such initiatives were piecemeal and largely ineffective.

Low-level interest in the political issues of the day led some electors to vote for parties with whom they profoundly disagreed. Lawrence Thompson met one lorry driver, famed in cafés along the A40 as a 'fervent protagonist of the Labour Party', who was hostile to trade unions and proposed sending striking dockers to Russia.[54] The Bristol survey discovered that when 'typical' Labour and Conservative propositions were put to electors, 27 per cent of Labour supporters agreed more with Conservative than Labour statements, whilst 7 per cent of Conservatives supported more of Labour's assumptions.[55] A similar discovery was made in Greenwich, where it was shown that many working-class voters disagreed with 'their' party. Asked whether they assented to five 'model' Conservative and Labour propositions, a majority found itself agreeing with two Conservative statements and only three Labour proposals.[56] No wonder the authors of this study remarked on the 'extent of common opinion, even on "controversial" issues, between those who support different political parties'.[57] Therefore, even during the 1950 contest, with the highest turn-out in the democratic era, popular partisanship was less than total. In Bristol it was felt that 'The maximum proportion of voters whose vote was primarily decided by an issue or issues cannot have been more than ten per cent, and may have been much smaller.' [58] It appeared that 'if voting behaviour were determined by attitudes to published policy statements alone, the Greenwich candidate for Labour might have lost his seat.'[59] The corollary of this state of affairs was that supporters of opposing parties shared many similar attitudes, including support for capital punishment, hostility to Jews and maintaining wage differentials between the sexes.[60] Instead of demonstrating accurately how much electors differed in their views, party allegiance actually obscured a large area of common ground.

Because of this pronounced lack of interest in the issues, the intention of Labour and Conservative constituency campaigns was simply to mobilize already existing or latent support. They were not designed to convince or persuade doubters and waverers through reasoned argument. In Bristol the parties canvassed with the sole purpose of locating supporters and ensuring they turned out on polling day. Consequently, campaigns made few converts and succeeded only in hardening already existing loyalties, forcing electors to take what was essentially a crude, dichotomous choice.[61] Each general election campaign, therefore, was not intended to arouse electors' interest in politics or make them any more informed than they had been before. Yet the public still—in the main—voted, having been persuaded to make the effort.

Perhaps the greatest difference between 1950 and other elections was that Labour and the Conservatives had brought their organizations to 'a pitch of preparedness which probably has no equal in the history of British politics'.[62] Both organizations enjoyed an unprecedented membership which could be relied upon to bring out the vote; both increased their vote. The much-improved Conservative showing was attributed to the mobilization of more 1945 non-voters rather than its success in demonstrating the superiority of its case to erstwhile Labour voters.[63] Furthermore, whenever Labour suffered a reverse at the polls, the cause most widely blamed by supporters was related to 'organization': either the Conservatives were better than before or Labour was worse. Thus the 1947 municipal elections were assessed in this light, as were the general elections of 1950 and 1951.[64] Bluntly, elections were primarily contests between activists in which many voters were dragged yawning into the polling booths.

The full extent of popular political ennui was already apparent to some Labour supporters before the first flush of heady enthusiasm had dissipated in the summer of 1945. PEP had long recognized the problem and tried to discover suitable means of surmounting it, especially in relation to municipal affairs. Particular blame for lack of interest in local decision-making was attributed to the feeling amongst voters that political activity was pointless because it would change nothing: 'They' would not allow it.[65] More fundamentally, the emergence of an increasingly passive and privatized culture was also accused of causing a decline in political interest. By the 1940s few people spent their leisure time outside the home; moreover, those who escaped the bonds of domesticity were mostly mere spectators, at football matches or the cinema.[66]

PEP appreciated the difficulty of encouraging the masses to take an interest in politics under such circumstances. As an initial step, however, it hoped to enhance activity in municipal affairs amongst members of voluntary associations, who were assumed to have developed 'a sense of the wider community which is an essential preliminary to more direct participation as citizens . . . [and have] practical experience of dealing with the machinery of democratic Government'. Unfortunately, it was found that even this select group exhibited a morbid contempt for 'politics'. Amongst such people was noted a

> profound mistrust and fear of anything to do with political life . . .. It is held that people are only in local politics for what they can get out of it and the idea of disinterested service is laughed at. The party machine receives much criticism.[67]

In spite of the organization's best efforts, the 1940s saw no increase in political interest. Moreover, the advance of commercial leisure accelerated whilst the voluntary sector continued to decline. By the early 1950s no more than 1 per cent of Derby's citizens were voluntary workers.[68] As Mass-

Observation concluded in 1947, the hope of wartime radicals to breathe life into an 'active democracy' was fast receding into the background.[69]

As a means of overcoming mass political apathy most progressives turned to 'education', whether it was defined as propaganda, advertising, public relations, or simply information. Whatever its form, the object was essentially the same, i.e. to tear down apparently irrational thoughts and thereby enable the individual to accept 'the appeal of facts'. In order to distinguish itself from its Fascist counterpart, this form of left-wing propaganda was to be morally uplifting: it would be truthful, wary of emotionalism and conducive to individual responsibility.[70] An appropriately educated trade unionist would be less likely to take strike action; once aware of the function of local government, electors would vote in municipal elections in increasing numbers; workers, after being informed of the true situation, would increase output.[71] John Hawgood made the exemplary progressive case for education as a way to ensure the full flowering of that 'active democracy' seemingly germinated during the war. He proposed that government open the channels of communication to explain its actions: parliamentary bills needed to be couched in less obscure language, press conferences made more frequent, the price of *Hansard* reduced, and 'education for citizenship' initiated by the Ministry of Education.[72] Many hopes were pinned on the role of public relations in promoting this active responsible democracy. During the 1940s public relations came to possess a democratic mantle, largely because of the way the war had forced those in power to keep the public 'in the picture', thereby ensuring their co-operation and consent.[73] Edward Hulton, proprietor of *Picture Post*, declared that progressives wanted the wartime Ministry of Information to continue. 'Has not the Government which has been elected by the people,' he asked, 'got the right, and duty, to put its case to them?'[74]

Despite being recently described by William Crofts as 'innovatory', the Labour government's application of such techniques was half-hearted and largely incompetent.[75] There were a number of external constraints on the use of propaganda by government, among which were cost, constitutional misgivings, Civil Service hostility, and the vigorous opposition mounted by the Conservative press. As a consequence, between August 1945 and February 1947 government public relations staff was cut by three-quarters, whilst the transformation of the wartime Ministry of Information into the Central Office of Information in March 1946 marked the official downgrading of propaganda's importance.[76] This is not to say that government did not make use of publicity. However, efforts were largely confined to necessary explanation, as in the case of the introduction of the National Health Service and the National Insurance Acts in 1948.[77]

Most members of the Labour Cabinet were by no means unhappy at the demise of public relations during this early period of power.[78] Clement Attlee, not exactly an ideal subject for the publicist's arts, confessed to being 'allergic to the press', and was considered the most reluctant Prime Minister since Lord Salisbury to 'play up to the public'.[79] Although Attlee appointed Francis Williams as the first prime ministerial adviser on public relations, Williams's role was to ensure the Labour leader was not burdened by such trivialities.[80] It was in response to such hostility and lassitude that Williams-Thompson wrote: 'No institution, to my mind, has been more culpable than the British Labour Party in deluding itself that the goods it has to "sell" need no advertisement.'[81] As a result, even the elemental principle of planning was left unexplained and undefended: the government's legislative programme assumed the appearance of a confusing incoherent flurry of White Papers.[82]

This was, perhaps, an overexaggeration. The Labour Party, as opposed to the Labour government, was not so complacent as to neglect propaganda completely. The party had a press and publicity department, which produced and distributed pamphlets, leaflets and posters to the constituencies, primarily in relation to election campaigns. Moreover, by 1951 the party's research department was issuing the *Town and Country Post*, published every other month, which dealt with local and national issues. This journal, derogatorily described as 'frankly designed for the lowest common denominator of the electorate', reached a circulation of 500,000. This department also produced infrequent illustrated magazines that enjoyed runs of up to one and a half million copies.[83] Labour also owned the *Daily Herald*, which, as might have been expected, enthusiastically promoted its proprietor's case.[84] Unfortunately, the *Herald* was one of the least successful daily national newspapers. The paper's 1950 circulation of 4.75 million or 12.8 per cent of adults was the highest it achieved during this period, yet it was still less than half that of the aggressively Conservative *Daily Express* and one quarter of that enjoyed by the salacious Sunday *News of the World*.[85]

In addition, at least some prominent officials and supporters recognized the decisive importance of propaganda. In 1945 Morgan Phillips, Labour's newly appointed General Secretary, proposed that every ward appoint a press officer. By keeping people informed, Phillips thought Labour could avoid recreating the 'gap of understanding' which emerged so disastrously between leaders, rank and file and the electorate during the 1929–31 administration.[86] During 1946 he wrote a series of articles in *Labour Organiser* which elaborated on this theme.[87] The Fabian Margaret Cole underlined his argument when she warned that although 'the ordinary voter has consciously voted for a change . . . he cannot understand without explanation; nobody is going to put up with being uncomfortable after the war unless he is told why.'[88] Within a few weeks of Labour taking office, the *New Statesman* informed Ministers that by not keeping the public in touch with developments, they were 'in danger of letting the enthusiasm engendered by the polling results evaporate in misunderstanding and apathy'. Due to the party's extensive reform proposals Labour could not afford to appear aloof but had to be in sympathy with the people. It could do this only by opening up the channels of communication: 'The affairs of State must be projected into the people's homes, into their everyday experience.'[89] Francis Williams reiterated this point by stating that Labour could not implement radical change 'without the active understanding and collaboration of many millions of ordinary men and women. Nor is their passive support sufficient. Positive cooperation is needed.' This could be achieved only by keeping the public properly acquainted with government thinking.[90]

Despite these warnings, Labour completely failed to meet the challenge. Phillips's proposals appear to have come to little. A 1947 article on public relations in *Labour Organiser* had to begin by carefully defining that term for the benefit of obtuse activists.[91] Despite being able to avail itself of the free distribution service provided by the National Film Association, by 1951 Labour had only produced one short film to be shown to local constituencies.[92] Compared with the Conservatives, Labour's propaganda was hidebound, something that can partly be attributed to the latter's relatively meagre income. As National Executive member Alice Bacon complained in 1948, to finance a national poster campaign cost £100,000; the party's annual income was only £130,000.[93] In contrast, the Conservatives spent almost £1 million on publicity between 1948 and 1951. Yet, more important than cost was the Conservative enthusiasm to employ any method likely to win voters back, whether it be direct mail techniques or training national officials for television appearances.[94] In the face of these innovations, the National Executive's definition of what constituted propaganda effort remained limited to the nineteenth-century idea of arranging speakers for local meetings.[95]

The cause of the Labour leadership's insouciance towards the new methods of propaganda lay in that peculiar amalgam known as Labour socialism which coalesced during the 1890s. Members of the Cabinet, most of whom were in their sixties or even seventies, remained under its spell.[96] To those such as Attlee, active in the party almost since its foundation, 'the emergence of the Labour Party as a great political force is still something of a miracle.'[97] To such people Labour was the agency of revealed truth whose victory was inevitable because it was to be 'the outcome of economic and social conditions'. Therefore, Labour's opponents had either been deceived or were morally deficient.[98] It was the party's self-appointed role to educate the public to distinguish between right and wrong. As Aneurin Bevan declared in 1944, whereas the Tories appealed to 'the subjective attitudes of the electorate', Labour's task was raise the people up to the heights of objective truth.[99] As the party was an electoral machine, the people would show they had reached the correct level of consciousness by voting Labour. Once they had performed this sacred rite, the party could press on with creating the new Britain and the new Britons, confident they had been permanently won as adherents to the cause. Like riding a bicycle, it seems, voting Labour was something never forgotten. Thus, many such Labourists saw 1945 as the moment of final consummation. After the trials of the 1930s the people had been won for socialism; by voting Labour they demonstrated their full support of its proposed reforms. To the Labour leadership, therefore, government and party had little need for propaganda, especially the new-fangled sort.[100] Henceforward, it would be a matter of drafting the appropriate legislation.

Even after 1945 many in the leadership and rank and file continued to look to members as the principal bearers of the Labour message. As Herbert Morrison told activists at the 1948 Party Conference, they were missionaries for the cause.[101] Although Attlee paid lip-service to the necessity for sophisticated propaganda, he still thought that the key to a Labour victory remained the moral conduct of individual members. As he wrote in 1937, 'The thing which will secure the triumph of Labour will be the demonstration by Socialists *in their lives* that they have a high ideal and live up to it.'[102] Alice Bacon told Party Conference delegates in 1948 that 'If the individual members of the Party are active in their places of work and recreation, then we have a most effective medium of publicity.'[103] A year later a delegate called for the revival of the 'old evangelical spirit', for Labour 'to go back to the street corner where we came from, to go back to the doorstep, to the factory gate, and to express what is truly within us'. Another bemoaned that 'There has been a falling away from the time when the spirit was keen and enthusiastic and when everyone was not only a propagandist but very often more or less martyr in the cause of Labour.'[104] This call to 'go back to the street corner' had also been made by the Assistant District Organizer for the north-west region in 1947.[105] As late as 1950 Coventry MP Richard Crossman proposed the revival of Clarion bicycling clubs so that members could do good works in Conservative strongholds such as neighbouring Warwick and Leamington.[106]

By no means all members remained enamoured with street corner meetings or attached to the martyrdom of membership. The 1946 Conference passed two resolutions which criticized both government information and party propaganda in spite of National Executive disapproval. An Ormskirk delegate felt that many of those who voted Labour in 1945 were turning back to their old allegiances, not as a consequence of government policy, but 'due to a lack of making policy manifest to the general public'. A member from Orpington echoed earlier warnings by pointing out:

> It is not enough to pass laws and to debate issues just within the walls of Parliament. There must be a great campaign of information calculated to stir the imagination of every man and woman in these islands, including those who voted against us.[107]

Such calls were renewed in 1947 when fifty-three resolutions were submitted to the Conference, calling for a greater effort to 'tell the people the facts'. The delegate who moved the eventual composite resolution described this as the government's greatest failure, indeed, 'it may be in the minds of some of you its only failure.' Government was too timid, he declared, and, as others had done the previous year, the failure to emulate the example of the wartime Ministry of Information was highlighted.[108]

The Labour leadership became interested in the possibilities of government propaganda only when it seemed imperative, not to widen the bounds of democratic activity, but to ensure its own political survival. As economic prospects grew ever darker during 1946, turned almost terminally black in 1947 and remained shrouded in contrasting shades of grey until the early 1950s, the government sanctioned a series of initiatives to explain why Britain faced such a crisis and outline Labour's proposals for recovery. It was in the wake of the climactic events of 1947 that Morrison informed the Labour Conference:

> Ballot-box democracy, where the people go and vote—if they can be bothered and persuaded and shoved around to go and vote—every few years and do nothing much

in between, is out of date. We must have an active, living democracy in our country and we must whip up our citizens to their responsibilities just as we canvass them in elections or just as the air-raid wardens did in the war. The individual counts more, and the individual will count more and more as our Socialist programme goes forward. Too many of our so-called democratic institutions are little better than shams which are run by small minorities in the name of large bodies of citizens who take not the least practical interest. In some cases this leads to cliques or sinister groups getting control of impressive-looking organisations and exploiting them for wrong reasons—as the Communists are so fond of doing. But even where this does not happen it is wrong and demoralising to put up with low standards of citizenship.[109]

For a machine politician who, whilst leader of London's Labour Party during the 1930s, had methodically prevented grass roots initiatives and arrogated all power to the centre, this was a remarkable statement.[110] However, it should be borne in mind that Morrison's comments were made during a speech devoted to finding ways of increasing productivity. His vision of active democracy was that of a society in which individuals worked harder for their elected representatives. A closer relationship between rulers and ruled meant, in this instance, a more efficient work-force: it did not imply a government more open and willing to take account of popular initiatives.

Labour's ambition during this fraught period was to inform the public about the urgent need to improve productivity and increase the number of exports in order to pay for imports.[111] Once in possession of these 'facts', it was assumed that the people would respond by working harder. The exercise largely failed. One major point of criticism was that the language used appeared to be designed for the erudite minority rather than the general public. Even the 'Battle for Output' pamphlet, ostensibly a popular version of the 1947 Economic Survey, produced widespread confusion and misunderstanding.[112] This particular technical flaw was merely one aspect of the campaign's basic misconception. The public was confronted by slogans and empty exhortations issued from the few at the distant summit of power who blithely expected them to be obediently followed. They were not. This failure was especially pronounced amongst the work-force, supposedly Labour's natural constituency. Williams-Thompson went so far as to describe the 'Work or Want' campaign as 'psychologically disastrous', given the way it succeeded in alienating those it had been intended to spur on to greater efforts. Meetings with trade unionists uncovered much resentment and numerous misunderstandings aroused rather than assuaged by the campaign. As one said, 'one group of people always has worked and wanted—another group has never worked and never wanted.' By the end of the campaign, the very word productivity provoked widespread derision.[113] As a consequence, by the time the productivity campaigns had been concluded, at least one-half of all adults remained stubbornly ignorant of the country's need to export more goods.[114] The government's failure was echoed by that of the Labour Party itself which initiated a 'Tell Britain' campaign designed to increase membership. The efficacy of this effort can best be gauged by the fact that Labour lost nearly 6 per cent of its members during the year in which the effort took place.[115] In 1946 Francis Williams had hoped that centrally directed information would weaken 'they' and 'we' attitudes confronted in another context by PEP.[116] It is possible that by further arousing popular resentment of those in power, Labour's campaigns actually reinforced such ingrained sentiments.

After this brief spurt of activity during 1947–8, the government drastically reduced the flow of economic propaganda. Disappointed with its failure to arouse the public, ministers were also forced to prune back expenditure by the very financial crisis they had sought to explain. It was just at this moment that the Conservatives and other opponents of further nationalization began to mobilize their forces ready for attack.[117]

There is some doubt that Labour's failure to present its case in a coherent and understandable form exacerbated the extent of the party's defeat in the 1951 general election. Many contemporaries placed too much faith in the effect of public relations, which, even when it was competently practised, could not guarantee success.[118] The positivistic belief among adherents of the persuasive power of the 'facts' also betrayed a defectively simplistic view of popular attitudes. Even so, in 1952 Arnold Rogow pointed to Labour's failure to 'educate on behalf of its program' as one of the causes of its eventual loss of power.[119] This was later endorsed by Ralph Miliband who contrasted the government's desultory and timid public defence of nationalization with the more aggressive activities of groups such as Aims of Industry.[120] Although H.H. Wilson questioned whether anti-nationalization propaganda on its own had turned the tide against Labour, he suggested that it nevertheless served to increase the government's difficulties.[121] Whilst Crofts has also raised doubts about the general validity of Rogow's claims, he has agreed that Labour's misuse of propaganda allowed the anti-nationalizers to reinforce hostile attitudes in the minds of already disaffected groups such as middle-class housewifes.[122] In contrast, Henry Pelling has completely dismissed the notion that propaganda influenced public attitudes.[123] Therefore, Labour would probably not have avoided defeat in 1951 even if it had followed the programme outlined by progressives such as Hawgood.

It is unlikely that on its own 'education' could have overcome popular disengagement from the political system. Whilst the existing structure of political life remained intact, along with the cynicism it provoked, voters would have remained impervious to any attempt to disabuse them of their prejudices. Words on their own would not have been enough whilst the distribution of power remained so uneven.[124] In any case, Labour's programme was based on the use of a monolithic state apparatus in which popular initiatives were deliberately left at a minimum. The party's 1945 proposals made no mention of changing the relationship between rulers and ruled; nor was its victory based on a groundswell of support for such a project. Labour's reforms were based on parliamentary legislation and relied on the manipulation of the existing constitution. Therefore, it is highly speculative to conclude that popular attitudes acted as a constraint on the Attlee government. This is because, voting apart, the Labour leadership had never placed too much importance on them. According to Mass-Observation, voting Labour in 1945 was one of several last efforts on the part of at least some of the electorate to make a better world. In 1947 it wrote, 'Much more than party or country depends on the next year or two of Labour Government. It can underline, accelerate, or possibly transfigure, the disillusions of so many Britons.'[125] Two years later G.D.H. Cole made much the same point: according to him Labour needed to 'change the mood of the people to one of more hopeful and far-seeing activity and effort'; it had to free them of their confusion, unreason, tiredness and lack of enthusiasm.[126] If this was the case, Labour failed to grasp the opportunity. During the party's period in office, the set of confused attitudes which gave rise to popular political disengagement remained wholly intact.

This chapter has sketched an outline of the problems confronted by those who felt that the war and the Labour victory had presented them with an opportunity to create a new type of politics. There is little evidence that either event had raised the political consciousness of many voters, most of whom remained largely uninterested in the mechanisms of democratic life. That the economic hardships endured after 1946 did not cause a move against Labour in 1950 and 1951 was remarkable—the party actually increased its proportion of the total vote to an unprecedented 48.8 per cent in 1951. However, this was by no means indicative of continued enthusiasm for the Labour cause. Even within its supposedly traditional working-class bastions, the party was supported by a largely lethargic body of electors, reluctant to be convinced of the virtues of nationalization or the necessity for increased productivity, but also afraid of the Conservative alternative. As *Picture Post* noted after the 1947 Jarrow by-election, the first to take place after the initial wave of austerity, 'the Government retains the loyalty of its supporters, but has lost a great deal of its popularity.'[127] This distinction, although fine, needs to be kept in mind by all those historians who too easily conflate the Labour vote with mass enthusiasm for its programme of reforms. If asked what they thought of the Labour government during the late 1940s, many Labour voters might well have replied, 'Don't know and don't care.'[128] For them, calculating the chances of a score draw at Old Trafford still seemed a more rational use of leisure time than studying the reasons behind the proposed public ownership of the cement industry.

Notes

1. J.B. Priestley, *Four Plays*, 1944 p. 255; *Picture Post*, 19 August 1944.
2. Thanks are due to Nick Tiratsoo and Tony Mason for their comments on earlier drafts of this chapter.
3. R. Samuel, 'The lost world of British Communism', *New Left Review*, No. 154 (November–December 1985) 8–9. See also F. Bealey, J. Blondel and W.P. McCann, *Constituency Politics. A study of Newcastle-under-Lyme*, 1965, pp. 405–6.
4. E. Hobsbawm, 'The formation of British working class culture', in his *Worlds*

of Labour. Further studies in the history of labour, 1984, pp. 176–93; M. Young and P. Wilmott, *Family and Kinship in East London*, Pelican edn, Harmondsworth, 1986, p. 94.

5. E. Hobsbawm, 'The forward march of Labour halted?', in M. Jacques and F. Mulhern (eds) *The Forward March of Labour Halted?*, 1981, pp. 1–19.
6. For a critique of this approach, see T. Jeffrey, 'The suburban nation. Politics and class in Lewisham', in D. Feldman and G.S. Jones (eds) *Metropolis. London. Histories and Representations since 1800*, 1989, pp. 189–216.
7. For a discussion of some of the issues, see D. Butler and D. Stokes, *Political Change in Britain*, Pelican edn, Harmondsworth, 1971, pp. 91–157; and T. Forrester, *The Labour Party and the Working Class*, 1976, pp. 12–29.
8. T. Harrisson, 'The public's progress', in A.G. Weidenfeld (ed.) *The Public's Progress*, 1947, p. xii.
9. V. Randall, *Women and Politics*, 1982, pp. 56–7.
10. R. Miliband, *Parliamentary Socialism*, 2nd edn, 1979, pp. 272–4.
11. J.B. Priestley, *Out of the People*, 1941, pp. 85–8. This was also the hope expressed in F. Williams, *Ten Angels Swearing . . . Or Tomorrow's Politics*, 1941, pp. 1–19.
12. J.A. Hawgood, *The Citizen and Government*, 1947, p. 9.
13. Political and Economic Planning [hereafter PEP], 'Active democracy—a local election', *Planning*, vol. 13, no. 261 (January 1947) 1.
14. The Tom Harrisson Mass-Observation Archive [hereafter MO], file 2270A.
15. MO, file 2257.
16. T. Harrisson, 'Who'll win?', *Political Quarterly*, Vol. 15, no. 1 (January –March 1944) 21–32.
17. Derived from D. Butler, 'Electors and elected', in A.H. Halsey (ed.) *Trends in British Society Since 1900*, Table 8.1, p. 235.
18. R.B. McCallum and A. Readman, *The British General Election of 1945*, Oxford, 1947, pp. 30–1, 43 and 258.
19. J. Blondel, *Voters, Parties and Leaders*, Pelican edn, Harmondsworth, 1969, p. 53.
20. The phrase is taken from A.H. Birch and P. Campbell, 'Voting behaviour in a Lancashire constituency', *British Journal of Sociology*, vol. I, no. 3 (September 1950) 206.
21. A.F.J. Chorley, 'Local elections ahead!', *Socialist Commentary*, Vol. 10, no. 10 (October 1945) 197.
22. Labour Party National Executive Committee Minutes [hereafter *LPNEC*], memo by M. Phillips, 'Report on municipal elections 1947', 26 November 1947.
23. A. Marwick, *British Society Since 1945*, 1982, p. 75.
24. R. Murphy, *Realism and Tinsel. Cinema and society in Britain 1939–48*, 1989, pp. 88–9 and 191.
25. 'Lest we forget: Fame is the Spur': J. Richards and A. Aldgate, *Best of British. Cinema and society 1939–1970*, Oxford, 1983, pp. 75–86.
26. Murphy, op.cit., 94.
27. Ibid., 95.
28. Mass-Observation, 'Film and public: chance of a lifetime', *Sight and Sound*, vol. 19, no. 1 (January 1951) 349–50.
29. T. Cauter and J.S. Downham, *The Communication of Ideas. A study of contemporary influences on urban life*, 1954, pp. 100–5; T. Harrisson, *Britain Revisited*, 1961, pp. 100–101.
30. Editorial comment, *Socialist Commentary*, vol. 16, no. 9 (September 1952)

194.
31. PEP, *British Trade Unionism*, revd edn, 1955, p. 45.
32. J. Goldstein, *The Government of British Trade Unions*, 1952, pp. 197–9; PEP, *Trade Unionism*, op. cit., 40–2.
33. B. Darke, *The Communist Technique in Britain*, 1952, pp. 50–8.
34. *Picture Post*, 21 May 1949.
35. G. Hodgson, 'The steel debates', in M. Sissons and P. French (eds) *Age of Austerity 1945–51*, Penguin edn, Harmondsworth, 1964, pp. 306–29.
36. The following discussion is based on *Future*, vol. 5 part 2 (April 1950) 13–17; vol. 5, part 3 (June–July 1950) 15–19; and vol. 5, part 4 (August–September 1950) 29–33.
37. Unless otherwise stated, polls referred to are taken from G.H. Gallup, *The Gallup International Public Opinion Polls. Great Britain 1937–75*, vol. 1, New York, 1977.
38. *Picture Post*, 21 May 1949.
39. *Picture Post*, 28 August 1948, 4 December 1948, 26 February 1949.
40. F. Zweig, *Men in the Pits*, 1948, pp. 157–61.
41. G.D.H. Cole, *A History of the Labour Party from 1914*, 1948, pp. 465–6.
42. R. Williams-Thompson, *Was I Really Necessary?*, 1951, pp. 33–53.
43. R.S. Milne and H.C. MacKenzie, *Straight Fight. A study of voting behaviour in the constituency of Bristol North-East at the general election of 1951*, 1954, pp. 88–9.
44. S.B. Chrimes (ed.) *The General Election in Glasgow, February 1950*, Glasgow, 1950, p. 43.
45. Mass-Observation, *Voters' Choice*, 1950, pp. 5 and 13.
46. Milne and MacKenzie, op.cit., 87 and 96.
47. M. Benney and P. Geiss, 'Social class and politics in Greenwich', *British Journal of Sociology*, vol. 1, No. 4 (December 1950) 320.
48. M. Benney, A.P. Gray and R.H. Pear, *How People Vote. A study in electoral behaviour in Greenwich*, 1956, p. 108.
49. Ibid., 47.
50. *Labour Organiser*, vol. 26, no. 307 (October 1947) 10.
51. *LPNEC*, Phillips memo, op.cit., 26 November 1947.
52. *LPNEC*, 'Report on the municipal elections', 27 June 1951.
53. *LPNEC*, 'A note on education in the Labour party', 18 September 1946; memo by H. Morrison, 'Party education', December 1950.
54. L. Thompson, *Portrait of England: news from somewhere*, 1952, pp. 99–101.
55. Milne and MacKenzie, op.cit., 108–9.
56. Benney and Geiss, op.cit., 321–2.
57. Benney et al., op.cit., 142.
58. Milne and MacKenzie, op.cit., 139.
59. Benney and Geiss, op.cit., 323.
60. H.J. Eysenck, 'Primary social attitudes as related to social class and political party', *British Journal of Sociology*, vol. 2, No. 3 (September 1951) 204–5.
61. Milne and MacKenzie, op.cit., 71 and 107.
62. H.G. Nicholas, *The British General Election of 1950*, Oxford, 1951, p. 22.
63. T.P. Jenkin, 'The British general election of 1950', *Western Political Quarterly*, vol. 3, no. 2 (June 1950) 179–83.
64. T.S. Newton, 'Labour's electoral record', *Socialist Commentary*, vol. 12, no. 7 (April 1948) 149; P. Williams, 'The next battle', *Socialist Commentary*, vol. 14, no. 3 (March 1950) 61; *New Statesman*, 31 May 1952 and 7 June 1952.
65. PEP, 'Active democracy', op.cit., 7–8 and 11–13.

66. PEP, 'Clubs, societies and democracy', *Planning*, vol. 13, no. 263 (March 1947) 4–7.
67. PEP, 'Watling revisited', *Planning*, vol. 14, no. 270 (August 1947) 79–80.
68. Cauter and Downham, op.cit., 105.
69. Mass-Observation, *Puzzled People*, 1947, pp. 120–6.
70. A.B. White, *The New Propaganda*, 1939, pp. 295–307.
71. Editorial comment, *Socialist Commentary*, vol. 13, no. 7 (July 1949) 158; A. Flanders, 'The good trade unionist', *Socialist Commentary*, vol. 14, no. 2 (February 1950) 35; J. Grundy, 'Non-voting in an urban district', *Manchester School*, vol. 18, no. 2 (1950) 98–9; PEP, 'The plan and the public', *Planning*, vol. 14, no. 269 (June 1947) 54; N. Anderson, 'Socialism without salesmanship', *Fortnightly Review*, vol. 159, no. 4 (April 1946) 273–4.
72. Hawgood, op.cit., 58–60 and 118–22.
73. F. Williams, *Press, Parliament and People*, 1946, pp. 78–81; H. Hopkins, *The New Look*, 1964, pp. 18–20.
74. *Picture Post*, 20 October 1945.
75. W. Crofts, *Coercion or Persuasion? Propaganda in Britain after 1945*, 1989, pp. 11 and 250.
76. A.A. Rogow, 'The public relations program of the Labour government and British industry', *Public Opinion Quarterly*, vol. 16, no. 2 (Summer 1952) 201–4; Crofts, op.cit., 18–26.
77. T. Wildy, 'Publicity and social planning', paper delivered at the Institute of Contemporary British History Third Annual Conference, 1990.
78. R. Williams-Thompson, *Tell The People!*, 1956, p. 17; Crofts, op.cit., 19.
79. R. Fraser, F. Owen and K. Martin, 'How to tell the people. A discussion on the British government's public relations', in A.G. Weidenfeld (ed.) *The Changing Nation*, 1947, p. 93; F. Williams, *Nothing So Strange*, 1970, p. 215; MO, file 2476.
80. Williams, *Nothing*, op.cit., 215–16.
81. Williams-Thompson, *Tell the People!*, op.cit., 17.
82. Ibid, 18.
83. *LPNEC* Minutes, Policy and Publicity Committee, 16 April 1951.
84. Labour Party Annual Conference Report [hereafter *LPACR*], 1948, pp. 30–1.
85. *The Hulton Readership Survey*, 1947–51.
86. *LPNEC*, Report by M. Phillips, 'Party development', 26 October 1945.
87. *Labour Organiser*, vol. 26, no. 287 (January 1946) 4–5, vol. 26, no. 290 (April 1946) 4–5, vol. 26, no. 291 (May 1946) 2–3, and vol. 26, no. 297 (December 1946) 5–6.
88. M. Cole, *The General Election of 1945 and After*, Fabian Research Series, no. 102, 1945, pp. 17–26.
89. *New Statesman*, 22 September 1945.
90. Williams, *Parliament and People*, op.cit., 86–7.
91. *Labour Organiser*, vol. 26, no. 307 (October 1947) 18.
92. *LPNEC* Minutes, Policy Subcommittee, 25 June 1951.
93. *LPACR*, 1948, p. 128.
94. R. Vicker, *How an Election Was Won*, Chicago, 1962, pp. 26–42, 87 and 93–4.
95. *LPNEC*, memo 'Party propaganda', 20 November 1946; memo 'Party propaganda', 28 January 1948; 'Report on propaganda activities', 21 March 1951.
96. K.O. Morgan, *Labour in Power*, Oxford, 1984, pp. 7–9.
97. C.R. Attlee, *The Labour Party in Perspective*, 1937, p. 10.
98. Ibid., 15; S. MacIntyre, 'British Labour, Marxism and working class apathy in

the nineteen twenties', *Historical Journal*, vol. 20, no. 2 (June 1977) 484–5.
99. Quoted in M. Foot, *Aneurin Bevan*, vol. 1, 2nd edn, 1975, p. 499.
100. *New Statesman*, 7 December 1946.
101. *LPACR*, 1948, p. 130.
102. Attlee, op.cit., 280–6 (emphasis added).
103. *LPACR*, 1948, p. 128.
104. *LPACR*, 1949, pp. 115 and 117.
105. *Labour Organiser*, vol. 26, no. 309 (December 1947) 8.
106. *LPNEC*, memo by R.H.S. Crossman, 'Problems facing the party', 16 April 1950.
107. *LPACR*, 1946, pp. 128–31.
108. *LPACR*, 1947, pp. 182–5.
109. *LPACR*, 1948, p. 132.
110.. M. Clapson, 'Localism, the London Labour party and the LCC between the wars', in A. Saint (ed.) *Politics and the People of London. The London County Council 1889–1965*, 1989, pp. 140–1.
111. Crofts, op.cit., 27–8.
112. Mass-Observation, 'The language of leadership', *International Journal of Opinion and Attitude Research*, vol. 1, no. 2 (June 1947) 56–9; Rogow, op.cit., 206–8.
113. Williams-Thompson, *Necessary*, op.cit., 98–111.
114. Crofts, op.cit., 39–45.
115. *LPACR*, 1948, pp. 112 and 126–8.
116. Williams, *Parliament and People*, op.cit., 125–6.
117. Rogow, op.cit., 213–14.
118. MO, file 2478.
119. Rogow, op.cit., 204.
120. Miliband, op.cit., 301–2.
121. H.H. Wilson, 'Techniques of pressure—anti-nationalisation propaganda in Britain', *Public Opinion Quarterly*, vol. 15, no. 2 (Summer 1951) 238–42.
122. Crofts, op.cit., 217.
123. H. Pelling, *The Labour Governments 1945–51*, 1984, p. 217.
124. A similar critique of the idealistic nature of the progressive strategy is made in R. Williams, *Culture and Society*, Penguin edn, Harmondsworth, 1963, pp. 314–18.
125. Mass-Observation, *Puzzled People*, op.cit., 151.
126. G.D.H. Cole, *Labour's Second Term*, 1949, pp. 5–6.
127. *Picture Post*, 24 May 1947.
128. The phrase is taken from Mass-Observation, 'Don't know, don't care', in A.G. Weidenfeld (ed.) *The Adventure Ahead*, 1948, pp. 56–61.

8 Labour and the reconstruction of Hull, 1945–51

Nick Tiratsoo

At the general election of 1945, Labour '"painted the Humber red"', winning all four of Hull's parliamentary seats where previously it had held two. The defeated candidates included Richard Law, the respected Minister of Education in the Caretaker government.[1] A few months later, there was cause for further celebration on the Left as Labour took control of the local city council. The party and its supporters were jubilant. Labour had run Hull between 1934 and 1938, but made little impact. Now, however, the portents were much more favourable. The party was in good shape, having kept up its organization and the publication of its paper, the *Sentinel*, all through the war. Moreover, the particular complexion of the problems facing Hull seemed to encourage a belief that real reform might at last be achievable. The city had suffered greatly during the hostilities, but the legacy of the death and destruction was not all negative. Indeed, as Labour took office, no less a person than Sir Patrick Abercrombie, the country's most eminent town-planner, was preparing a plan to show how Hull might be rebuilt on more modern and socially equitable lines. This chapter looks at how the hopes of 1945 fared over the following six years.

The justification for such an exercise is twofold. Very little has been written about Labour's local performance in the post-war period,[2] and so what follows will perhaps shed some light on a neglected dimension. At the same time, Hull's story is of interest because it may be used as a test case for various wider theories about reconstruction in Britain. To be specific, the narrative that follows offers an opportunity for evaluating some of the arguments presented in Corelli Barnett's much praised *The Audit of War*.[3] Barnett suggests that in wartime debates about reconstruction, 'New Jerusalemists' triumphed over realists, an ascendancy confirmed at the elections of 1945. However, this, it is argued, proved disastrous, since what

Britain needed was not homes and hospitals—these could come later—but rather industrial investment to make good war damage and replace surviving archaic plant. Labour is accused in this view, therefore, of leading the country down the wrong fork, and so paving the way for years of decline. Does what happened in Hull support Barnett's powerful thesis?

In 1939, Hull was Britain's third port as well as a major centre of the fishing industry, and this, together with its proximity to Germany, meant that from fairly early on in the war the city was quite severely and frequently bombed. The raids of March and May 1941 were especially serious, destroying the shopping centre, many factories and warehouses in the docks and much housing.[4] The extent of the destruction shocked inhabitants and visitors alike, but it was also pointed out that Hull's situation had some positive features: there was now an opportunity to right the wrongs of the past and rebuild the city in a planned way so as to make it both more efficient as an organism and a pleasanter place to live in.

The most important local pressure group for planned reconstruction was led by Max Lock. Lock, ex-student and member of staff at the Architectural Association and activist in the Modern Architecture Research Group, had originally come to Hull as Head of the School of Architecture at the College of Art.[5] In mid-1941, however, he had resigned from this position and, supported by a Leverhulme grant, had set out to compile a full-scale survey of the city in order to provide a basis for its eventual rebuilding.[6] As this work proceeded, no chance was lost to propagandize for planning in general and 'a bold and comprehensive approach' in particular. Lock argued that freed from the burden of the 'unintended, unplanned inhumanities' of its past chaotic growth, Hull could become a very different city, one which reflected 'the real needs of the community'. In detail, this meant, amongst other things, reorganizing industrial areas so that they were segregated from living quarters; providing extra, more modern housing, and grouping it in neighbourhood units so as to promote 'community' feeling; increasing amenities and open space; and improving the communications network, principally by removing an inner crescent of railway which necessitated constricting level crossings on all roads radiating out from the city centre (an idea which had been canvassed before the war).[7] Lock's prescription for Hull's main waterfront area facing the Humber, at this time a tangle of dilapidated warehouses, conveys the flavour of his proposals:

> The major operation here would be the reintroduction of life and breathing space. . . . Like the Viennese, we should be maintaining a green girdle in the heart of the city . . . as well as making use of the heaven-sent gift of a south fronting river bank, that universally enviable amenity our hard-working forefathers were far too busy to conserve.[8]

These views were, of course, fairly radical, but they quickly won quite wide support in the city. The editor of the conservative *Hull and Yorkshire Times*, for example, agreed that the coming years would provide 'an opportunity for planning in the public interest such as may never occur again'.[9] Ordinary citizens, too, seemed on the whole sympathetic, turning up in quite large numbers to the various planning exhibitions that were put on in Hull during 1942 and 1943.[10] Finally, it was apparent that key members of the local council, including the Town Clerk and a majority of members in both the ruling anti-socialist Municipal Affairs Group (MAG)[11] and the opposition Labour Party, had been at least influenced by Lock.[12] Thus, there was agreement in late 1942 to make planning for reconstruction a more central part of the council's work, a decision which led to the appointment of two eminent consultants, the leading town-planner and the leading architect of the day, respectively Sir Patrick Abercrombie and Sir Edwin Lutyens.[13] A few months later, in an equally significant move, the council responded to some of Lock's admonitions on housing and surveyed the existing stock. This led to the revelation that Hull needed 32,000 units of accommodation, 13,000 units as a matter of 'vital urgency'. After some discussion, formal acceptance was given to a target of building at least 5,000 units in the first year of peace.[14]

Nevertheless, if Hull was beginning to clarify its ideas about reconstruction, it was by no means certain that the decisions being taken at this time were all necessarily acceptable in Whitehall. Reith, the first and most radical Minister responsible for reconstruction, had been enthusiastic about Lock's Leverhulme project,[15] and his successor agreed with the appointment of the planning consultants (though Hull was informed that Abercrombie would have many other commitments).[16] Moreover, W.S. Morrison, the first Minister of Town and Country Planning, seemed equally to be in sympathy with the general direction of developments, consenting to open a prestigious exhibition of Lock's work at the Housing Centre in London during July 1943.[17] Yet against this, Hull found that over matters of detail, responses were very much less satisfactory. Pleas for future financial aid to hasten reconstruction at the war's end were met with evasion, and one councillor concluded that trying to negotiate with Whitehall on this subject was '"like trying to swim through a sea of glue"'.[18] Nor did a visit from the Advisory Panel, an official body set up to liaise with local authorities over reconstruction planning,[19] provide much reassurance. The panel arrived in Hull in the middle of October 1943, and was given a series of presentations emphasizing how badly the city had suffered and how much it was planning to do. Neither point was received with very much sympathy, however, and in its later deliberations the panel concluded that Hull had overestimated its real housing needs, and anyway should be concentrating more on its industrial future.[20] This evaluation was neatly summarized in a later briefing paper presented to the panel:

> The Corporation contend that housing provision must precede that for industry and trade. But if local building resources are so taken up, will not this be to put the cart before the horse? . . .. Over 80 per cent of Hull's houses are occupiable: less than 80 per cent of its factories and business premises are workable. This argues for the mixing of industrial and housing building.[21]

During the early months of 1944, there were further signs to worry the proponents of radical reconstruction. Again, official attitudes gave cause for concern, as when the government, acting on Board of Trade advice, defeated a Bill from Hull which would have allowed the Corporation some power to plan local economic development by sanctioning the municipal purchase of land for industrial building.[22] Moreover, scepticism about planning was on the increase in the city itself. Lutyens had died at the turn of the year, provoking a certain amount of worried comment about possible delays that this might cause in the completion of the overall plan.[23] At the same time, some of Abercrombie's initial pronouncements about how he saw the future of Hull—for example, his assertion that 'it was no use having industry if people were not living in comfortable suroundings easily related to industry'[24]—proved more controversial than might have been expected a year or two previously. Was the consultant about to repeat the 'extravagant' approach which marked his recently published plan for Plymouth? asked bodies representing commercial and industrial interests. If so, this would prove disastrous, since whatever was suitable elsewhere, in Hull the priority must be the securing of a prosperous economic future.[25] The local *Daily Mail* took up this theme with vigour:

> This is no time to be thinking about beauty spots and sports palaces, but of sites for factories and facilities for imports and exports. There must and will be healthy residential areas, fine schools, and playing fields . . . but we must have employment and wages, otherwise the amenities will be useless.[26]

Inevitably, division over this issue soon carried over on to the council. The MAG underlined its general sympathy with the views being expressed by 'responsible' bodies like the Chamber of Commerce and Shipping: the Hull of the future, as a leading member put it, should be 'a city and a port and not a cheap edition of Blackpool'. Against this, Labour warned of the powers of vested interests, and argued that having commissioned a plan, the council should not prejudge what it might contain.[27]

In November 1944, one of Abercrombie's assistants visited Hull, and the city was given its first real preview of how the consultant's mind was working. The perspective being employed, it seemed, was both expansionist and ambitious. Hull would have a thriving future because of its proximity to predicted growth markets like Scandinavia and the USSR. Consequently, the city's dock facilities and internal communications system needed to be improved. At the same time, it was clear that Abercrombie had accepted many of Lock's points about the need to make Hull a better place to live in. The result was a fairly radical collection of measures: a redesigned city centre, featuring a semi-pedestrianized shopping area built away from the present shattered site; segregated industrial zones; more open space and lower density housing; the abolition of the constricting level crossings; and a plan to open up the city's hinterland to bigger ships by 'dockizing' the River Hull (a narrow waterway which currently formed a cluttered harbour off the Humber).[28]

Very little of this met with much enthusiasm from interested parties. The council agreed to examine the proposals and display them at an exhibition,[29] but elsewhere responses were often hostile. The *Daily Mail* felt that ratepayers would 'sit back nearly breathless' after examining the recommendations, and predicted considerable modification to the Abercrombie scheme in the future.[30] Retailers rejected the idea of building a new shopping centre, because most owned the freehold sites of their damaged or destroyed premises and did not want to become tenants either of the council or of a property company.[31] Finally, river interests were especially incensed. Companies with property on the Hull had traditionally stored raw materials in adjacent barges, unloading cheaply (because river craft enjoyed an ancient exemption from tonnage dues) as and when they needed supplies. If the river was to be opened up, that is straightened and deepened, advantageous wharfage arrangements and even some of the waterfront property itself would be a thing of the past.[32]

Under pressure from these groups, the MAG too adopted a critical stance. Thus, in January 1945 the council announced that specialist consultants (Rendel, Palmer and Tritton) had been engaged to evaluate the River Hull proposals. Some weeks later, the City Engineer was commissioned to draw up an alternative scheme for the central area.[33] Both investigations produced conservative conclusions. The expert opinion on the Hull was against 'dockizing' because of the cost and inconvenience ('the scheme involves the displacement of a large percentage of existing mills and other industries which would be left without water-frontage or would have their access to the river seriously impaired'),[34] while the local official unsurprisingly came down in favour of simply rebuilding the centre and the shops in their existing positions. Labour denounced this latter plan as a capitulation to vested interests, but this did not prevent the MAG from ensuring that it became official council policy.[35]

Meanwhile, alongside these deliberations, there was also considerable debate in London about the Abercrombie proposals, as various ministries produced their own evaluations. Here, opinion was at best lukewarm. Thus, an early judgement at the Ministry of Town and Country Planning concluded that the consultant's ideas were 'very ambitious . . . what one might term "ideal" ', and noted that little consideration seemed to have been given to buildings still standing in the central area.[36] However, it was at the Board of Trade that officials were most perturbed. The belief in this department was that uncertainty about the city's future shape, directly stemming from the controversial nature of the Abercrombie scheme, had already proved damaging in that many firms were being deterred from making definite plans about rebuilding. Moreover, the situation in Hull was having a knock-on effect, since warehouses throughout the West Riding were having to cope with materials which in normal times would have been stored in the city.[37] The question was how this muddle could be resolved.

One solution which was canvassed from Hull centred on making Humberside a Development Area, but Dalton was unwilling to take this step because he was conscious of the number of such designations that had already been made.[38] Given this constraint, the Board eventually settled on a policy of trying to give industrial rebuilding as wide a priority as possible, regardless of any overall planning proposals. Of course, this kind of approach was not necessarily popular elsewhere in Whitehall, particularly in departments charged with securing social ends, and the Ministry of

Health was strong enough to ensure that in the overall government strategic planning for Hull, house and factory-building were given equal weight.[39] But by mid-summer 1945 the Board had won some powerful allies, not least amongst the civil servants of the Ministry of Town and Country Planning, where opinion was tending more and more to the belief that 'in the interests of Hull's economy it . . . [might] be necessary to throw overboard some of the planning principles incorporated in the Abercrombie proposals.'[40]

Nevertheless, despite all of this, supporters of radical reconstruction had no reason to be completely without hope. Labour's triumph at the general election augured well, since the party was committed to the idea of planning, and optimism was further encouraged when Silkin, the new Minister of Town and Country Planning, visited Hull and apparently guaranteed sufficient financial support for a comprehensive approach ('Mr. Silkin thinks that the State will make itself responsible for damage').[41] Even the situation on the local council looked less bleak than it had done, as Labour was able to force through a motion rescinding commitment to the City Engineer's plan for the central area, on the casting vote of the Mayor.[42] All eyes were now on the forthcoming local elections, which would see the ordinary people of Hull finally brought fully into the equation.

In the run-up to this contest, both the main parties clarified their positions on reconstruction. The MAG's policy was summed up in the slogan 'Prosperity through full employment'. The group emphasized that it had very much backed Abercrombie's original appointment, but because of the changing circumstances, what was needed in the future was a much more 'practical' approach than the consultant seemed to be proposing, related both to Hull's ability to pay and to its most pressing problem, the need to rebuild local industry. Too much planning, it was argued, would simply stifle the kind of private enterprise which alone could guarantee progress: 'We don't want people to be told, when they apply for business sites, that they can't have them because they would be in the middle of a football field.'[43]

Labour presented itself as being in favour of a very different set of aims.[44] Its main priority was housing, and the need 'to provide a self-contained permanent dwelling for every individual family at the earliest possible moment'. Other claims on resources, from factory and warehouse owners, would be subordinate to this end: 'We realise that industry also has its building programmes, *but the people must be housed first*, and industry can continue to carry on for a further short period in its present state, inconvenient though it may be'.[44] There followed policies on health and education and then a detailed statement about reconstruction in general. The council had appointed Abercrombie, Labour repeated, and it must wait until his plan was fully prepared. The MAG was being pressed by its supporters to jettison the consultant and 'pass a plan which will disturb them as little as possible' but they were not 'concerned with the city as a whole . . . only . . . the interests of "Big Business" '. In the event, it was this programme that proved the most compelling, and with 54 per cent of the vote, Labour romped home with 50 seats to their opponents' 34.[45]

The time was now right for some stocktaking in order to see how best the party's strategy could be set in motion. The new administration knew that the scale of the problems it faced was enormous. Hull could justifiably claim to be Britain's worst-bombed city, since raids had been both widely damaging (no district was untouched) and fairly frequent right to the war's end.[46] In all, 2 million square feet of factory and warehouse space (12 per cent of the 1939 total) was in ruins, while the city had also lost over 5,000 houses (nearly 6 per cent of the pre-war stock) and most of its big shops.[47] Overall rateable value in April 1946 stood 8.3 per cent down on the equivalent figure for 1940 (see Table 8.1). In addition, the indirect consequences of the war had been almost as calamitous. Thus, Hull's population was now one-fifth smaller because of the impact of the call-up and the direction of labour, while its fishing fleet, comprehensively requisitioned, had been nearly halved by enemy action.[48] Nor were there any real compensating advantages from the war effort—no new naval bases or 'shadow factories', yielding rate income and providing employment, because of the proximity to Germany. The relationship between needs (for example, a housing list over 7,000 applications long)[49] and resources to satisfy them was therefore well out of balance.

On the other hand, the political situation before the council seemed quite favourable. Of course, local and national pressure to prioritize industrial rebuilding remained much in evidence, and was strong enough to ensure that in the first test case about making good warehouses on the part of the River Hull that Abercrombie wanted restyled, it was the private firm concerned and not the council that received sanction in London.[50] Yet, against this, there were a number of more hopeful signs. Labour interpreted the local election result as a clear mandate to put its policies into practice, and was further encouraged by the interest shown in an exhibition of Abercrombie's proposals put on locally during February 1946.[51] Moreover, Silkin's public pronouncements still gave cause for hope, and suggested that the Board of Trade's line might not necessarily always win in the new government. Indeed, on a second visit to Hull, the minister was positively effusive about Abercrombie—'This was the plan of the people of Hull'—and quite unequivocal about how his administration saw the city's future:

> I should like to assure you of my sympathy and my support and that of the Government in all your efforts . . . we will give you such help as you may reasonably need in the performance of that task . . . be determined and ambitious for your city. The long and glorious story of Hull has many pages still to be written if you will only write them.[52]

In the light of this encouragement, Labour decided that it should push ahead with its manifesto programme. It was agreed, first, on the priority issue of housing, to try to build 5,500 units at a cost of £4.4m over the next three years.[53] At the same time, Labour councillors reaffirmed their belief in some of Abercrombie's key ideas for town-planning. The Ministry of War Transport and the LNER let it be known that they were against the abolition of the inner railway system, since the alternative (linking the main station to the high-level, outer railway ring by means of an incline) would be

Table 8.1 Hull CB: details of local government income, 1940–51

	(1940)	1945	1946	1947	1948	1949	1950	1951
Population	317,800	229,640	245,740	278,190	289,240	294,200	296,400	302,100
Rateable value (£)	1,804,870	1,627,848	1,654,861	1,683,757	1,765,617	1,719,775	1,747,958	1,794,931
Rate (s. d.)	–	20/6	20/6	21/6	23/10	21/-	19/-	21/2
Incomes from rates (£)	–	1,529,961	1,576,411	1,710,745	1,959,371	1,761,656	1,597,873	1,810,746
Net committee requirements (£)	–	1,882,571	2,040,619	2,464,604	2,704,432	2,320,193	2,306,058	2,475,496
Gov't grants (£)	–	350,851	451,585	769,240	732,736	753,462	553,824	642,149
Net loan debt (£m.)	–	11.2	11.2	12.2	12.7	13.5	14.4	15.4

Notes: 1. Figures relate to year ended 31 March unless otherwise stated.
2. Rateable value figures compiled from valuation list at year's beginning to 1947, then from valuation list at year's end.

Source: City . . . of . . . Hull, *Abstract of Treasurer's Accounts* 1940–51.

both expensive and operationally difficult. However, the council would not drop the idea, and suggested it be fully evaluated by consultants before any decision was taken.[54] Commitments were also made to pursue the new shopping centre and River Hull parts of the scheme.[55] In fact, on the latter issue, Labour mounted something of an offensive, repeating the warning that vested interests were at work:

> The River Hull, which should be the life blood of the city . . . was a disgrace. It had been allowed to go to rack and ruin. They (the Chamber of Commerce) had squeezed every penny they could get out of [it] . . . and had never been prepared to put a penny into its maintenance . . . 'We,' he said, 'believe in planning and in the resources of the city being used for the benefit of the people.'[56]

Finally, discussion began on the question of how the local council should actually start central reconstruction. Existing legislation allowed authorities to apply for Declaratory Order areas, within which they would have enhanced powers of compulsory purchase and considerable financial backing from the centre. But it was by no means certain from the statutes how widely the boundaries to such areas could be drawn, and what the minister responsible (the Minister of Town and Country Planning) would allow or not. None the less, Hull decided, again, to be ambitious and ask for 3,000 acres. The aim was to make the whole of the central area 'the property of the people' so that the value of any improvements 'instead of going into the private pockets of the owners, . . . [would] come into the pockets of the ratepayers'.[57]

However, over the following months, there were a number of signs that such optimism and ambition would not necessarily be enough to guarantee any real progress with reconstruction. Opposition from vested interests to the council's plans for Hull was, if anything, getting stronger, in that it had become more cohesive (with the Chamber of Trade, the Retailer's Advisory Committee and the Property Owners Protection Association agreeing to form a 'united front' against the local authority), better directed (the Chamber was employing a full-time organizer and a solicitor to promote its case), and considerably shriller ('"The Socialist proposal to acquire land and property years before any redevelopment is possible, and to appropriate the income from these properties, is robbery, naked and unashamed"').[58] Nor were there any indications that the government intended to help the city in the way that Silkin had promised. Thus, the scheme to abolish the level crossings had to be dropped after the consultants had costed it, because the Minister of War Transport made it clear that he favoured a much cheaper alternative (raising some of the radial roads over the inner railway), even if this did play havoc with the coherence of Abercrombie's projected overall central layout.[59] More significantly, in day-to-day decision-making about *current* resource allocations, it was clear that the Board of Trade view—against Abercrombie and for industrial building at all costs—continued to be most influential. Typically, therefore, when the Ministry of Health protested that not enough building labour was being used on housing in Hull (51 per cent of the total available were employed in this sector, as opposed to the 60 per cent recommended by a Cabinet guideline), no action was taken, because production departments did not want to jeopardize the local industrial projects they were sponsoring.[60] The direct outcome of this was a very low rate of housing completions (see Table 8.2), and with the return of Service personnel, a growing waiting list of over 30,000 people.[61]

Table 8.2 Hull C.B.: municipal housing completions, 1946–51

Year (to 31/12)	Cumulative total of units completed: Permanent	Temporary
1946	26	1,287
1947	248	2,103
1948	653	2,457
1949	1,231	2,457
1950	1,766	2,457
1951	2,842	2,457

Source: annual *Housing Return.*

Nevertheless, in spite of all this, Labour ended 1946 still relatively full of hope. In part, this was because of the publication in October[62] of the full printed version of the Abercrombie and Lutyens plan.[63] Abercrombie much later remembered this as '*probably* the best post-war report' with which he had been associated,[64] and it certainly made an impressive volume. All the ideas that had been floated in the previous years were included, but this time fully explained and justified, and in enough technical detail to impress the experts of the specialist press.[65] In addition, the various parts were grounded in a vision which had much in common with Labour's own thinking. The consultants' perspective was expansionist and coloured by a desire for greater social justice: they wanted to make Hull 'a great Civic Community', not merely rebuild an old industrial centre.[66]

In addition, Labour could draw some satisfaction from the November local elections. The MAG had launched its own broadsheet journal, *Freedom* (subsequently *The Hull News*), in April 1946 and was beginning to look a very credible opponent, approaching the polls with a manifesto ('"Clean Up Hull"') which promised 'homes for the people', 'improved shopping facilities without delay', 'full employment' and the scrapping of the 3,000-acre Declaratory Order application. When the results were declared, however, it was clear that the electorate's sympathies of 1945 were still basically intact, for although the Group had been able to increase its vote in some of the wards, it was Labour that emerged with an augmented council majority.[67]

Yet if the events of late 1946 provided something of a tonic, their effort was to be very short-lived. For in the early months of the following year, the council found itself sliding towards a crisis of dimensions which were entirely new. Its basic problem revolved around finance, and the legacy bequeathed by the wartime destruction of rateable value.[68] In April 1946 Labour had increased the rate by 1s. to 21/6d., but this had proved barely enough to balance the books, even allowing for a special central government grant of £285,000 given in recognition of the city's smaller total valuation. However, the outlook for 1947–8 looked very much bleaker. Inflation was rising, and the council also faced larger servicing payments, as its loan debt increased to cover the growth in expenditure on housing and rebuilding schemes. On the other hand, it was by no means clear that assistance from the centre would be continued at its present level, since the government had plans to alter the system of local authority finance. The obvious solution was to raise the rates still further, but the council knew that room for manoeuvre here was much less than it might appear. A high rate would deter industry and commercial interests from remaining in Hull. Much worse, it would clearly hit working-class Labour supporters disproportionately badly, since low-valued domestic properties made up about 50 per cent of the rate base.[69] In the end, therefore, the only choice possible was to keep the increase in the annual rate charge as low as possible—a figure of 23/10d. was decided upon—and prune projected expenditure to the bone. The prospects for a rolling programme with larger and larger budgets, as had been implicit in earlier housing plans for example, began to look distinctly remote.

To make matters worse, the council could hardly point to any great compensatory progress on other fronts. Relations with the government's planning apparatus remained strained, since decisions continued to go against the local administration. The pattern was set early on in the year over a case concerning one of the firms on the city's Citadel Estate. Abercrombie had earmarked this area for flats and public gardens, and suggested that existing users, mainly the timber trade, should be moved to one of the new industrial zones. This was not to the taste of the companies occupying the site, and one, in a test case, sought to obtain extended planning permission to protect its premises. The council offered a five-year remission period only, but this was not upheld on appeal to the Minister of Town and Country Planning. The logic used by Silkin in making his judgement was by now becoming depressingly familiar to councillors:

> the diversion from industrial use of the Citadel Estate as a whole would, in any circumstances that can reasonably be foreseen, seriously interfere with one of the principal activities of the port, which could not be so economically or effectively carried on elsewhere in the industrial area.[70]

In June, the minister's stock fell even further in this quarter, with the announcement of his verdict on Hull's first batch of spot compulsory purchase area applications. Again using the 1944 legislation, the council had decided it wanted four sites totalling about 185 acres, including one, on Anlaby Road, which was to be turned into the city's first new neighbourhood unit. However, Silkin was willing to grant only 51 acres in all, and only 32 per cent of the Anlaby Road application in particular. These decisions provoked consternation in the local Labour party, who saw them as 'extremely disappointing' and 'a serious blow to the replanning of the city'.[71] Activists were particularly disheartened because no logic could be detected behind the minister's thinking, except a desire to avoid controversy[72] and secure economy. Thus, even a ministry official had to concede that the Anlaby Road adjudication 'looked absurd when viewed on the ground'.[73] In these circumstances, the MAG had good reason to be jubilant: Hull's predicament proved, it claimed, both Labour's national incompetence at running the economy and its local delusions about the potential benefits of planning.[74]

Meanwhile, the Chamber of Trade and its allies continued to harry away at Abercrombie's central area proposals at every opportunity. One initiative involved circulating a petition in favour of keeping the main shops in their pre-war sites, and this was quite successful in that 30,000 signatures were collected. At the same time 'the united front' sought to disprove the argument that it was simply a combination of narrow interest groups by engaging W.R. Davidge, a past president of the Town Planning Institute, to prepare an alternative scheme to match Abercrombie's. This went on display in Hull during October and was predictably conservative, being shaped by the dictum that 'Considerations of cost and availability of materials must come foremost in any plans for redevelopment'.[75]

Given the scale of these various problems, and in the knowledge that the November council elections were approaching, Labour recognized that it would now have to offer some concessions. Accordingly, the 3,000 acre Declaratory Order application was dropped, and the Chamber of Trade informed that the council would negotiate about the central area, and drop its insistence on Abercrombie pure and simple. These moves did not have the desired effect, however. Property and shop-owners saw them as a sign of weakness, and redoubled their campaign for the Davidge proposals.[76] On the other hand, for many ordinary people in Hull the key issues, anyway, lay elsewhere. Labour had made promises, it was felt, but few were being honoured. The rate was high, yet there were no tangible signs of reconstruction in the city.[77] Permanent housing completions had barely reached 200 in 1947, while the council waiting-list remained static at around 11,000 applications (see Table 8.3).[78] Moreover, the wider economic difficulties being experienced across the country had caused a significant growth in local unemployment levels.[79] On all these counts it was easiest to blame Labour, the party that had, after all, control of all the levers of power.

The full extent of the change in popular attitudes became evident on election night. Labour's vote had fallen from 52 per cent of the total in 1946 to only 45 per cent. This meant that its majority on the council was now just eight. The party's *Sentinel* blamed 'apathy . . . and the "tight" times', but one of the local newspapers was perhaps nearer the mark when it attributed the defeat in part to some of the electorate's irritation at their drab, overcrowded and still war-ravaged living conditions.[80]

Between 1948 and 1951 there was little real change in the established pattern of reconstruction matters. One bright spot for the city administration, it is true, was Westminster's long-awaited reform of local govern-

Table 8.3 Hull C.B.: Housing waiting-list, various dates, 1945–53

Date	No. on waiting-list
15/9/45	7,675
13/4/46	11,692
6/7/46	11,056
17/5/47	11,146
14/2/48	11,795
19/2/49	13,896
19/11/49	13,343
8/5/50	14,367
1953	15,927

Sources: 1945–49: *HYT* date as stated;
1950: Hull City Council Housing Com., 8 May 1950, 2327;
1953: *The Architects' Journal*, 8 July 1954.

ment finance. Yet although this measure paved the way for rate cuts in 1948–9 and 1949–50 and allowed augmented borrowing, it was not enough to counteract the influence of some already existing and very effective constraints on the desired course of development.

The key problem for the council was the fact that the Board of Trade's pre-eminence in colouring official policy about Hull was becoming ever more pronounced. What this meant in practice was that whenever civil and industrial goals clashed, it was the latter that tended to receive official sanction. Thus, the outcome of spot planning appeals continued to follow a familiar pattern. One typical case occurred in early 1948, when a company in Little Humber Street sought security of tenure guarantees for its premises. The council was reluctant to grant this claim because Abercrombie had scheduled the whole area as a riverside park with lido and theatre, but the Minister of Town and Country Planning in the end favoured the firm. The *Daily Mail* rammed home the message that ' "Realities Before Idealism" ' had once again been proved to be the order of the day.[81]

More serious even than this, in the council's view, was the fact the Board's hand could also be detected exerting strong pressure in resource allocation. Thus, while official restrictions and 'unavoidable' shortages of building labour and materials continued to restrict the municipal housing programme,[82] there was a big increase in the number of Industrial Development Certificates issued locally over the period.[83] The results were inevitable. Though progress with housing was better than in the immediate post-war years, annual totals never reached what had been planned. Meanwhile, some 3 million square feet of factory space was being added to Hull's overall capacity.[84]

Developments over Abercrombie's controversial proposals for the city centre illustrated all the council's problems in a microcosm. It had been decided, eventually, that the local authority's best course of action would be to apply for only a 228-acre Declaratory Order area, and most of this was granted by the minister at the beginning of 1949.[85] However, this order was not a complete solution, since important issues relating to layout and ownership remained to be settled: were shopowners to rebuild on their pre-war sites, as they wanted, or would the local authority engage in wholesale land purchase within the 228 acres and insist on a new commercial centre in line with Abercrombie's recommendations? These questions continued to provoke acrimonious debate during 1948 and 1949, but in the end it was the council that was forced to back down. Again, pressure from Whitehall proved crucial. For it was now made very clear from departments that any further delay in planning would not just be inadvisable but actually disastrous: resources were about to be freed for the rebuilding of all blitzed centres, and if Hull prevaricated it was unlikely to get its fair share, which in turn might encourage exasperated retailers to go elsewhere. Given this frightening potential scenario, the council had no option but to agree, therefore, both that the shopping centre should remain on its pre-war site, and that municipal involvement there—in terms of land purchase or project development—should be strictly limited. This was a significant defeat for Labour and Abercrombie, as the MAG were quick to point out.[86] What made the situation even more unpalatable to those around the council was the fact that when allocations of steel and then capital sums for central reconstruction were finally made, Hull's share tended to be disappointing, so that by 1951, despite all the concessions, progress with the new blocks was hardly spectacular.[87]

The magnitude of these various problems inevitably modified political feelings in the city, and further strengthened the rightward shift in public opinion which had first been observed in 1947. There were no local elections during 1948, but a Conservative recruiting campaign, which boosted membership in just one of the four local constituencies to a level twice as high as Labour's city-wide total, promised changes.[88] Internal divisions hurt the MAG in 1949, but over the next two years it made significant gains so that by 1951 Labour had only a minority of elected councillors.[89] The underlying trend was also reflected in parliamentary contests, with the Conservatives being able to win back two seats in the 1950 election and then consolidate their gains the following year.[90]

How far, to sum up, had Hull Council been able to achieve its aims in the years 1945–51? Certainly, Labour supporters could be pleased with the 2,842 permanent and 2,457 temporary houses built over this period, and the administration's wider achievement of having provided accommodation for about 7,000 applicants from the waiting-lists. They could also point out, on the subject of housing, that council rents in Hull were well below those in equivalent cities, because of the chosen level of rate-derived subsidy. Finally, it was a source of some pride that, despite all the difficulties, seven major building projects had at least been started in the central area by early 1951 (see Table 8.2).[91]

Nevertheless, it was admitted that in the end this record was frankly disappointing. Housing had always been Labour's major preoccupation, yet the scale of provision over these years was nowhere near that promised in the early programmes. A waiting-list nearly 16,000 applications long in May 1951 told its own story.[92] Again, the limited building that had been started in the city centre could in no way disguise the scale of the reverses experienced by the council in more general planning matters. Most of Abercrombie's proposals had been simply abandoned, while those still theoretically intact (like the River Hull scheme) hardly seemed likely to be implemented. Indeed, the consultant's stock had fallen so low that when the city's Development Plan appeared in the early 1950s, it contained only 'a few details' of the original blueprint and 'none of the main concepts'.[93] Nor, finally, did a comparative perspective offer much comfort. Several of the similarly-sized blitzed cities (including Conservative Portsmouth) had built more permanent housing units than Hull over the period,[94] while most were further advanced with their central reconstruction.[95]

What had gone wrong? Contemporaries offered a variety of explanations. Abercrombie believed that the major responsibility for what had happened lay with the ministries in London.[96] Many others, of course, blamed the council for lack of vigour in pursuing its aims and for incompetence in handling the local commercial and industrial interests.[97] More than a few civil servants sympathized with this view, if only because they judged Hull's elected leadership to be of insufficient calibre (they were, one official concluded, 'pitifully inadequate, frustrated, combative, believing they are making the pace, in fact lagging behind').[98] On the other hand, there was also a feeling in Whitehall that Abercrombie was the real culprit. Some were irritated at the amount of time the consultant took to put his plan together, and felt he was not really being honest in blaming the delay on the paper shortage and technical problems.[99] Moreover, the finished article was generally thought to be technically unsatisfactory, too radical and 'remote from reality'. Consequently, the argument ran, though the council might be guilty of incompetence, most of what had happened was the fault of the planner. As one senior figure in the Ministry of Town and Country Planning put it: 'I think it only fair to them [the Council] to say that they have sought professional advice at a very high level and at considerable cost, only to be led into wild schemes incapable of fruition.' From this viewpoint, it was simply a 'tragedy' that Abercrombie and Hull had ever come together.[100]

Evaluating these different explanations is not easy, but the following points seem worthy of mention. First, in relation to the argument that the Labour council should have been more dynamic, it can be accepted that key elements in the leadership were badly prepared for the tasks confronting them on election to office, since the party had done little thinking about reconstruction during the war (the *Sentinel*'s coverage, for example, was limited to one article about Soviet town-planning, one explanation of Abercrombie's thinking and little else).[101] On the other hand, the party's room for manoeuvre over the following years was never really very great because of Hull's particular political complexion. The basic fact was that Labour's ability to maintain itself in power remained fairly problematic. The party gained narrow majorities in terms of votes at the 1945, 1946 and 1949 local elections, but there were several bastions of working-class Conservatism in the city which were never breached,[102] and constant eddies of popular anxiety about the rates and austerity in general. Moreover, an active and politically astute opposition party waited in the wings for any slip. In this situation, radical moves against, say, the commercial lobby were out of the question. Equally, challenging decisions made in London had to be handled very carefully: unwise words would not only damage Labour's national credibility, but might also give the impression that the party in Hull was somehow out of step with national priorities, even oblivious to the need for local industrial regeneration. Given these restrictions, it is difficult to see how the council could have pursued its ends in any other way than the one chosen.

Second, then, what of these ends? Was the council's fundamental mistake its original commitment to an unworkable plan? Taking the case against Abercrombie piece by piece, it can be conceded, first, that things would no doubt have been easier for Hull if the plan had been delivered earlier—if, in other words, the consultant had not been pressed into taking on so many other projects at around the same time.[103] However, excepting this, little else raised by Abercrombie's critics is in any way justified. The proposition that his ideas were either too radical or too ideal to be put into practice carries little weight. The planner was, of course, interested in creating a better future. Yet neither this aim, nor the methods that were advanced to achieve it, could really be called exceptional in terms of the existing town-planning consensus.[104] In addition, and as his critics very well knew, Abercrombie stressed that he expected his plan to be implemented bit by bit, over a number of years, and not all at once.[105] Much of the Civil Service reaction, therefore, seems rather disingenuous, and perhaps stemmed less from careful appraisal and more from a vague feeling that what was being proposed was simply too good for a northern, working-class port. The following private evaluation, emanating from the Ministry of Town and Country Planning at the end of 1945, illustrates the kind of prejudice that might be found lurking just below the surface of officialdom:

> [Hull] is and always must be a rather grey and ordinary city doing a very ordinary job. I feel it is no use trying to replan such a place so ambitiously as places like Bristol . . . that have dramatic features and some colour or tradition. In the case of Hull one has got to concentrate on making it an efficient and seemly place to do its ordinary job.[106]

Given all of this, it is difficult not to conclude that Hull's predicament was essentially Westminster-made. The problem, in other words, lay neither with the Council nor with Abercrombie, but with the national priorities pursued by central government. Ministries were not always agreed on what was best for Hull, but when it came to practical policy-making, it was usually the Board of Trade's view that triumphed. The consequence was a series of decisions over siting controversies and resource allocations, which blatantly favoured industrial as opposed to civil reconstruction.

Writing of the period around the ending of the Second World War, Barnett has argued:

> It was Britain's own free choice—the choice of governments and electorate alike—to relegate the physical recreation of her industrial base to a very poor second place in

her order of building priorities. Instead of starting with a new workshop so as to become rich enough to afford a new family villa, John Bull opted for the villa straightaway—even though he happened to be bankrupt at the time.[107]

For Hull at least, however, the situation was very much more complex. The local Labour party was attracted to Abercrombie's vision of a new city, as was a substantial section of the electorate. However, others in Hull wanted nothing more than a return to the pre-war status quo. At national level, too, there was more division than consensus. Some members of Attlee's government at first accepted the need for radical reconstruction; yet this view was not popular amongst civil servants, even in ministries like Town and Country Planning. Moreover, it clashed with priorities being pursued by the strong production departments, particularly the Board of Trade. The result was a pattern of reconstruction where, inverting Barnett, workshops predominated but villas were notable only for their relative absence.

Notes

1. *Hull and Yorkshire Times* [hereafter *HYT*], 28 July 1945 and 11 August 1945.
2. Though see S. Goss, *Local Labour and Local Government*, Edinburgh, 1989; and N. Tiratsoo, *Reconstruction, Affluence and Labour Politics: Coventry 1945–1960*, 1990, for two recent attempts to rectify this lacuna.
3. Barnett's book, published in 1986, is of sufficient calibre to have won great respect amongst senior members of Mrs Thatcher's Cabinet: see e.g. *The Independent*, 18 January 1990.
4. T. Harrisson, *Living Through The Blitz*, Penguin edn, Harmondworth, 1978, pp. 263–6.
5. Biographical information on Lock's career to this date is neatly summarized in the Housing Centre's *Hull Regional Survey*, 1943, p. 1.
6. *Hull Daily Mail* [hereafter *HDM*], 8 July 1941.
7. *HDM*, 18, 22 and 29 July 1941; HLG 79/256: [unsigned] memo, 'Hull Regional Survey. Draft Copy, May 1942': *HYT*, 6 June 1942; and *The Architects' Journal*, 29 July 1943.
8. *HDM*, 29 July 1941.
9. *HYT*, 30 August 1941.
10. *HDM*, 27 January 1942; and Hull City Council Housing and Town Planning Committee, 27 September 1943.
11. The MAG was a coalition of Conservatives and Independents welded together by their dislike of socialism (for a flavour of the group's thinking, see reports of its AGMs in *HYT*, 21 June 1941 and 18 September 1943). At this time it held a very narrow majority on the Council.
12. HLG 79/259: Town Clerk's Office 'Memorandum on the effect of the war upon the city . . .', February 1942; and BT 64/310: R.K. Kelsall, 'First Appendix to the report on the economic activities of Hull', January 1943, p. 21.
13. For Abercrombie, see G. Dix, 'Patrick Abercrombie 1879–1957', in G. Cherry (ed.) *Pioneers in British Planning*, 1981, pp. 103–30. Lutyens' career is summarized in *The Times*, 3 January 1944.

14. HLG 79/259: 'Report of the Special Sub-Committee . . .', May 1943, pp. 1–9; Hull City Council Housing and Town Planning Committee 10 May 1943 (24).
15. HLG 79/261: note M. Harris – B. Gillie (n.d.).
16. Hull Local Studies Library Acc. L711, 'Report of deputation . . . 5th June, 1942'; HLG 79/256: memo by G.L. Pepler, 'County Borough of Hull', 5 November 1942.
17. *The Architects' Journal*, 29 July 1943.
18. *HYT*, 6 February 1943.
19. For the Advisory Panel, see J. Hasegawa, 'The replanning of the blitzed city centre in Britain', unpublished Ph.D. thesis, University of Warwick, 1989, esp. pp. 29–34.
20. HLG 79/256: minutes nos. 10 and 11. Advisory Panel (n.d. but October 1943).
21. HLG 79/259: APCC 24, 'Notes by Dr. Sykes on Hull', 19 November 1943.
22. *HYT*, 22 April 1944; material in BT 64/3481; and *Hansard*, vol. 399, 98–122, 18 April 1944.
23. *HYT*, 8 January 1944.
24. Quoted in *HYT*, 4 September 1943.
25. *HYT*, 3 June 1944, 8 July 1944.
26. *HDM*, 7 July 1944.
27. *HDM*, 7 July 1944, *HYT*, 3 June 1944.
28. *HYT*, 11 November 1944.
29. Ibid.
30. *HDM*, 7 November 1944.
31. *HYT*, 6 June 1942, 29 July 1944, 10 February 1944.
32. *HYT*, 10 February 1945; HLG 79/261: letter W. Barr – Sir P. Warter, 16 May 1945; M.P. Fogarty, *Prospects of the Industrial Areas of Great Britain*, 1945, p. 268.
33. *HYT*, 20 January 1945 and 31 March 1945.
34. Hull Record Office Acc. TC1/14/1, 'Report on River Hull proposals', by Rendel Palmer and Tritton, May 1945.
35. *HYT*, 2 June 1945 and 9 June 1945; and *HDM* 3 August 1945.
36. HLG 79/261: note by C. Cameron to H. Gatliff, 15 December 1944.
37. HLG 79/261: memo '. . . Hull . . . replanning proposals. Notes of Discussion held on 12th June, 1945'; and letter E.R. Voyce – Gatliff, 24 July 1945.
38. *The Yorkshire Post*, 6 April 1945.
39. BT 208/1: Regional Distribution of Industrial Committee 5th Meeting (35), 16 April 1945; and 7th Meeting (50), 11 May 1945.
40. HLG 79/262: min. H. Wells – J.A. Stewart et al., 15 June 1945.
41. *HDM*, 26 September 1945.
42. *HDM*, 12 October 1945.
43. *HDM*, 3 October 1945 and 19 October 1945.
44. *HDM*, 16 October 1945.
45. *HYT*, 3 November 1945.
46. HLG 71/2222: memo 'Building priorities in blitzed cities. Regional comments', (n.d. but 1948), pp. 9–10.
47. Ibid.; U. Aylmer Coates, 'Development plan for . . . Hull. Written analysis', 1951, p. 6; and Hull City Council Housing Committee 23 September 1946 457.
48. *HYT*, 30 March 1946.
49. *HYT*, 15 September 1945.
50. See material in HLG 79/263, a file solely concerned with this case.
51. *HDM*, 13 and 21 February 1946.

52. *HDM*, 20 February 1946.
53. *HDM*, 12 March 1946; and *HYT*, 16 March 1946.
54. *The Times*, 26 February 1946; M.H. Jackson 'Problems of planning and reconstruction in . . . Hull', *The Journal of the Institution of Municipal Engineers*, vol. no. 8 (February 1948), esp. 403–4; and HLG 79/262: note Gatliff – E.S. Hill, 15 March 1946.
55. *HYT*, 6 April 1946 and 4 May 1946.
56. *HYT*, 9 February 1946.
57. *HDM*, 22 July 1946 and *HYT*, 31 August 1946.
58. *HDM*, 27 April 1946; HLG 79/260: 'Hull and District Chamber of Trade. Statement . . . 14th January 1949', pp. 1–2; *HYT*, 12 October 1946.
59. HLG 79/262: letter Town Clerk – Secretary, Ministry of War Transport, 2 August 1946.
60. BT 170/2: East and West Riding Regional Board for Industry, 9th Meeting (Minute 96), 3 September 1946; and 10th Meeting (105), 1 October 1946.
61. *HYT*, 6 July 1946.
62. *HDM*, 16 October 1946.
63. E. Lutyens and P. Abercrombie, *A Plan for the City and County of Kingston Upon Hull*, London and Hull, 1946. My own copy of this document is dated 1945; subsequent page references are to this volume.
64. Letter from Sir P. Abercrombie, *Town and Country Planning*, vol. 23, no. 139, (November, 1955), 538.
65. See e.g. *The Architects' Journal*, 31 October 1946; R.L. Reiss, 'Plan for Kingston Upon Hull', *Town and Country Planning*, vol. 14, no. 56 (Winter 1946–7) 170–5; and R. Meadows, review in *Journal of the Town Planning Institute*, vol. 33, no. 2 (January–February 1947), 52–6.
66. Abercrombie and Lutyens, op.cit., 3.
67. *HDM*, 15 October 1946; *HYT*, 2 and 9 November 1946.
68. The financial data upon which the following paragraph partly rests is summarized in Table 8.1.
69.. Hull City Council, *Abstract of the Treasurer's Accounts*, Hull, 1951, p. 11.
70. *HYT*, 18 January 1947 and 26 April 1947.
71. *HYT*, 21 June 1947.
72. The minister had recently seen one of his decisions regarding Plymouth quashed in the courts, because he had apparently interpreted the 1944 Act's statutes, over what was or what was not war-damaged land, too liberally; and he was determined that this should not happen in Hull: *HDM*, 20 February 1947, *HYT*, 21 June 1947.
73. HLG 79/269: unsigned memo 'Visit to Hull on the 17th and 18th June, 1947', 20 June 1947, p. 1.
74. *HYT*, 21 June 1947, *The Yorkshire Post*, 26 June 1947.
75. *HYT*, 15 March 1947, 24 May 1947, 31 May 1947, 16 August 1947; and HLG 79/268: W.R. Davidge '. . . Hull. Chamber of Trade. Report on central shopping area and improvements', n.d., p. 6.
76. HLG 79: note by W.B. Vince, 1 July 1947; and *HYT*, 6 December 1947.
77. For a description of the city at this time, see HLG 71/222: 'Building priorities . . .', n.d. but 1948, pp. 9–10.
78. *HYT*, 17 May 1947 and 14 February 1948.
79. *HYT*, 4 January 1947 and 24 January 1948.
80. *HYT*, 8 November 1947; *The Hull Sentinel*, no. 241, November 1947, 2.
81. *HYT*, 3 January 1948, 24 April 1948; and *HDM*, 24 April 1948.
82. E.g. *The Yorkshire Post*, 9 March 1948; and HLG 101/516: memo by J.

Stobart, 'Blitzed area—Hull C.B.', 29 November 1950.

83. Between 1945 and 1948, about 1,252,681 square feet of factory space was licensed in Hull. From July 1948 to December 1951, 143 IDCs (for buildings over 5,000 square feet only) were issued, covering projects totalling about 2,650,000 square feet (BT 177/185: Board of Trade, E. and W. Ridings, memo 'Kingston-Upon-Hull. A survey . . .', September 1948, Appendix E; and calculation from material in BT 1802–1805).
84. Calculation from material in BT 177/185: Board of Trade . . . memo . . . September 1948, Appendix E; and *The Times*, 8 October 1952.
85. *HYT* 15 January 1949.
86. HLG 79/260: min. M.B. Tetlow – Gillie, 14 March 1951; *HDM*, 19 December 1950; *Hull News*, no. 62, February 1951, 1.
87. See e.g. for reaction to one allocation ('Affront to Hull'), *HDM*, 16 May 1950.
88. Membership of the SW Hull Constituency Conservative Party was reported to be 4,000 in August 1948; total Labour party membership in the city at this time was about 2,000 (*Hull News*, no. 35, 16 August 1948 6; Labour Party, *Annual Report for 1950*, p. 246).
89. *HYT*, 12 May 1951. Labour kept control of the council, however, because it had a greater number of aldermen.
90. W.S. Craig, *British Parliamentary Election Results 1950–1970*, Chichester, 1971, pp. 172–6.
91. *HDM*, 8 May 1951; the Institution of Municipal Treasurers and Accountants, *Housing Statistics 1950–51*, 1952, pp. 6–17; and H.F. Alston, 'The redevelopment of the central area of Kingston Upon Hull', *The Journal of the Royal Institution of Chartered Surveyors*, vol. 84 no. 1 (July 1954) esp. 45.
92. *HDM*, 8 May 1951.
93. D. Rigby Childs, 'Hull', in *The Architects' Journal*, 2 July 1953, 6.
94. Completions by local authorities between April 1945 and December 1951 were as follows:

	Permanent units	*Temporary units*
Hull	2,842	2,457
Coventry	2,986	1,099
Plymouth	5,070	2,250
Portsmouth	3,428	1,400
Southampton	2,266	1,746

Source: Cmd. 8458, Min. of Housing and Local Government, *Housing Return . . . 31/12/1951*, Appendix B.

95. D. Rigby Childs, 'A comparison . . .', *The Architects' Journal*, 8 July 1954.
96. *Town and Country Planning*, vol. 23, no. 139 (November 1955) 538.
97. Silkin, amongst others, felt that the council was very undynamic: see HLG 79/266: minute by Gatliff to M. Jenkins, 18 January 1946; and memo by Voyce, 'Ministers' visit . . . 19/2/1946 . . .', n.d.
98. HLG 79/266: memo by Gatliff, 'Hull. A personal impression', 14 February 1946, p. 1.
99. See material in HLG 79/261, esp. note by Wells, 27 September 1944.
100. HLG 79/266: memo by Gatliff, 'Hull . . .', 14 February 1946, pp. 1–2; and HLG 79/260: min. by Tetlow, 14 March 1951.'

101. *The Hull Sentinel*, no. 191, September 1943, p. 1; and no. 209, March 1945, p. 5.
102. There were 21 wards in Hull at this time. The MAG held 4 of these continuously between 1945 and 1951, and 4 more continuously after 1946. It never succeeded in 8 of the wards, though it came close, on occasion, to winning 3 of them (calculated from material on election results in *HYT*).
103. For an idea of Abercrombie's various commitments in the final year of the war, see *Town and Country Planning*, vol. 12, no. 48 (Winter 1944–5) 173.
104. A. Ravetz, *Remaking Cities*, 1980, pp. 19–59.
105. Abercrombie and Lutyens, op.cit., 79–80.
106. HLG 79/261: H. Gatliff, 'Notes on a visit to Hull, 12th November, 1945', 5 December 1945.
107. Barnett, op.cit., 246–7.

9 The tide of history. The reconstruction of Conservatism, 1945–51

Bill Schwarz

On the evening of 26 July 1945 there occurred something very like a burlesque rendition of an English, or Home Counties, *grande peur*. The occasion was the announcement of the results of the general election and the discovery of the Labour Party's unprecedented parliamentary majority. As with all such social dramas historians should take this theatricality seriously, even if this is precisely how the participants, as historical actors, refused to take themselves. Extravagant gestures abounded: sentimental valedictions to maids and valets, a succession of last feed-ups at the Savoy Grill, desperate communications, *sotto voce*, with friends and relations contemplating the hardships of a refugee existence in the exclusive white redoubts of the Empire.[1] A febrile sensibility possessed the guardians of the old colonial order—subsequently given literary representation by an Evelyn Waugh or an Angela Thirkell—fearful that they were about to be condemned to uniformity and a regime of 'spam, black-outs and Nissen huts'.[2] Fatalistic subjection to the perceived indignities of democracy and an unforgiving modernity predominated in conservative cultures in the conviction that the tide of history had finally turned. A rare exception of contemptuous defiance was demonstrated with *élan* by an adolescent Nicholas Fairburn, who, fantasizing a heroic future as a *maquis* leader, took out all the windows of his local Co-op bakery.[3] The historical evidence suggests he was something of a lone figure. Panic existed, but people looked to their larder, not to the lamppost; Major Clement Attlee was not a figure to chill the blood of even the most insouciant upholders of privilege. The predominant expression of fear—however genuinely experienced—could only cohere as farce. Those with a predilection for Marxism might like to see this as a redramatization, staged within the collective memory of the Engish upper classes, of some prior political tragedy. I am more persuaded, however, to see evidence here of the deep habituation of Home Counties England to the ceaseless comedy of manners purveyed by the West End stage in this period, communicating to its audience a precise social code for every occasion.

Inside the Conservative Party, overall, the range of response was more modulated. Churchill himself, on the eve of the election results, was shaken by a dreadful presentiment. As he told his surgeon-in-waiting, Charles Moran:

> I dreamed that life was over. I saw—it was very vivid—my dead body under a white sheet on a table in an empty room. I recognized my bare feet projecting from under the sheet. It was very life-like. . . . Perhaps, [he mused], this is the end.[4]

Confirmation of 'the end' came early in the morning of the 26th with the announcement of Harold Macmillan's loss of Stockton. Thereafter seats tumbled. By the close of day some 60 per cent of the old Tory Parliamentary Party had gone, through either resignation or defeat.

While reflecting on the measure of this catastrophe, what clearly stung senior Tories—with sufficient intensity to recur in memoirs years after—was the apparent impertinence of their opponents on the hustings, and an uncalled-for triumphalism in the chamber during the first flush of victory. To Anthony Eden, suffering the loss of his son in the closing days of the war, the election was 'the dirtiest and cheapest' he had ever experienced.[5] For David Maxwell-Fyfe—admittedly not a man blessed with the sweetest of temperaments—'There was an irresponsibility about the 1945 election which made it unique in my experience', an irresponsibility on the part of Labour which continued into the opening sessions of Parliament. However, Maxwell-Fyfe was content to note that more tasteful behaviour, appropriate to the national legislature, was soon acquired, save for 'an obnoxious type of new Labour MP who seemed to attend the House solely for the pleasure of jeering at his opponents, and subjecting them to a stream of derisive interruption and mocking laughter in debate'.[6] Accustomed as we should be by now to the retrospective rehabilitation of Labour folk-devils, especially those of proletarian origins, this identification of Labour MPs of 'a new type' itself suggests something new; most of all, it hints at the presence of a stratum of traditional intellectual—Dalton would be one of the first and most prominent examples—attracted to Labour and consequently reviled by their own class as turncoats. In 1945, for a type of Tory habituated to rule, the triumph of Labour was all the more galling as it brought Dalton and his ilk to power.[7]

The transition from Churchill to Attlee signalled not only the curbing of a titanic ego and the end of rule by eccentric personalism, but also the political survival of a social class rather more domesticated and less ostentatious than hitherto—the shift in perception which could allow *Spring in Park Lane* (1948), for example, to be released as a quaintly anachronistic romantic comedy, and *Brief Encounter* (1945) be received as the very distillation of an emotionally intense, realistic provincial drama: the suburbanization of tragedy. Attlee represented what for Baldwin was a pose, and for Churchill an embarrassment: the realities of middle-class England strapped for cash (as they saw it) and 'making do' without the full complement of live-in domestic servants. Clement Attlee—Haileybury, Oxford and settlement in Limehouse, ending his days in Cherry Cottage, Great Missenden—would have found incomprehensible and faintly distasteful Churchill's boast that however impoverished he had been, there had never been a day when he could not have indulged himself and a friend in a decent bottle of champagne apiece: not for Churchill a dry sherry before lunch on Sunday. In this respect Paul Addison is right to draw attention to the social significance of Churchill's journey to the Palace—by means of his chauffeur-driven Rolls—compared with Attlee's, who made the same journey shortly after in the family Standard Ten, driven (on this occasion without mishap) by his wife, the long-suffering Vi.[8] This social divergence between the two is caught nicely in Churchill's realization that Attlee had no 'man' to travel with him to Potsdam, so Churchill offered him his own.

Of course this social divergence represented a deeper political convergence, which Churchill knew well enough even when he blustered and lost his temper. 'He is an admirable character, but not a man with whom it is agreeable to dine', declared Churchill.[9] However, whether a dinner companion or not, Churchill never much doubted that Attlee was sound on the two great issues: the Constitution and (as a worthy product of Haileybury), the Empire. In fact, Churchill's attitude to Attlee was not so very different from his attitude to Eden. Both he found weak, and he could never quite resist imposing a bullying, sadistic edge on his relations with them. Eden, as the more proximate of the two, suffered the more deeply. Indeed, during the war Eden and Attlee forged an axis in the War Cabinet in order, according to Attlee, to 'put a brake on Winston's wild ideas'.[10] For his part, Eden remained respectful of Attlee: 'I can't remember him ever making a point which I felt came from him as leader of the Labour Party.'[11] This shared history, deeply rooted in the crisis of the nation, can only have been reassuring to those who feared the worst.

Moreover, certain aspects of life before Labour remained intact, as natural features of the political landscape. Churchill saw nothing amiss in the leadership of his party—not yet having assumed the unattractively professional nomenclature of Shadow Cabinet—meeting in the Savoy each fortnight for business to be conducted in as convivial, and as familiar, an environment as possible. Nor did it seem odd that even after the election almost a third of Tory MPs had attended the same school. Whatever the indignities of living with Labour, there is a greater sense of tactic than of panic conveyed in Lord Woolton's recollection: 'I made up my mind that we would call the Government "the Socialist Party".'[12] The view from the private chambers of the Savoy was not altogether fearful.

Even so, despite the determination of pragmatists like Woolton to put the Tory Party back into political shape, the scale of the party's defeat should not be underestimated. There is, I think, a lack of perspective in much current historical reconstruction of the period 1945–51. Looked at from the point of view of the Labour Party, as it is most often, we know that by 1947 the hopes of two years earlier had collapsed. However, the disasters Labour inflicted on itself do nothing to mitigate the scale of the defeat suffered by the Conservative Party. Similarly, in retrospect we know that the Tories were back in business by 1951, and the constitutional wheel was once more turning on its supposedly natural pivot of the two-party system, rotating between the two great parties of state. Indeed, so confident did Tories themselves become in the wake of this recovery that the more imaginative of them could look back to the defeat of their party in 1945 and (so we are to believe) *welcome* it, as a stern reminder to the more selfish of their ranks that Labour deserved its turn too. Thus Rab Butler (or more probably his sister, who drafted the bulk of the memoirs which carry his name), with a matchless aura of confidence, explained that

> thirty years of almost uninterrupted power, such as we had exercised either alone or in coalition, must be regarded as unnatural in a properly functioning democracy. Such democracy does not necessarily require, like a tennis match, the regular alternation of service and defence; on the contrary, it is frequently strengthened by a lengthy continuity of experience in administration. But just as its post-war periods of office have mellowed the Labour Party, educating it out of many callower socialistic assumptions, so the Conservatives, when thrown into opposition, were provided with a healthy opportunity and a compelling motive for bringing their policies and characteristic modes of expression up-to-date. The adaptations and adjustments of both sides were, on a long-term view, of benefit to the country.[13]

This of course is artful rubbish. So far as one can judge these things, I am sure that Butler had a vision of the world which could transcend narrow party political advantage. Retrospective rationalization is another matter, however. His judgement here comes after thirteen years of Conservative dominance, 'lengthy continuity of experience' indeed. The deepest fear in 1945 was not that the Conservative Party had missed its turn—any politician can live with that—but that it would never get another. At the end of his career the hypnotic alternation of party may well have appeared to Butler as natural as day following night; in 1945 no one could be so sure.

This is not to give credence to Churchill's jibes about Labour's totalitarianism, or to the belief that Stafford Cripps—brainwashed by his spell in Moscow—was about to transmogrify into Felix Dzerzhinsky. The issue resolves not around dictatorship but democracy. As a prominent Conservative has reiterated, mass democracy is historically a relatively recent implantation in British society.[14] From the late 1880s we can see the protracted reconstruction of Conservatism—under the unwelcome tutelage, as I understand it, first of Joseph Chamberlain, and then of Lloyd George—into a political party able to exist in the prevailing conditions imposed by a mass electorate. Chamberlain's vision was of a mass populist party of the Right, whose governing dynamic was a recharged imperialism; briefly, and with less confidence, Lloyd George shared a similar view. The formal programmes of both these projects were defeated, and in consequence the Conservative Party retreated into a more defensive, pragmatic rule from above, dominated strategically by an anti-socialist coalitionism and only hesitantly (under Baldwin in the 1920s) embracing the exigencies of two-party constitutionalism. Thus for all his artifice, Butler was right to emphasize the long periods of Tory-controlled coalitionism which dominated the earliest moves to mass democracy in Britain: 1916–22, 1931–40 and 1940–5. By 1945 the Conservatives had had very little experience of competing in the open political market with what was now indubitably its main contender, an active and professionally organized Labour Party. Understandably, when this did occur, bringing with it such dramatic consequences, the experience was unnerving, suggesting the possibility—as Churchill feared in his dream and sometimes in his waking life—that 'the end' was to hand, and in this context the personal attributes of Labour's leader were neither here nor there.

It is for this reason, I think, that the Tories began to be so exercised during the war about those civic and government-sponsored institutions which were becoming overenthusiastic about the virtues of citizenship and mass democracy. The BBC, the Army Bureau for Current Affairs, the cavortings of independent MPs and so on threatened, in their combined effect, precisely to open out the workings of civil society and to function as a bridgehead for the deepening democratization of the state. A not untypical response came from Maurice Petherick, Tory MP for Penryn and Falmouth, who in December 1942—in the aftermath of Beveridge—wrote to Churchill's PPS complaining about ABCA:

> I am more and more suspicious of the way this lecturing to and educating of the forces racket is run . . . for the love of Mike do something about it, unless you want to have the creatures coming back all pansy-pink.[15]

Yet what is so intriguing about the predominant radical and populist discourses of the war is how rudimentary was their sense of democracy, their authors feeling impelled to explain the nuts and bolts of electoral practice to what otherwise might be an indifferent or ignorant constituency. This was especially so when women were addressed, unambivalently positioned as novices in the imperatives of constitutionalism. The *Daily Mirror* is revealing in this respect, progressing before the war from instructions for its female readers on 'how not to mix old vermilion lipstick with fuchsia rouge', to exhorting them 'to act politically, in 1945, for the sake of home and family'. On 12 June 1944, with the Normandy landings under way, the paper implored its readers in elementary tones:

> And I don't mean the X that we used to put on a picture postcard to show which was our room in the hotel on the sea front.
>
> THIS X is the one that goes on the ballot paper against the name of the man or woman you want to vote for, because you think he or she is the candidate who expresses *your* views . . .
>
> At the next Election, every man and woman over twenty-one will be able to write that X. And anyone who doesn't will be betraying the principles for which our men are fighting today.
>
> Why? Because if you are too lazy to use your vote you give a chance to others, not so lazy, but perhaps more unscrupulous, to get into power to run *your* life.

It was the job of women in particular to take things in hand, if necessary by chivvying their husbands:

Your man, serving in the Forces, *must* vote at the next General Election. By fighting for his country he has won the right to have a say in its peace time running . . . .. It's more likely that your man will bother if *you* ask him to. Write *NOW* and get him to get hold of the form.[16]

The war mobilized the political expectations of a generation, and exerted potentially disruptive pressures from below on the established party system. The language of constitutionalism was an effective part of the Tory repertoire; the language of democracy triggered rather more unpredictable possibilities.

There is some evidence—as in earlier moments in the history of Conservatism—that there were those who were prepared to contemplate the disappearance of the Tory Party in order to safeguard the longer-term future of a broader, more effective Conservatism. It is common for historians to observe that the foremost leaders of the party in this period—Churchill and Eden—were indifferent to domestic affairs, and could never quite adjust themselves to the parochial concerns of a declining nation in peacetime. While true, it is also the case that both Churchill and Eden, at different moments, felt a repugnance for the party they led. In June 1945 Eden wondered, in the privacy of his diary, what hopes there were to achieve anything 'through the sordid medium of Tory party politics'.[17] Leadership of the party never prevented Churchill from blowing hot and cold about the political imbeciles who surrounded him, yearning for the days of his personalized special relationship with Roosevelt when the management of party politics could be left to the time-servers.[18] Even Rab Butler despaired of the pigheadedness of Tory back-benchers, noting in his diary at the time of the Beveridge Report that many of them harboured 'a feeling that Beveridge is a sinister old man, who wishes to give away a great deal of other people's money'.[19]

With anxieties such as these it is not surprising that a significant clutch of senior Tories hoped for a continuation of coalition government, at least until the defeat of Japan, preferably for longer. *The Times*, still then a significant political force and not always in these years well disposed to Conservative opinion, favoured this view.[20] The virtue of this strategy, as its adherents saw it, would be to continue a tried and tested solution which, they hoped, would place a brake upon the socialist ambitions of the Labour Party, constraining Labour from within as it were. Little wonder that Attlee loomed so large in these deliberations as the figure—given his accommodating anti-partisan record since 1940—on whom the Conservatives would depend. If this strategy were to be realized, its proponents banked on the possibility that a coming confrontation with Labour might be postponed until a more propitious moment, or even avoided altogether.

Tories wary of this view—including the great majority of the back-benchers—saw a different possibility. The very purpose of coalition, as it had been articulated at least since the coupon election of 1918, was anti-socialism. Given the extraordinary transformations wrought by the war in extending the role of the state, combined with the ceaseless promises from Tories of every stripe that extensive social reform would be the priority once hostilities had ceased, there did seem to be a distinct possibility that to continue government by coalition in these conditions could only bring about socialism by stealth, and moreover a socialism apparently legitimated by the presence of Conservatives in government. Far from neutralizing the doctrinaire elements of the Labour Party, the tide of history had swung so far against the Conservatives that, so this reasoning continued, the Tory Party would be drawn unwillingly into the practicalities of socialist reconstruction. As we shall see, even after the electoral defeat of 1945, the issues which underpinned these alternative strategies re-emerged in modified form to divide the party. Either way, however, in the months leading up to the general election the Conservative Party lost the initiative. Irrespective of the hopes held by Churchill and Eden—and indeed by Attlee—the Labour Party decisively reordered the balance of political forces, making the break from coalition, and bidding for single-party government. The wartime Coalition was both made and unmade by the Labour Party. There was little the Conservatives could do.

Prior to Labour's exit from the wartime coalition, a contingent or passive integration of the old Tory Party into some larger national coalition—transforming it in practice while maintaining the rhetoric of customary allegiances and ritual—was not an unintelligent notion for Tories to contemplate, even if political realities made the likelihood of this occurring extremely slim. Yet to leading if quirkily dissident Conservatives, who had experienced five years of accommodation with Labour at the apex of the wartime Coalition, the idea certainly held a measure of appeal. In the aftermath of the election, however, formal moves to revamp the Conservative Party, organizing it as the nucleus from which to launch a new, more progressive and socially less exclusive political party, looked patently absurd and failed to make an impact. Thus in the summer of 1946 Harold Macmillan went on the stomp, choosing the not exactly plebian locations of Hatfield and Chatsworth to launch, in his words, 'a new democratic party'. The response was negligible, inspiring Low to produce a cartoon depicting the enthusiastic new democrat with the caption 'Re-christening of Blimp'.[21] A year later, with his curiously immovable aristocratic sentiments still intact, Macmillan was at Hawarden Castle in cahoots with Charles Gladstone grandiloquently announcing it time to bury the historic divide between Tory and Liberal.

What Macmillan's venture failed to appreciate was the degree to which the Conservative Party had *already* become the representative of the broad coalition of anti-socialist forces. Churchill's caretaker government of the summer of 1945 included seven 'non-political' figures, and four Liberals, all of whom had become virtually indistinguishable from their Tory colleagues. After the election, of the 213 opposition members only 189 were designated Conservative: the remainder was made up of Ulster Unionists, National and Liberal National candidates. Even after the election the Conservatives continued to attract political figures who hesitated to see themselves strictly as Tory. Before the final count had been completed Lord Woolton declared his intention of joining up, thereby jettisoning his erstwhile faith in the ideals of Fabian socialism. Indeed, a new political generation came to the

Conservatives less out of regard for any high Tory principles than from anxiety about doctrinaire socialism. Thus of the 1950 intake of MPs one can note—pretty much at random—that Charles Hill (more famous as the Radio Doctor, an inveterate campaigner for the party) insisted on standing as a Liberal and Conservative candidate; Reginald Maudling was rather attracted by the concept of National Labour; and Robert Carr was closer to much of the Labour programme than to Conservatism, until he fell into conversation with a man 'in a roadhouse' one lunchtime who happened to be the Tory agent for Barnet.[22]

Yet in the aftermath of the election, as the rump of anti-socialist opinion gathered under the Tory banner, it was clear that the reversal suffered by the Conservative Party was not merely electoral. There is a sense in which the culture as a whole had shifted—that the popular radicalism generated by the war had transformed the very categories of democracy, citizenship and welfare, leaving Conservatism broken and incoherent. This is a difficult argument to pursue. It requires investigation to turn from high politics to popular culture. It needs to draw from some elements of what is currently characterized as discourse theory in order to appreciate the degree to which the political field itself was reconstituted on a more popular axis. And, perhaps most tricky of all, an analysis cast in these terms not only has to reconstruct popular sentiment as lived, but also grasp the ways in which it *came to be represented* in the higher reaches of the state. It is not possible to develop these points here. Some work in this vein already exists.[23] All I can do is to propose the hypothesis that from 1940 such a popular radical culture did in fact exist in Britain; that the election of 1945 reflected this shift in cultural life; and that by 1947 radical populism from below had all but run aground—undone, as I see it, by the dual demands of the Labour government's statism and by the Cold War.[24]

What is at issue here is the question of cultural power. This is difficult to verify or quantify at the best of times; elections, for example, although obviously crucial, do not necessarily correlate in any simple way to deeper relations of cultural power. However, essentially my argument—uncontentious enough—is pitched against an overly psephological reading of 1945, emphasizing instead the sharp loss of cultural power suffered by Conservatism during the 1940s as a whole.[25]

It would be possible to locate this shift in terms of social geography. Thus the Tory loss of Birmingham, for example—depending in some instances on dramatic switches in political allegiance—represented not simply a quaint swing of the electoral pendulum, but the unmaking of the historic tradition of provincial Unionism inaugurated by Joseph Chamberlain in the 1880s. Manchester and Leeds became Labour cities for the first time, clearly suffering from an influx of 'pansy-pink creatures' from the forces. So, more surprisingly, did York, Lincoln and Winchester.

Or it could be grasped in terms of personalities. To take a single example: Edward Hulton, the proprietor of *Picture Post*, supported the Labour Party in 1945. On two previous occasions, in 1929 and 1931, he had stood unsuccessfully as a Conservative candidate. His support for Neville Chamberlain lasted until the very last moment. Rather swiftly, through the medium of the 1941 Committee and through contact with figures like Kingsley Martin, Michael Foot and A.D. Lindsay, his allegiance turned. *Picture Post* itself functioned as a decisive organizer of social-democratic opinion. Throughout the war Hulton maintained a benign distance from the periodical which carried on its cover the subheading Hulton's National Weekly. His first major intervention in its workings, revealing in both timing and substance, occurred at the beginning of 1947 when he accused Tom Hopkinson, his editor, of peddling 'Sovietism'—a marked shift from the days of Stalingrad. Things came to a head in 1950 when Hulton sacked Hopkinson for attempting to publish copy (filed by James Cameron and Bert Hardy) critical of the UN forces in Korea. A year later Hulton was back in the Tory fold, though maintaining a spirited campaign against the brand of Conservatism espoused by Churchill and Beaverbrook.[26]

Or finally, in attempting to gain some measure of the collapse of a whole Conservative culture, there is the range of emergent debate about social rights and welfare—particularly but by no means exclusively focused on the Beveridge Report—about which plenty has been written. To be as succinct as possible I shall point only to the issue of the public schools. As we know from subsequent history, no established political party has come close to imposing any kind of challenge to these institutions of what are—to everyone's admission—redoubts of class privilege. However, in 1942, and for some little time thereafter, it is apparent that Churchill (schooled at Harrow) and Butler (Marlborough) were on the point of conceding, if not their extinction, then at least a radical modification of the basic market principle which underlies their existence. Privately, they believed the case for their continuation into the post-war world was lost.[27] To discover this from the perspective of the 1980s or early 1990s—when private schooling has enjoyed a new renaissance and when to question its privilege and authority is to reveal oneself possessing a cast of mind equivalent to Beria, or worse—is indeed a startling index of historical change.

Yet having said all this, a mesmerizing quality of the Conservative Party is its capacity to recover from appalling situations, reconstruct itself while pretending nothing much is happening, and represent itself to the world at large as a historic and entirely uncontentious feature of English civilization—in the hope that people will vote for it, but not notice it. Conservatives are attracted by the Conservative Party because, pragmatically, it works: it wins elections and distributes power accordingly. Even the trauma of 1945—equal only to 1846 or 1906—did not incapacitate Conservative political workers. Reconstruction developed on two fronts: organization and policy.

These developments are well documented in the secondary literature and do not require elaboration here.[28] Maxwell-Fyfe was charged with investigating the state of party organization. His interim report appeared in October 1948, and the final version the following July. Three principal reforms were recommended: the training and payment of party agents throughout the country; and the unequivocal endorsement of independent constituency associations in selection of candidates. (In retrospect Maxwell-Fyfe came to regret this last proposal. In his view it encouraged the selection of too many dull, local worthies confirmed, as he saw it, by the intakes of

1955 and 1959. Mrs Thatcher, we might recall, was elected in 1959.)[29] In addition Central Office was overhauled and the Research Department expanded. The Young Conservatives replaced the Junior Imperial League—in the hope, we are led to believe, of modernizing the image of Tory youth.[30] Lord Woolton was appointed Chairman of the party in July 1946, and secured a steady rise in individual membership, which nearly doubled from the end of 1947 to June 1948. More than half a century after Randolph Churchill's melodramatic interventions in the National Federation, the Conservative Party slowly transformed itself into a functioning organization adequate for a mass electorate.

Matters of policy were clearly more divisive. A striking indication of the party's incoherence lay in the degree to which its ideologues were forced to respond to discussion generated from outside the party itself. The experience of the war—imposing from above economic recovery, ensuring full employment and the active mobilization of the entire national population, and the impromptu appearance of new welfare services—posed a severe challenge to Conservative faith in the market. From the moment the war economy took off, intense debate burned through the Conservative ranks, polarizing an already demoralized party. A sizeable body of Tory opinion viewed the war economy as a necessary and temporary evil, to be packed away the moment victory was achieved. As much through party management as through a process of zealous conversion, this position came to be contained within the Conservative Party, subordinated to a more electorally attractive variant of 'progressive' Conservatism which heralded the virtues of the mixed economy and the welfare state.

However, this essentially strategic recomposition of the party could not have been achieved without the existence of a nucleus who were indeed philosophically persuaded by the new Conservatism, who invented it, fought for it and who wore it with evangelical excitement. This was a relatively junior cohort—many of whom experienced for the first time in their lives an intermittent, rough egalitarianism in the forces—who delivered to the party managers the raw material for new official policies: even in the Tory Party there are occasional hints of rebellion from below. This nucleus cohered in the organizational guise of the Tory Reform Committee at the beginning of 1943, just when the ideological balance of forces inside the Coalition had been thrown into confusion by the debates on the Beveridge Report. Although there were precedents, it was fundamentally the Tory Reform Committee which incorporated into Conservatism the spirit of social democracy, attempting to fashion it in a Tory image.

The Tory reformers received an important boost in May 1944 with the publication of the government's White Paper on Employment Policy, which for long had been incubating in a variety of anonymous governmental subcommittees. Whatever the internal coherence—or incoherence—of the White Paper, it created for the progressives inside the Conservative Party the elements for a distinctively Tory programme, and a distinctively Tory version of the mixed economy. First, it appeared to offer to progressive opinion of all shades the technical means by which, through state management, full employment could be secured. This was a psychological break of the first importance. It is again with a sense of shock that one returns to the decaying, parsimoniously produced broadsheets of the 1940s and can actually *see* the excitement with which the pamphleteers alighted upon their discovery that full employment lay within the means of human control. This realization provided the route for Conservatives to participate in the new politics alongside more orthodox social-democrats.

Second, the White Paper specified the conditions in which full employment could be secured in Britain. It advocated the need for a buoyant export trade in order to keep the balance of trade favourable; and it emphasized the importance of maintaining wage and price stability. In other words, ultimately the White Paper conceptualized an active role for British manufacturing, left free to manoeuvre in the market-place, and simultaneously pointed to the long-term dangers of wage drift and ever-strengthening unions. On these two issues—the regeneration of manufacturing and the need for a watchful eye to be kept on union power—a specifically Tory programme could cohere. Combined with hostility to out-and-out nationalization it dealt the Conservative Party a powerful hand.

Thus by the time of their electoral defeat the Tories were already evolving a language around the key issues of state intervention and social rights, which was sufficiently elastic to permit them a deal of strategic manoeuvrability. We can take the example of Quintin Hogg—a singular character, admittedly. Hogg was one of the tyros of the Tory Reform Committee, perhaps its most public propagandist. In a series of articles in the late summer and autumn of 1945, published in the *Daily Mail*, he reaffirmed his faith in the mixed economy and welfare state. While not blaming him for the defeat, he also included a harsh indictment of Churchill. Yet even in this context, just four days after the election results and desperate to disseminate amongst his demoralized colleagues the 'gospel' of a new Conservatism, Hogg referred to the unions as 'the most ruthless and most self-seeking of all the vested interests in the country'.[31] This, I think, conveys an indication of the specific timbre of the new Conservative thinking of the period.

A problem with the appropriation of a strategy with this degree of flexibility is that it can become the cause of confusion and further dissension. There was a celebrated occasion, entertaining for their opponents, when Conservatives used the correspondence columns of *The Times* to determine whether or not they were members of a social-democratic party.[32] It can also confuse historians. In an attempt to rectify the pieties of the party's official version of events, one historian deploys an engagingly brusque interpretation: 'comparing official party policy in 1951', he writes, 'with official *and* unofficial Conservative policy in 1945, *no revolution in party doctrine or policy took place in the six years of opposition*'.[33] I take the point. However part of the issue is the way in which unofficial policies of 1945 became the official policy of 1951. It is also necessary to grasp the largely symbolic dimensions of these debates in order to understand how the strategic recomposition of the party was achieved.

In these terms nothing is more relevant than the party's much vaunted *Industrial Charter* of 1947. This became the form of words in which Tories hoped to spell out the backbone of their new policies. In truth, against its detractors, it does provide a flavour of the new thinking. The document, in an overall context of commitment to a mixed economy, lays great emphasis on the individual and the consumer, on rewards and the importance of 'national housekeeping'. Swallowing hard, the authors feel compelled to remind the faithful about the official line on the unions: 'We desire to state quite clearly that the official policy of the Conservative Party is in favour of trade unions.' Nor were the authors shy about resorting to the occasional platitude ('Man cannot live by economics alone').[34] Butler himself, who nursed the *Charter* into being, was sceptical of its worth.[35] As Maudling recounts—and it is worth repetition—Churchill was, at best, negative:

> 'Give me five lines, Maudling', he said, 'explaining what the Industrial Charter says'. This I did. He read it with care, and then said, 'But I do not agree with a word of this'. 'Well, sir', I said, 'this is what Conference has adopted'. 'Oh well', he said, 'leave it in', and he duly read it out in the course of his speech, with the calculated coolness which he always accorded to those passages in his speeches, rare as they were, which had been drafted by other people, before he went back to the real meat of his own dictation.[36]

One might add, the *Charter* was passed at the Party Conference with a majority which would have proved embarrassing for a Guatemalan Field-Marshal.

Yet despite the platitudes and the stage management it did work to symbolize the unity of the Conservatives, registering a vague allegiance to the new philosophical principles. It became the basis on which Butler and the rest constructed a new alliance within the party—overcoming the disaster of 1945—which remained in place until the late 1950s. It is the crucial document signifying the recovery of the Conservative Party in the post-war period.

Yet these explanations for the recovery of the Tories are all derived from initiatives internal to the party itself. It is necessary to place these developments in a larger, global and imperial context. Again, given the constraints of space, this must be done with extreme compression.

The historiography which might highlight the connections between the extraordinarily volatile shifts in foreign affairs and the domestic fortunes of British Conservatism in this period simply does not exist. Historians seem content to focus on Winston Churchill at the Llandudno Party Conference of 1948, wishing he had been supplied with a blackboard in order to communicate the better his conviction that Great Britain lay at the centre of three defining concentric circles: the Empire, the anglophone Atlantic powers and Europe. However, it may yet prove that it was the shifting order of foreign relations which generated the dynamic underpinning of the Conservative recovery, providing Tory strategists with the cutting-edge as putative defenders of the West and the Empire, and touching deeply the organization of popular culture.

If India and Palestine were the dominating imperial issues during the Labour administrations, it was India which impinged most deeply on the habits of Conservatism, and threatened most to unhinge the emergent, fragile alliance within the party. Since the fashioning of a recognizably modern Tory symbolism, under the aegis of Disraeli, India had played a prominent role in the official mind of Conservatism, giving substance to the mystique of Empire. It also ran deep in the psyche of generations of Conservatives, gradually cohering in an authentic collective memory, accreted through a complex tissue of an infinite number of personal connections between the subcontinent and 'Home'. When Butler opens his memoirs by claiming that his life had stood on the 'tripos' of Cambridge, India and Conservatism he was—in his emphasis on the imperial dimension—wholly representative of his class and generation.[37] Given the intensity of emotional investment in India prevalent amongst Conservatives, it was potentially a divisive issue.

However, the Conservatives reaped the benefits of not being in office, thus avoiding condemnation as the prime mover in the destruction of Imperial India. As the magisterial chapter on Labour and India in this volume would suggest, Conservatives must have been thankful for that. Fundamentally, the Tory leaders, with the conspicuous exception of Churchill, were caught in the same confusion as their Labour counterparts, yet were even more powerless than they to break out from the ensuing political paralysis. Increasing resistance from India itself, culminating in the Quit India campaigns of August 1942, combined with the historic commitment to eventual emancipation from Westminster, imposed one set of pressures; traditional loyalties and the very concept of Empire imposed another. These contrary imperatives could not be reconciled. It is significant that in this context the Tory managers attempted to establish India decisively as a non-party issue, reviving in local form the customs of the Coalition. The main figures in the making of this pact were Attlee—understandably desperate to generate the maximum consent possible for policies which daily were slipping from his grasp—and Eden.

For his part Churchill determined on a tactic of frontal assault, keen precisely to intensify partisan politics, reliving his unflagging opposition to the Government of India Bill which had dominated his political being in the early 1930s and, I suspect, revelling in the remembered romance of his days as a young subaltern under the command of Sir Bindon Blood. The means he employed were varied and not always the most scrupulous. If, in Churchill's view, Attlee and the socialists were scuttling India, winding up Britain's imperial destiny, it was no more than many in his own party were prepared to countenance. In confronting both Attlee and Eden, Churchill found himself up against the old wartime alliance, although no longer able to call upon his authority as premier. The most remarkable aspect of this episode is the demonstrable weakness of Churchill himself—to the point where Eden or others would gently manoeuvre the ageing leader out of the chamber when contention over India looked likely to erupt.[38] Churchill's hopes of organizing a parliamentary revolt against the betrayal of the Raj failed to win even the romantics of his own party.

The speed and degree of the Tory capitulation on India is none the less surprising, and it would be instructive to possess more detailed investigation of the shifts in back-bench opinion. It would be worth exploring how accommodation on India was linked in the Conservative mentality to accommodation on domestic issues: how, in other words, the half-articulated but persistent belief that traditional Toryism was in danger of being swept aside by the tide of history encompassed not only a vision of enemies within the nation, but even more starkly of enemies without. Even so, there is no reason to suppose that any of the Conservatives who gave way on India relinquished their larger commitment to the maintenance of the British Empire. In this respect, whatever strategic divisions appeared over India, the Conservatives were still united in this period as the unequivocal party of Empire.

Indeed, the most subtle theorists of Empire in the late 1940s conceived what in essence was a *new* imperial role for Britain in the aftermath of the independence of India, requiring a strategic relocation of overseas power, particularly in the eastern Mediterranean and eastern Africa.[39] This, after all, comprised the vision from which was born the Central African Federation. The ranks of loyal imperialists in the Conservative Party could marvel at this recharged commitment to extend the life of the old Empire. Its greatest instigator, however, was another survivor from the wartime Coalition, the Labour Foreign Secretary, Ernest Bevin.

Bevin's record as Foreign Secretary has been extensively reviewed. One judgement, from a historian of centrist disposition and not prone to excessive opinion, notes 'the constant applause for Bevin's foreign policies from Churchill, Eden and the right-wing journals in Fleet Street'.[40] The supremacy of Bevin at the Foreign Office clearly signifies the degree to which imperial regeneration lay at the heart of Labour's programme from 1945. Nor was this a state of affairs which ever came to be seriously threatened by an anti-imperial politics arising from opposing elements in the Labour Party or from the wider Labour movement.[41] The consequences of this are clear. In matters of imperial policy the Labour governments marked an effective continuity with the policies of the wartime Coalition, a continuity organized around the dominating personalities of Attlee and Bevin, Churchill and Eden. This continuation of coalition by other means served to contain the Tory Right and the Labour Left, forging a front-bench consensus on matters of Empire. Yet the party which could articulate the politics of Empire with the greater conviction and with all the legitimacy of historic tradition, notwithstanding the new vocabulary of Commonwealth and partnership and so on, was undoubtedly that of the Conservatives. Where on domestic issues the Conservative Party was forced to contend with unfamiliar and often inimical policies, reconstructing old ways step by step—diffidently, occasionally uncomprehendingly, and as if by means of a political ventriloquism—on the Empire the party could reasonably present itself as the real thing. If in 1945 contending policies over market relations divided the ruling élite, the Empire brought it together again. Continuity in imperial politics dealt the Conservative Party a second powerful hand.

Independence for India in 1947, however, coincided with the onset of the Cold War, and the imperatives of Empire merged imperceptibly into a new Atlantic frame. US hostility to the old European colonial powers—so public a sentiment at the moment of the Atlantic Charter—transmuted into a less discriminating stance, in which any ramshackle old Empire could be recruited as a friend of freedom so long as it held fast the front-line against Soviet, and thereafter Chinese expansionism. The overextension of the imperial state in Britain could only exist in so far as it was underwritten by its economically more vital North American ally. The moment of reckoning arrived in February 1947 when, within a week, the British government pledged a timetable for Indian independence (a date soon radically brought forward), bequeathed control of Greece and Turkey to Washington, and (partly as a consequence of these external shifts) Truman discovered he had a Doctrine and Marshall a Plan. The evaporation of Britain's reserves, the vulnerability of its export trade, and the heavy costs of imperial revival conspired to draw Britain, inescapably it seemed, into the field-force of the US system, henceforth functioning as a minor satellite in the greater constellation coming to be known as the West.

Here, too, Churchill was at odds with his more cautious colleagues, deploying much earlier than they—at Fulton—the manichean scenario of a totalitarian East ready at a moment's notice to sink its teeth into the democratic, essentially pacific nations of the West. Eden, having not yet shed the modulated pragmatism of the FO which formed his early political career, was appalled, thinking that once again Winston had been unleashed without the appropriate minder to hand. On this occasion, however, Churchill was the more prescient, and by the time the Berlin airlift had run its course, the Churchill scenario was functioning as the politicians' commonsense. In this, entirely free from the taint of socialism of however a pale a hue, the Tories found their trump.

It is inordinately difficult to grasp at what levels the Cold War registered as an active force in the national culture, yet all the evidence suggests that by the end of the 1940s a naturalized sense of the division of the world between East and West was, in the truest sense of the word, hegemonic—tangibly present, but as unnoticed as the air we breathe. These mental reflexes, however, did not necessarily all work in spontaneous harmony with Conservatism. While suspicion or fear of Sovietism was prevalent, an old paternalist Tory Anglicanism could none the less find little comfort in North America as the way of the future. Yet the mental effects of this newly divided globe did much to discredit and neutralize the Left, including the Labour Party, and offered the Conservatives a concomitant potential for expanding the reach of their political project—as we have noted in the case of Edward Hulton. In terms of lived cultures—in a Britain still constrained by the petty privations of rationing—rambling, the Collected Works and Bulgarian folk-dancing could not easily compete in the popular imagination with Hollywood and zoot suits, Tin Pan Alley and bootlegged PX bounty. With the imaginative allure of America so proximate in British culture, fantasies of wealth could unsettle previously fixed structures of political expectation and allegiance.[42] The materialism signified by America, although doubled-edged, carried for the Conservatives an endorsement of a version of civilization which they too upheld. Shorn of its unspeakable vulgarities and given a suitably English articulation—as Butler and Macmillan were to show in the 1950s—this model of capitalism could produce a powerful popular register, allowing in 1951 the Conservative

Party to jettison Attlee's exhortations for yet another round of belt-tightening, and to promise in its place prosperity without limit.

The Conservative recovery depended on the containment and at least partial reversal of the radical populism of the war years. Particularly in the field of foreign and imperial politics the Conservative Party came increasingly to impose its own vision, defining the terms of debate. Moreover, compared to the confusion of July 1945, the Conservative Party was able in the later 1940s not only to contain the impetus of radical populism, but also to appropriate some of its distinctive motifs, creating an authentically popular register for its own political project. To be sure this emergent popular emphasis within Conservatism was relatively muted and passive, subsumed by a managerialist politics which decidedly did not aim to summon up popular activity from below. Yet the transformation of Conservatism in these years was largely constituted by its capacity to appropriate the language of the people, and compared to the collapse of 1945, it marks a significant political recomposition.

The favoured image for projecting this jaunty new Conservatism came to be that of a 'property-owning democracy', an idea resurrected from the 1920s when it had been introduced into the political language by an unjustly forgotten Tory politician of influence and unusual wisdom. The more mystical renderings of this concept conjured up the notion of England as a harmonious community of small producer—the final breath of a historically superseded and jaded Jacobinism—which was so far removed from the realities of a corporate, imperial power locked into the economic and military system of Bretton Woods and the United States. The deployment of this language established continuities with pre-war Baldwinism, although these could hardly be acknowledged. This idealized notion of community was represented in the wider culture in Michael Balcon's Ealing comedies—films which explicitly knocked old Toryism but which also can be seen as the sharpest cultural expression of the containment of 1940s popular radicalism.[43] It was given a feminine, domestic rendering by the British Housewives League—one of the few popular organizations in this period which swung categorically to the Right—and which produced a potent rallying cry of 'Home vs the State'.[44] It also found archetypal expression in the Marshalls of Guildford, the family featured in the 1949 official Tory publication *The Right Road for Britain*, who in retrospect possess an uncanny resemblance to the Roberts family of Grantham.

This realignment within the Conservative Party became consolidated after the 1950 election, marked by the arrival of 93 new Tory MPs, the majority of whom had never been close to the orthodoxies of pre-war Toryism: here the war functions as a decisive caesura. It was this generation in particular which developed the practicalities of the distinctively Conservative appropriation of Keynes and Beveridge.[45] Even so, the frustrations of opposition did not dimnish until the very end. Churchill despaired, knowing that Labour were on the run, but that the Tories were failing to press home their new-found confidence. After losing yet another division by a handful of votes, Churchill complained: 'It looks as if those bastards can stay in as long as they like.'[46] However, 'those bastards', although winning an increased numerical vote in the election of 1951, had reached a point of historic exhaustion. They had created a social system which the Tories were to exploit. The tide, slowly, was turning. Recounting the eventual victory nearly half a century later, I can still hear the note of triumph in the voice of one old Tory: 'We had 'em out!.'[47]

Notes

1. See A. Howard, ' "We are the masters now" ', in M. Sissons and P. French (eds) *The Age of Austerity*, Oxford, 1963.
2. Evelyn Waugh to Graham Greene, contrasting *Brideshead Revisited* to *A Burnt-Out Case*, in M. Greene, *Dreams of Adventure. Dreams of Empire*, 1983, p. 109. The reference to Angela Thirkell is particularly to her novel *Peace Breaks Out*, published in 1946.
3. N. Fairburn, *A Life Is Too Short*, 1989, pp. 65–6.
4. According to Moran's recollections of Churchill on 8 July, 'The election festers in his mind'. Lord Moran, *Winston Churchill. The struggle for survival*, 1968, pp. 310 and 280.
5. R. Rhodes James, *Anthony Eden*, 1986, p. 304.
6. D.P. Maxwell-Fyfe, Viscount Kilmuir, *Political Adventure. The memoirs of the Earl of Kilmuir*, 1964, pp. 137–8.
7. Evidence for the universal Tory belief in Dalton's opprobium runs through Ben Pimlott's biography, *Hugh Dalton*, 1985.
8. P. Addison, *Now The War Is Over. A social history of Britain, 1945–51*, 1986, p. 24.
9. K. Harris, *Attlee*, 1982, p. 244.
10. *Ibid.*, 208.
11. *Ibid.*, 253.
12. Lord Woolton, *The Memoirs of the Rt Hon The Earl of Woolton*, 1959, p. 335.
13. Lord Butler, *The Art of the Possible*, Harmondsworth, 1973, p. 128.
14. See, *inter alia*, Margaret Thatcher, *What's Wrong with Politics?*, 1968; and her *Second Carlton Lecture*, 26 November 1984.
15. Quoted in Addison, *op.cit.*, p. 17. And see N. Grant, 'Citizen soldiers: army education in World War II', in *Formations of Nation and People*, 1984.
16. A.C.H. Smith, *Paper Voices. The popular press and social change, 1935–65*, 1975, pp. 90–1.
17. Rhodes James, *op. cit.*, p. 304.
18. Truman, for one, resisted the spell of Churchill's charm. Of his first meeting with Churchill, he recorded: 'He gave me a lot of hooey about how great my country is and how he loved Roosevelt and how he intended to love me, etc etc': see R. Jenkins, *Truman*, 1986, pp. 73–4.
19. Quoted in K. Jefferys, 'British politics and social policy during World War II', *Historical Journal*, vol. 30, no. 1 (1987) 301.
20. The editor, Barrington-Ward, held an 'independent but not hostile' view of the Labour Party. The inimitable Woolton tried to prevail upon him, adumbrating the higher responsibilities owed by *The Times* to the nation:

    'I explained to him that, while it is the duty of the Opposition to oppose, it is the duty of *The Times* to get the best it can out of the Government of the day.

The King's Government has to be carried on'. (I. McDonald, *The History of 'The Times', vol. 5: Struggles in war and peace, 1939–66*, 1984, p. 129)

The Manchester Guardian boasted a rather different view. Two days before the election it had this to say about Churchill: 'Probably never in our political history has a party leader exhibited such a shameless determination to subvert the constitutional processes of an election to his own ends' (quoted in R.B. McCallum and A. Readman, *The British General Election of 1945*, 1947, pp. 185–6).

21. H. Macmillan, *Tides of Fortune. Memoirs, vol. 3: 1945–55*, 1969, pp. 289–90).
22. See H. Nicolson, *Diaries and Letters, 1930–39*, 1966, p. 406, for Maudling's early vacillations about party allegiance, and his subsequent justification. Information on Robert Carr from an interview with him, 18 June 1987, in which he elaborated 'My heart lay in what would subsequently be known as Gaitskellite Labour', and declared he favoured at this time 'a non Clause 4 socialism'. Carr, significantly, was PPS to Eden from 1951 to 1955.
23. I have in mind here most of all Angus Calder, *The People's War*, 1971; more specific insights could be derived from Mass-Observation. Revealing material on the BBC in the 1940s can be found in the various essays of Paddy Scannell and David Cardiff, appearing mostly in *Media, Culture and Society* throughout the 1980s: their findings have been extended and developed in the second volume of their *A Social History of Broadcasting*, forthcoming from Blackwell. Despite its emphasis on high politics, Paul Addison's *The Road to 1945*, 1977, is clearly relevant, especially his chapter 'Conservatism in eclipse, 1943–5'. Addison has been taken to task for placing too much stress, too early, on 'consensus' between Conservative and Labour. See Jefferys *op. cit.*, and also his 'R.A. Butler, the Board of Education and the 1944 Education Act', *History*, vol. 69, no. 227 (1984). Briefly one might note:

    1. the value of placing the roots of the post-war settlement in the events and consequences of 1940;
    2. the need to distinguish between different levels in the Conservative hierarchy, in the belief that those at the top had a rather more positive outlook on consensual politics deriving from the Coalition;
    3. the impact of the 1945 defeat in forcing the Tory Party to move more aggressively to the centre;
    4. as suggested below, the *distinctive* articulation of the Tory version of the post-war settlement.

    For an exhaustive account from which much of this derives, see K. Middlemas, *Power, Competition and the State, vol 1: Britain in search of balance, 1940–61*, 1986, and my own response, 'Conservatives and corporatism', *New Left Review*, no. 166 (1987).
24. I am conscious that this reads as unduly manichean: the complex, contradictory elements of this popular radicalism 'from below' would have to be brought out, most especially in relation to nation, race and Empire. The career of Michael Foot is telling in this respect.
25. The term itself, psephology, was coined in the period immediately following the 1945 general election.
26. For this latter phase, T. Hopkinson, *Of This Our Time. A journalist's story, 1905–50*, 1982, p. 251.
27. A. Howard, *Rab. The life of R.A. Butler*, 1987, pp. 119–22.
28. J.D. Hoffman, *The Conservative Party in Opposition, 1945–51*, 1964; and A. Gamble, *The Conservative Nation*, 1974.

29. Maxwell-Fyfe, *op.cit.*, 158.
30. For the full story, Z. Layton-Henry, 'The Young Conservatives, 1945–73', *Journal of Contemporary History*, vol. 8, no. 2 (1973).
31. Quintin Hogg, 'Defeat, but not catastrophe for Conservatives', *Daily Mail*, 30 July 1947. His notion of 'a new gospel' comes from a later article in the *Mail*, 11 September 1947.
32. *The Times*, March and April 1949. Note too, earlier but on the same theme, Ernest Marples' intransigent correspondence to *The Economist*, 30 August 1947.
33. Hoffman, *op.cit.*, 208, original emphasis.
34. Conservative Political Centre, *Industrial Charter*, 1947, pp. 3, 11 and 21.
35. Howard, *op.cit.*, 161–2.
36. R. Maudling, *Memoirs*, 1978, pp. 45–6.
37. Butler, *op.cit.*, 1.
38. It is worth recalling that Butler had been appointed by Baldwin to rally the constituency loyalists behind the 1935 Government of India Bill, and thus on the question of India was pitted directly against Churchill through this earlier period; and that Attlee, as well, was active in promoting constitutional reform for India in this earlier period.
39. For a consummate discussion, W.R. Louis, *The British Empire in the Middle East, 1945–51. Arab nationalism, the United States and postwar imperialism*, Oxford, 1984.
40. K.O. Morgan, *Labour in Power, 1945–51*, Oxford, 1984, p. 239.
41. The best general survey remains P.S. Gupta, *Imperialism and the British Labour Movement, 1914–64*, 1975. The contrast with the United States is striking, where the politics cast in opposition to British colonialism connected with a tough, indigenous Black politics: H.R. Lynch 'Pan-African responses in the United States to British colonial rule in Africa in the 1940s', in P. Gifford and W.R. Louis (eds) *The Transfer of Power in Africa. Decolonization, 1940–60*, New Haven, 1982.
42. C. Steedman, *Landscape for a Good Woman*, 1986.
43. J. Ellis, 'Made in Ealing', *Screen*, vol. 16, no. 1 (1975). It is worth noting that Eden's denunciation of unbridled capitalism as being a 'paradise for the spiv', made at the 1947 Party Conference, was directly echoed in Ealing's poetic defence of England and its welfare state—counterposed to a 'spiv's paradise'—in *Passport to Pimlico*, 1949. For Eden's comment, Conservative Political Centre, *The New Conservatism. An anthology of postwar thought*, 1955, p. 11.
44. The League started as a spontaneous women's organization in July 1945 under the direction of Irene Lovelock, a parson's wife from Selhurst in Kent. A major turning-point occurred in February 1946 when the Ministry of Food attempted to withdraw supplies of dried egg, thus precipitating in the Home Counties a rush of meetings called to denounce controls. According to Addison, 'With her staunch conviction that the interests of the patriotic middle class were being sacrificed for the benefit of feckless elements of the population, Mrs Lovelock—who had actually voted Labour in 1945—was one of nature's conservatives.' In the event, under the dominating figure of Dorothy Crisp, the League adopted a doctrinaire libertarianism, and women in local Conservative associations were enrolled *en bloc*. Addison, *Now The War Is Over*, pp. 40–4; B. Campbell, *The Iron Ladies. Why do women vote Conservative?*, 1987, pp. 76ff.
45. Note that Maudling's maiden speech (10 March 1950) dwelt on the dangers of inflation, and Macleod's (14 March 1950) on the need to reverse the principle of universalism in the NHS. In the aftermath of Mrs Thatcher, *The Economist* (22

December 1990) has endeavoured to revive Macleod as the appropriate Tory icon for our own day.

46. Quoted in Morgan, *op.cit.*, 412.
47. Interview with Lord Deeds, 10 May 1988.

10 'Responsibility without power' The Attlee governments and the end of the British rule in India

Nicholas Owen

The ending of British rule in India has been regarded as one of the most decisive achievements of the Attlee governments.[1] It marked the dismantling of the source and justification of Britain's imperial system east of Suez, precipitated 'a fundamental change in the nature of the Commonwealth', and defined 'a process of political evolution which led directly to the dismemberment of empire in Africa, the Caribbean and the Pacific in the fifties and sixties'.[2] For Cripps, the transfer of power was 'a great civilising experiment', the like of which had never before been attempted.[3] In Cabinet discussions, India ranked in importance second only to the economic situation.[4] Attlee himself thought it the decision for which he would best be remembered.[5]

However, Attlee's own account of the transfer of power is misleading. It represents Britain's withdrawal from the subcontinent as the long-expected and crowning stage of her imperial mission. The surrender of hegemony occurred, he wrote, 'without external pressure or weariness at the burden of ruling'.[6] Indian independence, he told the House of Commons, was 'not the abdication, but the fulfilment of Britain's mission in India'.[7] This was not merely self-delusion. It was the first stage in the creation of a myth of the end of British rule in India: the myth that Indian independence was a well-planned and timely act of generosity. This myth was not merely flattering to the politicians involved; it also served an important purpose in legitimizing the transfer of power.

Naturally, Attlee's self-serving account has found little favour with historians. It is now recognized that Labour's Indian policy was born as much of the economic and strategic imperatives of the late 1940s as of any longstanding commitment to Indian freedom.[8] Nevertheless, even if the transfer of power is no longer seen as an act of selfless emancipation, it is often presented as a great triumph of statesmanship. For Kenneth Morgan, this was an 'escape from empire' from which Attlee emerged as 'a liberator, the leader of his goverment and the architect of the new Commonwealth'.[9] Attlee's biographer, Kenneth Harris, is equally fulsome. 'From start to finish, he moved steadily and unshakeably, coolly and adroitly, according to his plan, stepping up the pace towards the end with fine judgement.'[10] The Conservatives had hoped that the British might remain in India to hold the ring while Hindus, Muslims and Princes settled their differences.[11] However, Labour brought a 'healing prescription' to the Indian problem: Attlee's extension of the principle of self-determination to colonial peoples. Thanks to his foresight, it has been argued, Labour extricated Britain from what might have been a costly disaster of more than Palestinian proportions.[12]

Historians more sceptical of Labour's motives have offered a different picture of the transfer of power. For Anita Inder Singh, Labour's imperial attitude reveals 'a woolliness and illusion about decolonization which was as strong as that of the Conservatives'.[13] Attlee's Indian policy is thus best seen as a clever attempt to win by judicious concession what could evidently not be held by force. The transfer of power was merely the last and most subtle move in the long game the British had been playing in India since the Mutiny: the striking and restriking of political bargains with indigenous allies whose support ensured the protection of British interests. The ending of constitutional sovereignty in 1947 was thus a piece of 'fancy footwork'[14] carried out in pursuit of the old imperialist ends: the preservation of the strategic and economic substance of the Anglo-Indian connection. Labour hoped, it is argued, that the swift granting of the nationalists' demands would secure a reservoir of goodwill on which Britain could draw informally long after the formal constitutional connection with India had ceased to exist. India's continued membership of the Commonwealth and the strengthened trade links that followed independence illustrate the partial success of this neo-imperialist strategy.

Labour ministers have thus been regarded either as far-sighted planners of colonial disengagement or as closet imperialists. Common to both these views, however, it is the imposition of a spurious logic upon Labour's Indian policy, and the neglect of the false starts and setbacks which characterized its evolution. In presenting decolonization as an orderly progression from plan to practice, they do more to rationalize than to explain Labour's policy. Morgan claims that Labour's contribution to Indian independence was the provision of a procedure and a timetable,[15] and Peter Hennessy has praised Attlee's Indian policy for its 'clarity of purpose'.[16] According to Howard Brasted and Carl Bridge, 'Labour persistently applied to the transfer of power conundrum the procedural cards Attlee had dealt it in the 1930s.'[17] Yet the evidence points much more to a series of attempts to reshuffle the imperial pack in the hope of finding a winning trick, until Labour finally threw in its hand in exasperation.

This should not be surprising. For the Labour Cabinet, the Indian problem was the art of the possible writ large. Following events at a distance, and faced with a crisis of bewildering fluidity, they were baffled by its complexities. Even members of the Cabinet's India Committee were ignorant of basic details. Wavell gloomily recorded that 'Addison . . . had no idea that the Sikhs lived in the Punjab, and Ellen Wilkinson had no idea that we only had some 500 British officials.'[18] The Earl of Listowel, a member of the India Committee throughout, and Secretary of State for India from April 1947, wrote that it was 'scarcely a team that could compare in knowledge or intellectual calibre with Churchill's'.[19] Moreover, Labour refused to rely solely upon the diplomacy of the supposedly reactionary India Office or defeatist Indian Civil Service. Instead, senior ministers set great store by their own personal diplomacy.[20] They relied heavily upon informal contacts with Congress, but failed to penetrate the purdah in which the Muslim League planned its strategy.[21] At critical moments, the Cabinet were 'thinking not about India but coal, electricty and Palestine'.[22] Pethick-Lawrence told the Viceroy that the inability of the Cabinet to supply a firm policy

> [did] not spring from any complacency or optimism on our part, nor from any acceptance of a policy of 'drift', but from the fact that the situation as we see it changes from day to day and any 'ultimate' policy decided on this week would almost certainly by force of events prove to be all wrong next week or the week after.[23]

Most significantly, Labour leaders were never free to make policy in isolation from a stifling tangle of constraints. At home, they were obsessed by the threat of parliamentary opposition and the potential unpopularity of a premature scuttle or show of force. Decolonization, to be successful, required the control of policy by small cliques of likeminded Cabinet ministers, and its isolation from the storms of political controversy it might arouse among the uninitiated. Congress politicians must not be encouraged to greater intransigence by the irresponsibilities of the Labour Left, nor Muslims and princes by Tory diehards. Futhermore, Labour faced the conundrum with practically no means of bringing pressure to bear upon the Indian parties. In India, conflict with Congress had alienated the sympathies of many Indians in provincial administrations. Indianization had been accelerated by the war and the suspension of home recruitment. As rivalry between Congress and the League intensified, administrators, the police, and even soldiers felt the tug of communal loyalties. Unsure of the resources at its disposal, Labour had to make do without the traditional methods of imperial rule: coercion, which became impractical, and collaboration, which was unforthcoming. Moreover, as Wavell had warned Churchill in 1944, the future of India was 'the problem in which the British Commonwealth and the British reputation [would] stand or fall'.[24] Its implications for Britain's international standing were tremendous. The solution of 'the Indian problem' depended on events far beyond Labour's control, even if political expendiency demanded that it pretend otherwise.

Labour came to power in 1945 with only the broad outlines of its Indian policy settled. Its election manifesto had merely offered the equivocal promise of 'the advancement of India to responsible self-goverment', and

India's future had not been an election issue.[25] It was true that Labour had been in favour of 'self-determination' for India since 1920, and could happily unite behind the slogan of 'India for the Indians', but this was largely because the slogan was sufficiently imprecise to allow it. Although Attlee had served on the Simon Commission, a body whose recommendations were outdated before they were published, he admitted that the experience had given him a distorted picture of Indian nationalism. Moreover, he had lost touch with the situation thereafter.[26] Labour had thus given little thought to the thorny details of the Indian problem. These included the provision to be made for the protection of minorities, and the nature and terms of the treaty Labour demanded as the price of independence. More importantly, many Labour leaders, including central figures like Bevin and Cripps, assumed India would achieve independence as a junior partner of the Dominions, and not unnaturally, their model of Dominion status was that of the inter-war years. Independent India would be a nominally sovereign state within the Commonwealth, bound to the mother country through ties of sentiment, security and economic dependence, and willing to accept British leadership in her external relations.[27] Labour's commitment to Nehru's ideal of unconditional independence was far less certain. In a letter to Cripps, Nehru wrote that he found 'a strange reluctance to use the word "independence" with all that it conveys. "Self-government" is used in the old way . . . This is not a minor matter of wording. It is basic.'[28]

Furthermore, although Labour had a long tradition of sympathy for Indian freedom, there was also a streak of paternalism.[29] Labour had a touching faith in the benefits Western socialist efficiency might bring to India. Before the First World War, Sidney and Beatrice Webb had called for the state to introduce 'rural socialism' in India, through a return to the collective agriculture which they imagined to be characteristic of the Indian village.[30] Although failure to understand the nature of India's communal rivalries had led some Labour MPs to the illusion that Congress was a kind of oriental Labour Party engaged in the class struggle, those MPs who had visited India often returned shocked by the harshness of Indian capitalism, scornful of the calibre of Indian Labour leaders and impressed by the work of the Government of India.[31] Many Labour thinkers itched to introduce planning or responsible trade unions to the Indian economy.[32] Even at the height of wartime civil disobedience, when the Indian political situation might have made such thinking redundant, it had still influenced the deliberations of the Labour leadership.[33]

Nevertheless, Labour's first moves seemed clear enough. The government was pledged to honour the terms of the Cripps Mission of 1942, a hastily improvised offer made in the aftermath of the fall of Singapore and the Japanese invasion of Burma.[34] This entailed immediate elections for a constituent assembly to be charged with the task of drawing up a new Indian constitution. In return for swift transfer of power, Labour hoped to establish a friendly successor government prepared to take part in Britain's Commonwealth defence system. It was, however, the fate of Labour ministers always to be one step behind the situation in India. They had failed to notice that the convulsive impact of the war upon Indian politics had rendered their plans obsolete.

In the first place, British prestige, upon which the Raj was largely based, was lower than ever. In 1939, the Viceroy had taken India into war with Germany without consulting a single Indian. Following the ignominious collapse of Burma, the British had begun a 'scorched-earth' retreat to Bengal, burning what they did not commandeer. In the subsequent famine, between one and a half and three million people died.[35] Wavell complained bitterly of London's indifference to the crisis. By November 1945, according to one of Cripps' Indian correspondents, there was 'not a single element in Indian public life on whose support the British Government [could] rely'.[36]

Worse still, the leaders of Congress thoroughly mistrusted Labour's motives.[37] The collapse of the Cripps Mission amid mutual recriminations had poisoned their hitherto close relationship with Cripps and Attlee. Nehru had blamed Cripps' 'insensitiveness and woodenness' for the breakdown, and attacked his 'anti-Congress, communal and reactionary attitude'.[38] In a letter to Evelyn Wood, he had written that Cripps had 'effectively succeeded in creating a tremendous revulsion against the British Government and all its works in India'.[39] For his part, Cripps had accused Congress of seeking dictatorial powers, and blamed Gandhi's last-minute intervention for the Working Committee's rejection of his plan. Although the detailed negotiations of 1942 had merely revealed the genuine points of difference between British socialists and Indian nationalists, the rejection of Labour's best offer discredited Congress in the eyes of British Labour leaders. For Dalton, they were 'starkly exhibited . . . as mere ridiculous word-mongers'.[40] For Attlee, the events of 1942 had revealed a degree of totalitarianism in the Congress Party, and that Muslim fears of Hindu raj were not ill-founded. In the aftermath of civil disobedience, he had retreated to the formulae of the Simon Commission, favouring an appeal to elected provincial politicians rather than the Congress leadership, who were no more than 'a brown oligarchy subject neither to Parliament nor electorate'.[41] Labour's acquiescence in the wartime repression of the 'Quit India' movement and consequent imprisonment of the Congress leadership had left a residue of bitterness. After Nehru's release, Cripps moved quickly to re-establish contact. However, in a private letter to Krishna Menon, Nehru revealed that his doubts remained:

> There is one thing I want you to know. I have not yet got over Stafford Cripps' behaviour just after his visit to Delhi in 1942. . . . [It] created a greater gulf between India and England than the action or inaction of any other individual in recent years.[42]

Unhappily for Labour, the Muslim League had also hardened its demands. Its standing enhanced by wartime collaboration with the Raj, the League was no longer satisfied with the paper guarantees promised in the Cripps' Offer. In 1940 it committed itself to the fight for a separate Muslim state, to include not merely the north-western Muslim-majority provinces, which Jinnah dismissed as a 'moth-eaten Pakistan', but also Assam and Bengal.[43] With elections in the offing, fierce competition for Muslim votes between Congress and the league forced Jinnah to play on communal differences.[44]

Of most of this Labour remained oblivious. At the first meeting of the reconstituted India and Burma Committee in August 1945, Labour ministers plunged enthusiastically into the Indian question. Bevin was anxious to show progress in India before meeting Molotov and Truman in September.[45] Cripps too was keen to take advantage of what he mistakenly believed to be 'the amazingly receptive mood in India'. Relying upon information supplied by Congress correspondents, he argued that Muslim feeling could safely be discounted since the Muslim League was in decline.[46] Indeed, until early 1946, in spite of evidence to the contrary, Cripps continued to believe Nehru's oft-repeated claim that, if ignored, support for Pakistan would crumble away.[47] It was agreed that the government should aim at implementing the Cripps Offer as vigorously as possible. 'As a gesture of real value', Wavell was to come home immediately for talks.

Labour's haste to settle the Indian question was also in part a response to pressure from within the party. Wavell observed that Attlee 'made it clear, without intending to do so, that the Cabinet was thinking more of placating opinion in their own party, and in the USA, than of the real good of India.' At the back of Cripps' mind were 'pledges to the party tail and fear of their pressure, instigated by Congress propaganda'.[48] Cripps feared that any apparent retreat from the principles of the 1942 offer would make agreement with Congress all the harder to achieve. On 6 September fifty-two Labour MPs signed a letter to newspaper editors, calling for the reconstruction of the Viceroy's Executive Council on a more representative footing.[49] Later that month, Pethick-Lawrence received a deputation of Labour MPs critical of the 'apparently leisurely policy' of the government.[50] Pethick-Lawrence stressed the government's good intentions, but pointed out that

> the problem was one of immense difficulty. . . . Action cannot be decreed from this country by a stroke of the pen. . . . Whilst they were anxious to make a suitable gesture, a new government cannot be introduced by a single word; a constitution must be built up and handed over in working form.

Pethick-Lawrence told Wavell that he thought he had satisfied his critics,[51] but he remained sufficiently concerned about back-bench opinion to propose that a parliamentary delegation should be sent to India to 'see the real thing'. The MPs should stay with reliable District Commisioners, should see the Indian Army, and 'not spend all their time talking to politicians'.[52] Not for the last time, Labour ministers were made aware of the interlocking of colonial and domestic politics. Not only might back-bench dissent push the Cabinet faster than it wished to go; its impact on Indian opinion and pro-Congress sympathizers in America might also reinforce the pressure.

Wavell was shocked by the naiveté of Labour's intensions. He bluntly informed the India Committee that the Muslim League, which contrary to Cripps' suppositions spoke for 99 per cent of the Muslim population, would boycott any constitution-making procedure unless Pakistan were conceded in advance. He therefore favoured Round Table talks in London with the leaders of Indian opinion before the summoning of the Constituent

Assembly.[53] Cripps regarded this proposal as 'disastrous'. It would be interpreted as abandoning the offer of 1942, to which opinion in the United Kingdom and America held that the government was committed. For Attlee, it was tantamount to the imposition of a constitution upon India by Labour and 'selected party leaders, the degree of backing behind whom was very far from certain'.[54] Despite this opposition, Wavell eventually secured a compromise. Before the Constituent Assembly was convened, he would consult representatives of the newly elected assemblies to decide how best to create the new constitution.

As Cripps had predicted, Congress was incensed by the delay. Patel told Birla that 'you can hardly distinguish between a Labour Prime Minister speaking and a Conservative with the exception of some plain and direct expressions of the Conservative.'[55] Congress was further enraged by the use of Indian troops to put down nationalist revolt in Indo-China and Indonesia, and the treason trials of members of the Indian National Army, which had joined the Japanese during the war.[56] By November 1945, Wavell feared Congress would launch a fresh 'Quit India' campaign if independence were not granted immediately after the elections. The choice lay between 'capitulating to Congress and accepting their demands . . . and using all our resources to suppress the movement'.[57] However, the threat of disturbances did not dampen Labour's misplaced zeal. Cripps continued to believe that the Muslim League's capacity for trouble was minimal. Chairing the India Committee in Attlee's absence, he proposed that it was possible to avert Congress insurrection by inviting Nehru and Jinnah to talks in London. The Viceroy should be asked to meet Gandhi, who, Cripps understood from his Congress correspondents, was willing to co-operate. Furthermore, every effort should be made to restore personal contacts to heal the fracture between Labour and the Indian people.[58]

In an astonishing display of wishful thinking, the Cabinet took up these proposals with enthusiasm. Aneurin Bevan called for reciprocal visits of trade unionists, and Ernest Bevin proposed the appointment of political advisers to the Viceroy, and stressed the need to 'press on with the economic and social development of India'. Renewed concern about improving the lot of the masses produced the suggestion that 'the Government of India should put themselves forward as the champion of the poorer classes.'[59] Attlee and Morrison were shocked to learn of the shortcomings of the Government of India's publicity arrangements. Their improvement, Attlee claimed, would allow Labour to 'reach the peasant over the head of the anti-British vested interests'. Morrison too called for the Government of India to set itself up as 'the poor man's protector and friend', since 'the leaders of the anti-British movement were all from the exploiting professional and money-lender classes whose policies did not serve the real interests of the masses.'[60] Some instinctively paternalist Labour ministers evidently had yet to reconcile themselves to Indian self-government. More worryingly, the Cabinet remained convinced that they still held the initiative in Indian affairs.

Attlee overruled Cripps' plan to invite the leaders to fresh talks, ostensibly on the grounds that it might be regarded as 'contrary to our declared policy of dealing with the elected representatives of the Indian people'. However, he was willing to allow that 'there might be something to be said for a representative of H.M.G. going out to India and talking to the leaders on the spot.'[61] Of course, this too was contrary to the policy of dealing only with elected representatives, but for Attlee it had the advantage that it kept negotiations firmly isolated from irresponsible British politicians. Better still, the dispatch of a Cabinet minister to India also diverted policy-making from the India Office and the Government of India.[62] Cripps was convinced that the India Office knew little of 'the real India'. Attlee, Pethick-Lawrence and Bevin were also agreed that Wavell, whom they imagined was in the hands of 'anti-Congress' officials, lacked the political skills to secure a settlement on his own.[63] Attlee thought the advantage of sending a minister would be that he would be 'divorced from the machine of Indian administration', and Pethick-Lawrence agreed that he might 'by-pass officialdom'.[64]

The decision to take matters into its own hands forced Labour, perhaps for the first time, to attempt to establish its priorities. A united India was Labour's preferred solution, for Pakistan, especially if conceded in the 'moth-eaten' and divided form, would be economically crippled and indefensible against attack from the Soviet Union or China. Even Jinnah's 'full Pakistan' would be destabilized by its recalcitrant Hindu minority and the hostility of independent Hindustan. Worse still, partition would entail the splitting of the Indian Army and the disruption of military communications.[65] Naturally, Labour ministers hoped that these difficulties might yet bring Hindu and Muslim politicians together, perhaps in some kind of federal solution. In the absence of such an agreement, however, Labour faced an acute dilemma. The League could not be coerced into joining an Indian union, because to do so would risk civil war in northern India and the breakup of the Indian Army, in which Muslims played a disproportionately large part. To connive at Muslim separatism, on the other hand, was to encourage Congress to incite a fresh civil disobedience campaign intent on ejecting the British before settling with the League. Either way, Labour risked losing the prize of India's 'stability and contentment', without which it could never play the role of Britain's defence partner east of Suez.

At its meeting on 14 January 1946, the Cabinet wrestled with the problem:

> On the one hand, it was argued that a pledge had been given in 1942 that India was to have independence after the war. If the succession governments were not able to stand on their own feet economically or for defence purposes, it would be for the appropriate international organisation to interest itself in them. On the other hand, it was felt that the pledge of independence was not a blank cheque. . . . We had a moral responsibility not to hand over the country to Indians without being satisfied that the succession governments were fully aware of the military and economic problems which a self-governing India would have to face and that they had concerted reasonable plans to meet them.[66]

Nevertheless ministers recognized that the risk of the latter point of view was that if no solution was reached which Britain could regard as reasonable, 'logically we should continue governing India even if it involved rebellion which would have to be suppressed by British troops.' This was clearly unacceptable, and had been ruled out by Attlee the previous September as 'a course which opinion in this country would not tolerate'.[67] The Chiefs of Staff observed that the 'primary political object' was 'to grant India independence if possible within the British Commonwealth'. Its advancement should not be jeopardized by 'classifying any of Britain's needs as essential'.[68] In the absence of Indian co-operation, Labour would be forced back to the first alternative: independence without preconditions.

After preliminary talks with Azad and Jinnah, Cripps drew up a memorandum suggesting two solutions.[69] The first proposed a three-tier federation of India, in which the provinces should concede such powers as they wished to subfederal governments, while foreign affairs, defence, communications and finance would be reserved to a federal centre. The second solution was the partition of India into Hindustan and the weaker 'moth-eaten' Pakistan. The choice reflected the weakness of Labour's bargaining position. Cripps could countenance neither a strong centre, useful for imperial defence but likely to incite the Muslims to resist, nor Jinnah's 'full Pakistan', which would forfeit the goodwill of Congress. In order to secure agreement, Cripps was prepared to abandon the requirement that the new Dominion should conclude a defence treaty with Britain, and even to avoid the implication that India would be required to remain in the Commonwealth. The Cabinet balked at this, expressing reservations which, as Wavell correctly noted, were 'obviously dictated by apprehension of what Winston and the Opposition might say'.[70] However, Labour's hands were tied. Although the Cabinet's preference, confirmed by the Chiefs of Staff, was for union within the Commonwealth rather than partition, it recognized 'the over-riding necessity . . . for some agreement'.

Cripps' proposals were unenthusiastically received in India. Although both sides formally accepted the three-tier scheme, they placed contradictory interpretations upon it. The Muslim League had been assured that constitution-making would be carried out in sections which could only be altered by the consent of both parties. Congress accepted Cripps' plan on the understanding that the provinces would have the right to opt out of their allotted sections. When Jinnah called for the rejection of the Congress interpretation, the mission prevaricated, anxious to avoid a breach with Congress. Failing to gain satisfaction, and convinced that Congress was determined to collapse the three-tier system into a centralised two-tier system, Jinnah withdrew the League's acceptance of the plan. The consequences of the breach were wholly calamitious. The League resolved to resort to direct action to achieve Pakistan, and in subsequent communal violence in Calcutta some five thousand people died. In an attempt to reconcile the League, Labour finally accepted its interpretation of the provision for grouping. A tortuous series of negotiations brought the League into the interim government in late October, but this was largely in order to continue the struggle for Pakistan from a position of influence. The coalition brought communal rivalries within constitutional bounds, but at the cost of paralysing central government.[71] In September 1946 Wavell told the Cabinet that he could not expect to maintain control for more than eighteen months. He feared that Congress, now co-operating in the interim government would, under threat of resignation, force him to acquiesce in the suppression of Muslim agitation. He recommended resort to a breakdown plan by which Britain would attempt to force the issue to a conclusion.[72] The Viceroy would declare Britain's intention to quit no later than March 1948. Meanwhile, power would be transferred immediately in the Hindu provinces, and Britain would retreat to the disputed Muslim territory in the hope of securing a settlement. The implicit threat of Pakistan would, Wavell hoped, force Congress to adopt a more helpful attitude.

Wavell's plan would have secured few of Labour's objectives. Pethick-Lawrence warned him that his proposed announcement would lead to an attempt to set up Pakistan by force 'either at once or in the wake of our departure'.[73] Congress would be keen to strike quickly in response. Withdrawal without a settlement would precipitate 'scrambling for position' and ensure that India was rent by internal disorder. The Chiefs of Staff had advised that it 'would not only fail to safeguard our strategic interests, but would inevitably lead to civil war'.[74] Worse still, retreat in India might be seen as 'evidence of a decline in British power and resolution', which would undermine Britain's prestige and prejudice her diplomatic efforts in the Middle East and Europe. 'Scuttle' in India might be regarded as 'the beginning of the liquidation of the British Empire'.[75]

As Labour ministers contemplated this dismal prospect, and their own inability to affect it, they became increasingly fearful of the domestic repercussions of any apparent 'scuttle'. Thus what finally forced the Cabinet to dismiss Wavell's strategic retreat was that it was 'not politically realistic': 'It would not be acceptable to Parliament and to public opinion that India should be left in chaos. [Indeed] . . . it would be an inglorious end to our long association with India.'[76] Since Wavell's plan obliged the Viceroy to surrender his statutory responsibilities, it entailed the repeal of the India Act of 1935, and Labour ministers were, with good reason, opposed to bringing proposals to Parliament until successor authorities emerged in India.

This was not because there was substantial parliamentary opposition to the principle of Indian self-government: on the contrary, most Conservatives were prepared to accept that India was indisputably set on the path to independence. However, they required that the transfer of power be unhurried, orderly and honourable.[77] Indeed, they had resolved in May 1946 to 'pillory' the proposals of the Cabinet Mission as 'obviously unacceptable and apt to lead to riot and bloodshed, which British troops will be called in to suppress'.[78] Later that year, as communal violence spread, Pethick-Lawrence had stressed to R.A. Butler the importance of the Conservatives refraining from taking sides with the Muslim League.[79] Butler's reply had not been entirely encouraging. Although Eden and he would not take this line, he could not answer for Churchill. Furthermore, if the government 'took sides between the two parties or yielded to one of them . . . the Conservative Party would violently react.' The Conservatives also felt 'obliged to stress strongly the claims of the Depressed Classes and other minorities in the final settlement'. This was worrying for two reasons. Not only did it impose strict limits on the support which Labour could expect if events in India forced it to make concessions to Congress, but it might encourage even greater intransigence on the part of the Muslim League and the minorities, now provided with a powerful voice at Westminster. Nor could Labour rule out the possibility that Churchill might choose to take up 'the Indian question'. Like an elderly volcano, Churchill was dormant yet still simmering. In early 1946, according to the Vice-Chairman of the Conservative Party, J.P.L. Thomas, Churchill had been planning to lead 'an anti-capitulation Indian campaign so we are back to 1930–33'.[80] Indeed, Attlee had already concluded that discussion of Wavell's plan with the opposition would be 'useless as long as Winston is functioning'.[81] Churchill remained fully capable of launching a popular onslaught upon measures much more radical than the modest advances he had denounced in the 1930s. Moreover, nearly 60 per cent of those questioned in a 1946 Gallup poll agreed that Britain should remain in India until a new constitution was established.[82]

Fear that 'the Indian question' would become a party issue thus overshadowed Labour's deliberations. Although, as John Darwin has argued,[83] British policy-makers operated in a 'self-centred metropolitan political culture impatient of the intrusion of external issues which might jeopardize . . . domestic political strategies and calculations', this political culture was only held in place by astute party management and tight control over the parliamentary and political agenda. Hitherto, Attlee had attempted to insulate Westminster from the Indian problem. Debates had been sedulously avoided where possible, and parliamentary questions side-stepped, tactics which infuriated Conservative peers.[84] To dampen awkward questions, responsible Conservative leaders had been briefed in advance of each new statement of policy.[85] However, the worsening Indian situation had steadily undermined this strategy. Throughout the autumn of 1946, as communal violence intensified, the Conservatives were provoked to further criticism. Moreoever, in a fruitless attempt to isolate Indian leaders from the disturbances, Attlee decided in November to invite Jinnah and Nehru to London. This provided ready means for opposition interference. Churchill made special arrangements to keep in touch with Jinnah by secret telegraph, and Simon provided the names of Conservative peers who were keen to raise Muslim grievances in Parliament.[86] These Conservative exertions caused considerable anxiety to Labour ministers. Alexander told the Cabinet that Eden had privately attacked the government for 'going too fast', and that 'this view might command some support in the country.'[87]

With the rejection of Wavell's breakdown plan at the end of 1946, Labour's Indian policy had again ground to a halt. The refusal of the Muslim League to co-operate in constitution-making and repeated demands from Congress for the resignation of the League ministers had produced deadlock in India. At home, Labour ministers were under pressure to say whether they would accept the decisions of the Constituent Assembly as binding upon all India, or merely upon those parts represented in it. The Conservatives were also anxious for confirmation that the Viceroy had not handed over to Congress ministers any of his responsibilities.[88] Simon wrote to Eden:

> The Indian situation is rapidly passing beyond our grasp and nothing but widespread and bloody murder will be the result. Wavell, in my opinion has disregarded his trust and is leaving Nehru and Company to run the Indian Government in complete defiance of the Government of India Act. . . . I fear we shall come out of this with the maximum of discredit.[89]

Churchill too was by now 'anxious to make [India] a party issue'.[90] In addition, the Viceroy himself made repeated pleas for a more definite policy. 'I do not think that half-measures or wishful thinking will get us any further', he had written to Pethick-Lawrence in late November.[91] The rejection of his breakdown plan forced him to 'put it on record that . . . the Cabinet's decision, or lack of decision, increases the risk to our nationals in India, and is likely to decrease the chances of a settlement'.[92]

Worse still, economic pressure was tightening on the Cabinet.[93] In the bleak midwinter of 1946–7, the Attlee government found itself in the grip of an interlocking crisis of economic stringency and strategic overcommitment. Britain's overseas responsibilities were not just a burden on the balance of payments. They also kept some 18 per cent of the working population away from the tasks of domestic reconstruction and the production of exports. In January 1947, to meet the crisis precipitated by Britain's reluctant attempt to make sterling convertible, defence spending was cut by 5 per cent. Two months later, the reduction of the length of national service from eighteen months to one year was only accepted by Montgomery on the assumption that troops would be withdrawn from India. This ruled out any chances of holding India in the event of civil war.[94] Attlee and Alexander toyed briefly with the idea of referring the whole problem to the United Nations, but soon recognized that this provided no guarantee that British interests would be protected, and might even permit a dangerous Soviet foothold in the subcontinent. Besides, the United Nations would almost certainly require British troops to enforce its decision.[95]

The Labour Cabinet thus found itself trapped in the worst of all postimperial crises: that of responsibility without power. The collapse of the London Conference had revealed to Attlee that 'it was impossible to be confident that the Indian parties had any real will to reach agreement.'[96] There seemed 'little realisation among Indian leaders of the risk that ordered government might collapse'. The aim of Labour's policy should now be to 'do anything . . . to bring home to them the heavy weight of responsibility which rested on them'.[97] Attlee, while rejecting the breakdown plan, was thus forced to accept Wavell's recommendation that only the announcement of a date for British withdrawal would break the Indian impasse. Even if no agreed constitution emerged, power would be transferred to 'responsible Indian hands' no later than June 1948.[98] To coincide with the announcement, Wavell was to be replaced by Mountbatten. In August 1946 Attlee had told the new Governor of Burma that there was 'no advantage in setting paper dates'.[99] In India in April 1946, Cripps too had concluded that 'One thing is absolutely certain. We can't leave this country without a settlement of some kind. If we did there would be bloodshed and chaos within a few weeks.'[100] Now for the first time, Labour was to admit the possibility that Britain would abandon her responsibilities in India whether or not Congress and the Muslim League came to terms.

This was Attlee's last card, and the decision to play it was neither one he could have made happily, nor one readily accepted by the Cabinet. Several ministers had expressed 'grave objections' to the proposal when it had been made by Wavell,[101] and Addison had called for public assurances that Britain would not withdraw from India in the absence of the creation of 'satisfactory forms of government'.[102] At Cabinet on 31 December, Attlee's proposals were criticized as tantamount to scuttle.[103] Ministers feared that such an admission of defeat would undermine Britain's capacity to contain nationalism in Burma and Malaya, and encourage the Soviet Union to take an interest in Indian affairs. Cripps objected on the grounds that it might prejudice the creation of a united India. On the day after the meeting, Attlee received an extraordinary outburst from Bevin.[104] Bevin stated categorically that he was 'against fixing a date'. He deplored the 'defeatest attitude' of Wavell and the Cabinet, which was 'completely letting us down'. India should be handed over 'as a going concern'. What Attlee proposed was 'scuttle . . . without dignity or plan'. Bevin was convinced that Labour would 'lose irrevocably when the public become aware of the policy of the Cabinet'. Morgan is thus certainly mistaken to claim that 'the Cabinet remained broadly united' behind Attlee.[105]

The Conservatives were also shocked by the reversal of policy. Coincidentally, Attlee had received a letter from Salisbury, accusing him of planning a premature and dishonourable surrender: 'Is this country to go down in history with the badge upon her of betrayal?'[106] When Attlee outlined his plans to Conservative leaders on 18 February, they protested that Labour's plan failed to allow for the postponement of the transfer of power if no responsible government or governments emerged.[107] For many Conservatives, Labour had departed from the condition of an agreed constitution.[108] The wartime Coalition's 1942 offer of post-war independence had been conditional upon satisfaction of Britain's pledges to the minorities and the princely states. In the eyes of Conservative and Labour leaders alike, Attlee now seemed prepared to waive the condition. The tradition of bipartisan advance was breached. In a confidential memorandum to the parliamentary party, Churchill encouraged MPs to make speeches attacking the 'cowardly abandonment of our duties . . . on the pretext of a failure of the Indian parties to reach political agreement':

> The party are [sic] resolved to oppose by every available means the casting away of Parliament's responsibility for the Government of India, in advance of any arrangements for that responsibility to be assumed by an authority or authorities able to discharge it.[109]

At the end of January the Muslim League finally refused to take part in constitution-making. Thereafter, Cabinet reservations were swiftly overtaken by resignation and despair. Attlee, replying to Bevin's criticisms, had written: 'I am not defeatest but realist. . . . If you disagree with what is proposed, you must offer a practical alternative.'[110] Bevin was unable to provide one. Even Alexander, who like Bevin hated the idea of leaving India,[111] and who had hitherto deplored deviation from the policy laid down by the Cabinet Mission, was forced to conclude that 'the Government had no alternative but to prescribe a date.'[112] In drafting the directive for Mountbatten, Cripps was prepared to omit any suggestion that India should be encouraged to remain in the Commonwealth, or to co-operate in defence with Britain.[113] It was only at the insistence of Mountbatten, prompted by Ismay, Chief of the Defence Staff, that this was included. It is hard not to see these as signs of panic. Within three days of deciding to set a deadline for Indian independence, the government had also announced withdrawal from Greece and the eastern Mediterranean, and the surrender of the Palestinian Mandate. The Indian problem too had simply become unbearably frustrating. At the end of that week, Dalton wrote:

> It would be a waste both of British men and money to try and hold down any of this crowd against their will. They must be allowed to find their own way, even through blood and corruption and incompetence of all kinds, to what they regard as 'freedom'.[114]

Under the circumstances, it is scarcely surprising that the Labour Cabinet came to see its problem as 'not so much a military as a political operation of great delicacy'.[115] Wavell's breakdown plan was little more than an admission of defeat, and would have sacrificed Britain's chances of influencing the outcome of the Indian crisis. However, the importance of Attlee's statement was not that it significantly improved these chances, but that it provided a politically acceptable means of retreat. Rather than a demoralizing and humiliating military evacuation, Attlee favoured the gradual devolution of power upon the interim government through the informal surrender of the Viceroy's power of veto.[116] This preserved the existing constitution intact, and thus protected Labour from parliamentary scrutiny. Wavell once wrote that 'the really fatal thing would be for us to hang on to responsibility when we had lost power to exercise it.'[117] What he failed to appreciate was that this was precisely what Labour had to do. Pethick-Lawrence put the point bluntly: 'Our policy, as we have conceived it, does certainly involve our remaining in India beyond the point at which we can control events.'[118]

The Cabinet therefore set about creating a rationale for its actions. At its meeting on 31 December, it had been noted that:

> withdrawal from India need not appear to be forced upon us by our weakness nor to be the first stage in the dissolution of the Empire. On the contrary, this action must be shown to be the logical conclusion, which we welcomed, of a policy followed by successive Governments for many years.[119]

Attlee was asked to redraft his statement in order to make this clear:

> There was . . . no occasion to excuse our withdrawal: we should rather claim credit

for taking this initiative in terminating British rule in India. . . . For these reasons it would be preferable that . . . the Statement should recall the main stages in India's evolution towards self-government, as a process to which successive Governments in this country had been committed ever since the end of the last war, and should present the transfer of control to an Indian Government or Governments as the final phase in this process of evolution.[120]

The India Committee's new draft, which was circulated to Cabinet on 4 January, combined wishful thinking and a disingenuous interpretation of recent history:

The association of the peoples of Great Britain and India has achieved much in its long history that is notable and enduring for good. The step now announced marks the climax in the long period of deliberate preparation and development which has been the dominating feature of this relationship for many years past.[121]

Mountbatten was critical of the new draft, fearing that 'the historical and rhetorical part' failed to give the impression of a 'new deal' for India.[122] However, Attlee advised him that it was needed 'to keep the Opposition quiet, and in order to explain the whole position to the people of the United Kingdom'.[123]

Historians have lately become aware of the way in which invented traditions and political myths have been employed by élites to hold societies together in times of crisis, and reinvented history used to justify controversial or unpalatable policies.[124] The end of empire is rich in such myths: Macmillan's 'sensing' of the 'winds of change', and Wilson's justification of retreat east of Suez are perhaps two more recent examples.[125] Few at the time shared the view of Paul Scott's Guy Perron that 'getting rid of India will cause us at home no qualm of conscience because it will be like getting rid of what is no longer reflected in our mirror of ourselves.'[126] For many, not only Conservatives, British India was still the embodiment of British power and self-esteem. Moreover, its loss played upon other less articulated resentments: of 'national decline' or of a Labour Party 'unfit to govern' the Empire. Imperial propaganda had created 'protected markets of the mind' which could be dismantled only slowly.[127] When independence came, Enoch Powell walked the streets all night 'trying to digest it. One's whole world had been altered.'[128]

Labour's myth was a useful sedative for such emotions. First, it attempted to depict Indian decolonization as uncontroversial and long-expected. Labour tried to undercut Conservative opposition by stressing that the new policy was merely the final stage of a long process set in train by a Liberal Secretary of State in 1919, and carried further by successive governments of every political colour. Differences between the steady progress to self-government envisaged by Montagu and Hoare and the headlong dash now favoured by Labour were to be obscured.[129]

Second, the transfer of power had to be seen as a deliberate, honourable and above all orderly process. Imperial responsibilities could only be transferred, never thrown away. Accordingly, Labour must pretend that Britain still exercised some control over the course of events in India. The India

Committee recommended that 'nothing should be said which would suggest that we are not in a position to prevent Indian parties from seizing power themselves.'[130] However, it was also important to give the impression that setting a date was the only alternative to chaos. The India Committee was insistent that

> It should be made plain that His Majesty's Government has only two choices:–
> (a) to maintain British Control in India by force for a substantial period such as 15 years; or
> (b) to fix and announce now a date for the transfer of power.
> The advice from India was that (a) was not practicable.

Labour was anxious to avoid charges of betrayal of the minorities and the states. It must therefore be made clear that they would have nothing to fear from Indian independence: 'We cannot now import the conception that Indian leaders are incapable of bearing [the] responsibility [of assuming authority].[131]

Finally, it must be suggested that since independent India would preserve its links with Britain through membership of the Commonwealth, decolonization was positive. Thus the common interests and outlook of India and Britain were emphasized and pious hopes for the future of Anglo-Indian relations expressed. Cripps claimed that Labour had 'blended in a single association of closely linked and equal nations . . . the age-long wisdom of the East and the modern experience and development of the West'.[132] The old daydream of the Commonwealth as a tightly-knit alliance of 'English-speaking peoples'—or White Man's Club—was quietly dropped in favour of a new fiction: that of a variety of cultures united in liberal constitutional advance. The enlistment of the crown in this enterprise, as Head of the Commonwealth, and, in the case of India, by association in the person of Mountbatten, provided a notable stamp of approval.

Wavell described Labour's appointment of Mountbatten as 'an unexpected one, but a clever one from their point of view'.[133] The decision was informed, however, by the same preoccupations that had characterized Attlee's policy since the failure of the Cabinet Mission. As early as December 1945, he had considered the dispatch of a plenipotentiary empowered to make a settlement without reference home.[134] Mountbatten was allowed to appoint his own staff and superimpose them upon the officials of Government House. In a secret codicil to his instructions, he was permitted to remove any member of the Indian Civil Service (ICS) who obstructed him.[135] Listowel, who replaced Pethick-Lawrence as Secretary of State in April 1947, was not even told of Mountbatten's powers.[136] All this reflected Cripps' and Attlee's mistrust of the officials of New Delhi and the India Office.[137] Their choice of Mountbatten, who had developed a close rapport with Nehru in 1946, reflected both their faith in personal diplomacy, and a canny sense of what would impress Westminster and the electorate. After all, it had been Churchill who had appointed Mountbatten Supreme Allied Commander in South-East Asia. He was not a party figure but a popular hero, which was precisely what the situation demanded: an 'imperial undertaker who never wore black'.[138]

Mountbatten's instuctions informed him that it was the government's 'definite objective' to realize 'a unitary government . . . if possible within the British Commonwealth'.[139] If this proved impossible to secure by means of the Cabinet Mission's plan, he was to recommend a procedure for transferring power. However, Mountbatten had not been in India long before he realized that Attlee's deadline for the transfer of power was not too early but too late. He told Cripps: 'We are sitting on a volcano which only an announcement of how we decide to transfer power can prevent from erupting.'[140] Indeed, Attlee's announcement had worsened communal violence, as rioting spread to the disputed provinces which the Muslim League claimed for Pakistan: the Punjab, run by a coalition of non-League Muslims, Sikhs and Congress, and the Congress-administered North-West Frontier Province. Although Mountbatten thought Pakistan 'sheer madness', and Jinnah 'a psychopathic case', he was forced to accept it in the face of the intransigence of the League.

Mountbatten's first attempt at a solution was aptly named 'Plan Balkan'.[141] Power would be transferred to provinces, or in the case of Bengal, Assam and the Punjab, sub-provinces, which would then be free to join a Hindustan Group, a Pakistan Group, or remain independent. Congress, frightened by the collapse of ordered government in the disputed provinces, at first raised only 'comparatively small points'.[142] In early May, the Working Committee accepted 'the principle of partition based on self-determination as applied to definitely ascertained areas'. It was even prepared to acknowledge that communal disorder made the partition of Bengal and the Punjab an 'urgent necessity'.[143] However, Congress feared that unless a strong centre was maintained, the transfer of power to provinces would merely encourage the fragmentation of India. Nehru insisted that only the immediate transfer of power to a Dominion status interim government could curb communal disorder and preside over the secession of those provinces which rejected the constitution.

The Cabinet, after discussing 'Plan Balkan', decided to revise it in order to extend the principle of self-determination to the states and those provinces which had already accepted the Cabinet Mission's procedure. Again, the Cabinet feared Conservative accusations of betrayal. Mountbatten was told that 'there must be a free choice if the scheme is to be consistent and defensible in Parliament.'[144] This qualification made the threat of 'Balkanization' quite explicit, and Nehru, complaining that the plan presented a 'picture of fragmentation and conflict and disorder', rejected it. Within two days, Mountbatten too had abandoned 'Plan Balkan' in favour of a new plan for partition into two Dominions. This gave the provinces a simple choice: they could join the existing Constituent Assembly, or join together in a new one. They could not stand out for separate independence.

However, Mountbatten's volte-face startled London.[145] The India Committee had been told that Nehru had more or less accepted 'Plan Balkan', and their own minor revisions did not seem to warrant its rejection. More worryingly, Nehru had told Mountbatten that the Labour Cabinet seemed 'to function in an ivory tower . . . isolated from realities in India'.[146] Attlee, in a draft telegram to Mountbatten, confessed himself 'very worried' by the turn of events. He toyed again with the idea of replacing Mountbatten with a minister with full powers and the minimum of reference home.[147] Confronted with Mountbatten's new plan, Attlee, Cripps, Alexander and Listowel were unanimous that 'the situation was now so confused that it was essential that either a Minister or Ministers should proceed to India to discuss the situation at first hand' or Mountbatten should be ordered home to explain.[148] Ismay told Attlee that only the latter course would be acceptable to Mountbatten.[149]

Labour ministers were unhappy with Mountbatten's new plan. In accepting the legitimacy of the existing Constituent Assembly, it seemed to Listowel to acquiesce in the Congress distortion of the Cabinet Mission scheme which Labour had been at pains to reject the previous December.[150] In its denial of the right of self-determination to the Indian states it broke earlier pledges, and laid Labour open to Conservative charges of treachery. Worse still, since Congress insisted upon a swift transfer of power in return for accepting partition, it cut short an already hectic timetable. In February, the Indian Committee had concluded that six months was 'an impossibly short period' for withdrawal from India.[151] Now it was told that legislation must be passed within six weeks and preferably without opposition. Crucially, however, Congress had accepted Dominion status within the Commonwealth as the price of independence. This secured the escape clause Labour needed: an agreed settlement in India which could be represented at home as a worthy achievement.

Ironically, the decisive events had taken place elsewhere. Labour's policy was rarely its own, and owed more to its fear of 'scuttle' or blood-bath than to its 'ideology' or its leader's far-sightedness. Only once Congress had come to accept partition as the only alternative to civil war was an agreed settlement feasible. Congress was prepared to accept Dominion status within the Commonwealth for the same reason: it allowed power to be transferred before new constitutions were drawn up. This change of heart was primarily a response to the rising tide of communal unrest rather than Labour's threat of withdrawal. To the last, as Nehru had once written to Cripps: 'On both sides, whatever our personal feelings in the matter, we have become the agents of powerful forces which we may influence somewhat but cannot control.'[152]

After the Cabinet had decided to quit India, Hugh Dalton wrote in his diary: 'If you are in a place where you are not wanted, and where you have not the force, or perhaps the will, to squash those who don't want you, the only thing to do is to come out.'[153] Dalton's peremptory assessment was rarely acted upon. Indeed, it is one of the paradoxes of post-war decolonization that the British should so often have clung to imperial responsibilities even when the diplomatic and material resources for meeting them had vanished. In Palestine, for example, despite having surrendered the political initiative to the United Nations in February 1947, Britain insisted on retaining sole responsibility for law and order with the capacity to preserve neither. Nor in India was the Cabinet able to apply Dalton's hard-headed calculation. Confronted with the early collapse of their pre-war policy under the pressure of communal rivalries, Labour ministers' self-confidence had ebbed away rapidly. Enfeebled by the depletion of Britain's resources and unnerved by the apparent intractability of the problem, they came to see the Indian problem as near-insoluble.[154] Nevertheless, when it had become painfully apparent that they no longer held the initiative in Indian matters, they continued to speak the language of responsibility, duty and obligation, rather than that of retreat and surrender.

Of course, Labour could take comfort from the fact that in some sense it had allowed Indians to determine their own constitution. It was wishful thinking, though, to pretend that partition amounted to anything other than a substantial defeat of its pre-war objectives. At violent odds over the partition of Kashmir from the start, the new Dominions were never able to take part in Britain's defence system east of Suez. Some careful constitutional chicanery allowed India to remain in the Commonwealth after it became a Republic in 1949, but this was a poor substitute for the close relationship for which Labour had hoped.[155] Nevertheless, even this result was better than many expected. Britain had come perilously close to a bitter and prolonged 'Indian crisis', and relief at the narrowness of her escape spilled over as ill-deserved praise for the Labour leadership. Thus despite the imperfections of the Indian settlement, Attlee was able to project it as a kind of triumph. As Nehru observed to the departing Wavell, 'some failures are greater than successes'.[156]

Notes

1. I am grateful to John Darwin, David Omissi, Andrew Adonis and David Butler for reading and commentating on earlier drafts of this chapter.
2. D.K Fieldhouse, 'The Labour governments and the Empire Commonwealth 1945–51' in R. Ovendale (ed.) *The Foreign Policy of the British Labour Governments 1945–51*, Leicester, 1984, p. 83.
3. *Hansard*, vol. 434, col. 506, 5 March 1947.
4. J.G. Darwin, *Britain and Decolonisation*, 1988 p. 79.
5. *News Chronicle*, 20 April 1959.
6. C.R. Attlee, *Empire into Commonwealth*, Oxford, 1965, p. 1.
7 *Hansard*, vol. 439, col. 2446, 10 July 1947.
8. R.J. Moore, *Making the New Commonwealth*, Oxford, 1987, p. 9–15.
9. K.O. Morgan, *Labour People*, Oxford, 1987, p. 142.
10. K. Harris, *Attlee*, 1982, p. 386.
11. N. Mansergh et al., *India: The transfer of power* (Hereafter 'TP'), 1970–83, vol. 5, doc. 188, War Cabinet India Committee Paper I(45)5 by Attlee, 9 January 1945.
12. C.R. Bridge and H.V. Brasted, 'Labour and the transfer of power: a case for reappraisal?', *Indo-British Review*, vol. 12, no. 2 (1987) 70–90.
13. A. Inder-Singh, *The Origins of the Partition of India*, Oxford, 1987, pp. 144–5.
14. B.R. Tomlinson, 'The contraction of England: national decline and loss of

empire', *Journal of Imperial Commonwealth History*, vol. 11, no. 1 (October 1982) 58–72.
15. K.O. Morgan, *Labour in Power*, Oxford, 1984, p. 227.
16. P. Hennessy, 'The Attlee governments 1945–51', in P. Hennessy and A. Seldon (eds) *Ruling Performance*, Oxford, 1987, p.41.
17. Bridge and Brasted, op. cit., 84.
18. Archibald Wavell, in P. Moon (ed.) *The Viceroys's Journal* (hereafter '*Journal*') Oxford, 1973, p. 395.
19. Listowel, 'The Whitehall dimension of the transfer of power', *Indo–British Review*, vol. 7, nos. 3–4 (1978) 22–31.
20. CAB 127/143: letter Cripps – Nehru, 12 December 1945; Bodelian Library Oxford, Attlee MSS dep35, letter Pethick-Lawrence – Attlee, 17 April 1946.
21. R.J. Moore, *Escape From Empire*, Oxford, 1983 pp. 78–9.
22. Wavell, *Journal* p. 241.
23. TP VIII 177, letter Pethwick-Lawrence – Wavell, 19 August 1946.
24. TP V 64, letter Wavell – Amery, 24 October 1944.
25. P.S. Gupta, *Imperialism and the British Labour Movement*, 1975, pp. 282–4.
26. C.R. Attlee, *As It Happened*, 1954, p. 65; *Hansard*, vol. 434, col. 764, 6 March 1947.
27. PREM 4/46/12: letter Cripps – Churchill, 29 November 1944.
28. TP VI 496, letter Nehru – Cripps, 5 March 1946.
29. G. Fischer, *Le Parti travailliste et la décolonisation de l'Inde*, Paris, 1966.
30. Niraja Gopal Jayal (ed.) S. and B. Webb, *Indian Diary*, Delhi, 1987.
31. G. Douds and H.V. Brasted, 'Passages to India: peripatetic M.P.s on the Grand Indian Tour 1870–1940', *South Asia*, vol. 2, nos. 1 and 2 (March and September 1979) 91–111.
32. Fischer, op. cit., 268–80.
33. TP VI 217 Cabinet India and Burma Committee minutes (hereafter 'IB Committee') IB(45)7, 19 November 1945; TP VI 244 Cabinet minutes CM(45)56, 27 November 1945.
34. R.J. Moore, *Churchill, Cripps and India*, Oxford, 1979.
35. Sarkar, *Modern India*, Delhi, 1983, pp. 388–413.
36. CAB127/147: letter Shiva Rao – Cripps, 20 November 1945.
37. CAB127/147: letter Shiva Rao – Cripps, 15 October 1945.
38. Letter, Nehru – Menon, 15 April 1942, reprinted in S. Gopal (ed.) *Selected Works of Jawaharlal Nehru*, Delhi, 1972–, vol. 10, doc. 23.
39. Letter Nehru – E. Wood, 1 May 1942, reprinted in Gopal, op. cit., vol. 10, doc. 30.
40. London School of Economics, Diary of Hugh Dalton (hereafter *Diary*), entry for 9 April 1942.
41. TP V 345 War Cabinet India Committee minutes I(45)14, 27 March 1945.
42. Letter Nehru – Menon, 3 September 1945, in Gopal, op. cit., vol. 10, doc. 7.
43. M. Gwyer and A. Appadorai, *Speeches and Documents on the Indian Constitution, 1921–47*, 1957, pp. 443–4.
44. Bodleian Library Oxford, MSS Attlee dep. 34/132–4, letter B. Richardson – Attlee, 25 March 1946.
45. Wavell, *Journal*, p. 165.
46. TP VI 33 IB Committee IB(45)1, 17 August 1945.
47. TP VI 217 IB Committee IB(45)7, 19 November 1945; TP VI 384, letter Nehru – Cripps, 27 January 1946.
48. Wavell, *Journal*, p. 169.
49. TP VI 97, letter Dobbie et al. – newspaper editors, 6 September 1945.

50. TP VI III, note of meeting between Pethick-Lawrence and deputation of Labour MPs, 17 September 1945.
51. TP VI 120, letter Pethick-Lawrence – Wavell, 21 September 1945.
52. TP VI 136, letter Pethick-Lawrence – Wavell, 9 October 1945.
53. TP VI 78 IB Committee IB(45)2, 29 August 1945; TP VI, 91 IB Committee Paper IB(45)10 by Pethick-Lawrence, 3 September 1945.
54. TP VI 78 IB Committee IB(45)2, 29 August 1945; TP VI 92 IB Committee IB (45)3 4 September 1945.
55. Letter Patel V.J. – G.D. Birla, 20 September 1945, reprinted in G.M. Nandurkar (ed.) *Sardar's Letters—Mostly Unknown*, Ahmedabad, India 1977, vol. 1, p. 174.
56. TP VI 248, Cabinet Paper CB(45)313 by Cripps, 28 November 1945.
57. TP VI 194, letter Wavell – Pethick Lawrence, 7 November 1945.
58. TP VI 217 IB Committee IB(45)7, 19 November 1945.
59. TP VI 244, Cabinet minutes CM(45)56, 27 November 1945.
60. PREM 8/58: notes of a meeting at Chequers, 23 November 1945.
61. TP VI 247 IB Committee IB(45)8, 28 November 1945.
62. TP VI 155, letter Cripps – Pethick-Lawrence, 22 October 1945; TP VI 262, letter Cripps – Pethick-Lawrence, undated but probably written 4 December 1945; Trinity College Cambridge, Pethick-Lawrence Papers MSS 5/63, letter Cripps – Pethick-Lawrence, 19 December 1945.
63. PREM 8/59: letter Attlee – Cripps and Pethick-Lawrence, 22 December 1945.
64. PREM 8/59: letter Pethick-Lawrence – Attlee, 26 December 1945.
65. TP VI 355 IB Committee IB(46)1, 14 January 1946.
66. Ibid.
67. TP VI 92 IB Committee IB(45)3, 4 September 1945.
68. TP VI 521, letter L.C. Hollis – D.T. Monteath, 13 March 1945.
69. TP VII 71, memorandum by Cripps, undated but probably written 8 April 1946.
70. PREM 8/541/3: f94 telegram Attlee – Cabinet Mission, 15 May 1946; Wavell, *Journal*, p. 269.
71. Moore, *Escape from Empire*, 168–83.
72. TP VIII 286, letter Wavell – Pethick-Lawrence, 8 September 1946.
73. TP VIII 379, letter Pethick-Lawrence – Wavell, 28 September 1946.
74. TP VII 509, Cabinet Defence Committee Paper DO(46)68, 12 June 1946.
75. TP VIII 528 Cabinet Paper CP(46)222 E. Bevin on 'Situation in India and its possible effect upon foreign relations'.
76 TP IX 181 Cabinet minutes CM(46)104, 10 December 1946.
77. *Hansard* vol. 341, cols 1523–37, 12 December 1946.
78. Nuffield College Oxford, Cherwell Papers J62/7, letter Cherwell – Churchill, 16 May 1946.
79. TP IX 105, memorandum of meeting between R.A. Butler and Pethick-Lawrence, 27 November 1946.
80. British Museum, Emrys Evans Papers Add. MSS 58240, letter J.P.L. Thomas – Emrys Evans, 26 March 1946.
81. PREM 8/541/6: f80, notes by Prime Minister, undated but probably written 20 September 1946.
82. G.Gallup, *The Gallup International Opinion Polls: Great Britain 1937–75*, New York, 1977, pp.125–6.
83. J.G. Darwin, 'The fear of falling: British politics and imperial decline' *Transactions of the Royal Historical Society*, 5th series, vol. 36(1986)27–44.
84. Wavell, *Journal*, p. 434; Nuffield College Oxford, Cherwell Papers J63/28,

letter Cherwell – Rankeillour, 7 November 1946.
85. TP VI 524, record of meeting of ministers, 13 March 1946; TP VIII 7 Cabinet minutes CM(46)65, 5 July 1946; PREM 8/541/6: f37, letter Attlee – Pethick-Lawrence, 28 September 1946.
86. M. Gilbert, *Winston Churchill 1945–65: Never Despair*, 1988, p. 292; letter Simon – M.A. Jinnah, 11 December 1946, cited in Moore *Escape from Empire* op. cit. 206–7
87. TP IX 151, Indian Conference in London ICL(46)1 Meeting of Attlee, Mission Ministers and Wavell, 4 December 1946.
88. Bodlean Library Oxford, MSS Simon 97/4–6, letter Simon to Churchill, 12 December 1946.
89. Ibid. MSS Simon 97/15, Letter Simon – A. Eden 7 February 1947.
90. Wavell, *Journal*, p. 390.
91. TP IX 87, telegram Wavell – Pethick-Lawrence, 24 November 1946.
92. TP IX 281, letter Wavell – Attlee, 17 January 1947.
93. R.F. Holland, 'The imperial factor in British strategies from Attlee to Macmillan 1945–63', *Journal of Imperial and Commonwealth History*, vol. 12, no. 2(January 1984) 165–86.
94. H. Tinker, 'The contraction of Empire in Asia 1945–8: the military dimension', *Journal of Imperial and Commonwealth History*, vol. 16, no. 2(January 1988)218–33.
95. TP IX 157, Indian Conference in London; ICL(46)6 Meeting of Attlee, Mission Ministers and Wavell, 5 December 1946.
96. TP IX 181 Cabinet minutes CM(46)104, 10 December 1946.
97. Ibid.
98. TP IX 213 IB, Committee IB(46)13, 20 December 1946.
99. Directive to the new Governor 29/8/1946, in H. Tinker (ed.) *Burma:the Struggle for Independence 1944–48*, vol. 1, 1983–4 pp. 970–2.
100. Diary of Sir Stafford Cripps: 'The Cabinet mission to India 1946', unpublished but copies held by Sir Maurice Shock and Nicholas Owen, p. 21.
101. TP IX 186, IB Committee IB(46)8, 11 December 1946.
102. TP IX 206, IB Committee Paper IB(46)52 by Addison 18 December 1946.
103. TP IX 235, Cabinet minutes CM(46)108, 31 December 1946.
104. TP IX 236, minute Bevin – Attlee, 1 January 1947.
105. Morgan *Labour In Power*, op. cit. 224.
106. Letter Salisbury – Attlee, 18 December 1946 cited in Moore, *Escape from Empire*, op. cit. 207.
107. TP IX 426, IB Committee IB(47)12, 18 February 1947.
108. Bodleian Library Oxford, MSS Simon 96/35–8, 'Note for Winston', undated but probably April 1947.
109. India Office Library and Records, Templewood Collection Eur MSS E240/79, memorandum on 'India', 20 February 1947.
110. TP IX 243, letter Attlee – Bevin, 2 January 1947.
111. Wavell, *Journal*, p. 397.
112. TP IX 421, Cabinet minutes CM(47)23, 18 February 1947.
113. TP IX 365, letter Attlee – Mountbatten, 8 February 1947.
114. Dalton *Diary*, 20 December 1946.
115. TP IX 245, IB Committee IB(47)1, 3 January 1947.
116. TP IX 262, Cabinet minutes CM(47)4, 8 January 1947.
117. TP IX 460, letter Wavell – King George VI, 24 February 1947; TP VIII 501 Letter Wavell – Pethick-Lawrence, 23 October 1946.
118. TP IX 94, letter Pethick-Lawrence – Wavell, 25 November 1946.

119. TP IX 235, Cabinet minutes CM(46)108, 31 December 1946.
120. Ibid.
121. TP IX 249, Cabinet Paper CP(47)1 by Attlee, 4 January 1947.
122. TP IX 376, letter Mountbatten – Attlee, 11 February 1947.
123. TP IX 378, undated notes by Mountbatten of a meeting on 11 February 1947 with Attlee and Ismay.
124. For example, E. Hobsbawm and T.O. Ranger (eds) *The Invention of Tradition*, Cambridge, 1985; R. Samuel and P. Thompson (eds) *The Myths We Live By*, 1990.
125. H. McMillan, *Pointing the Way*, 1972, pp. 116–17; J.H. Wilson, *The Labour Government 1964–70: A personal record*, 1971, p. 212.
126. Scott, *A Division of the Spoils*, 1977, p. 105.
127. J. Mackenzie, *Propaganda and Empire*, Manchester, 1984, p. 257.
128. B. Porter, *The Lion's Share*, 1975, p. 315.
129. For example, TP IX 426, IB Committee IB(47)12 minute 5, 18 February 1947; TP IX 459, IB Committee IB(47)13, 24 February 1947.
130. TP IX 213, IB Committee IB(46)13, 20 December 46; TP IX 216, minute Pethick-Lawrence – Attlee, 21 December 1946.
131. TP IX 459, IB Committee IB(47)13, 24 February 1947.
132. *Hansard*, vol. 440, col. 230, 15 July 1947.
133. Wavell, *Journal*, p. 419.
134. PREM 8/59, letter Attlee – Pethick-Lawrence and Cripps, 22 December 1945.
135. TP IX 365, letter Attlee – Mountbatten, 8 February 1947; TP IX 376, letter Mountbatten – Attlee, 11 February 1947.
136. Listowel, op. cit., 23–4.
137. For Cripps' attempt to have Abell, the Viceroy's Private Secretary, replaced, see TP IX 377, letter Mountbatten – Attlee, 11 February 1947.
138. D. Cannadine, 'Mountbatten', in *The Pleasures of the Past*, 1989, pp. 58–67.
139. TP IX 543, minute Attlee – Pethick-Lawrence, 18 March 1947.
140. CAB 127/139: letter Mountbatten – Cripps, 24 April 1947.
141. TP X 139, Viceroys Conference Paper 28, 14 April 1947.
142. TP X 257, minute E.C. Mieville – Mountbatten, 30 April 1947.
143. TP X 267, letter Nehru – Mountbatten, 1 April 1947.
144. TP X 394, telegram Ismay – Mountbatten, 10 May 1947.
145. TP X 410, telegram Mountbatten – Ismay, 11 May 1947; TP X 421–2, telegrams Ismay – Mountbatten and Mieville, 12 May 1947.
146. TP X 419, telegram Mountbatten – Ismay, 12 May 1947; TP X 428, draft telegram Attlee – Mountbatten, 13 May 1947.
147. TP X 435, minute T.L. Rowan – Attlee, 14 May 1947.
148. TP X 438, telegram Ismay – Mountbatten, 14 May 1947.
149. TP X 449, letter Ismay – Mountbatten, 15 May 1947.
150. TP X 475, IB Committee IB(47)71, 17 May 1947.
151. TP X 414, minutes of Viceroy's 31st Staff Meeting, 12 May 1947.
152. CAB 127/143: letter Nehru – Cripps, 3 December 1945.
153. H. Dalton, *High Tide and After*, 1962, p.211.
154. TP VIII 375, note of discussion between Pethick-Lawrence and Cripps, 27 September 1946; Trinity College Cambridge, Pethick-Lawrence Papers MSS 5/77, draft letter Pethick-Lawrence – Attlee, 2 April 1947.
155. Moore, *Making the New Commonwealth*, op. cit.
156. Wavell, *Journal*, p. 462.

11 Facing facts? The Labour Government and defence policy 1945–1950

Anthony Gorst

The defence problem would be relatively easy to solve if we could get as much money as we needed. We must however face the facts of the present financial position.

Emanuel Shinwell, Minister of Defence,
to the Chiefs of Staff, 11 May 1950.[1]

Despite their impressive war record against the Axis powers after 1942, the British armed forces required reconstruction after nearly six years of total war no less than any other part of Britain's society and economy. An imposing façade of seasoned forces totalling some five million men at the wartime peak equipped with modern weapons hid a structure that had begun to crack even before the end of hostilities as the combined demands of the war in Europe and the war in the Far East strained British capacities to the limit. However, this reconstruction could not be based on a return to a pre-war status quo, nor could it take place in a vacuum: British defence policy as a whole needed recasting in the light of changed post-war conditions and had to reflect both economic and strategic requirements. Advances in weapons technology, such as the atomic bomb, and developments in the international arena, notably the onset of the Cold War, might dictate an 'ideal' strategy, but this had to be balanced against the increasingly severe economic situation of the country.

The military argued that British defence policy and the size and shape of the armed forces ought to be governed by the need to simultaneously fulfil short-term occupation and counter-insurgency commitments and begin long-term preparations for the next war. However, the harsh reality was that this demanded a level of resources that the Labour government under Clement Attlee was both unwilling and unable to provide: the demands of the services, initially in terms of manpower and later in terms of finance, could only be met in full at the expense of other government commitments, notably welfare measures, which senior Labour ministers were not prepared to contemplate.

Attlee and his Minister of Defence Albert Alexander therefore faced an unenviable dilemma in evolving a settled post-war defence policy. On the one hand the breakup of the wartime alliance and the deterioration of the international situation after 1945 implied an unforeseen expansion of British military commitments, which was reflected in the financial and manpower allocations demanded by the Chiefs of Staff (COS) and the Service Ministers supported by the powerful figure of Foreign Secratary Ernest Bevin. On the other hand the Chancellor of the Exchequer (initially Hugh Dalton and then Stafford Cripps), the President of the Board of Trade (Cripps and then Harold Wilson), and the Minister of Labour (George Isaccs) constantly asserted that these demands competed with civil reconstruction and could not be fulfilled without disastrous consequences for the British economy.

Stark choices were therefore placed before the Attlee government in the annual budgetary battles in the main policy-making body, the Defence Committee, which shaped British defence policy: whether to give priority to civil or military reconstruction, whether to meet the short-term or the long-term requirements of the armed forces and whether to give priority to the demands of the Army, the Royal Air Force or the Royal Navy. The result was that the defence policy of the Attlee government was made up of a series of unhappy compromises. Pushed by the demands of the services it could not reduce the annual defence estimates to the target figure of £500 million per annum envisaged in 1945; but at the same time the armed forces maintained at such a cost were incapable of meeting either their short-term or long-term commitments, a disparity graphically revealed by the Korean War in 1950.

In the first two years of the post-war period the Attlee government had the greatest difficulty in producing a settled defence policy that reflected anything other than short-term constraints: this was acknowledged in both the 1946 and 1947 Defence White Papers.[2] On taking office on 26 July 1945, the Labour government had few ideas on an overall post-war defence policy beyond providing armed forces to back up British foreign policy. It is significant that the first substantive discussion of defence policy between Attlee (who was also the Minister of Defence until the establishment of a separate Ministry of Defence under Albert Alexander on 1 January 1947) and Bevin revolved around the administrative structure of Britain's higher defence organization and the need to reduce defence expenditure to the Coalition government figure of £500 million per annum rather than around the implementation of a long-term defence policy.[3]

This emphasis on the short-term was paralleled in the military. The COS entered the post-war era with no clear idea of the future: what post-war strategic planning there had been had simply served to illustrate the difficulties inherent in what was derisively called 'crystal ball gazing' by the higher echelons of the Foreign Office.[4] The COS were therefore reluctant to put forward a strategic blueprint on which a long-term defence policy could be based until all aspects of the problem had been considered; only then would the Joint Planning Staff (JPS) prepare a report on 'Future Defence Policy'. This process took until July 1947 and even then was fatally flawed precisely because despite all the evidence of the budgetary battles of 1945–7, the strategic concept evolved paid only lip-service to economic reality.[5]

In the meantime, lacking a long-term objective which would give it badly needeed coherence, British defence policy drifted with disastrous consequences for the Services. Pulled by the need to fulfil expanded occupation and counter-insurgency commitments in Europe, the Middle East and East of Suez as the Cold War gathered momentum, but at the same time unable to advance strategic arguments to justify demands for what seemed to be a disproportionate share of scarce resources, the Service Departments were vulnerable to arbitrary cuts by the Defence Committee and Cabinet on purely economic grounds. Defence policy therefore became little more than an extension of foreign and economic policy and the Services were to pay a high price for this lack of direction.

The dominant theme of the Attlee government was the need to reduce the resources allocated to defence as rapidly as possible: from VJ Day it placed incessant pressure on its military advisers to reduce their requirements in the interests of national economic recovery, accepting the risk of disorganized armed forces in the belief that war was unlikely in the near future. The production programmes, manpower requirements and financial estimates of the armed forces were all subject to the minutest scrutiny and the severest cuts from autumn 1945: at almost every meeting of the Defence Committee, the COS and their Ministers were faced with fresh demands for retrenchment from the formidable combination of Attlee, Dalton and Cripps.[6]

The issues involved were starkly revealed during prolonged and heated debates on the requirements of the armed forces which were submitted to the Defence Committee and Cabinet in January and February 1946, prior to the production of the first post-war defence programme for the financial year 1946/7. On 11 January 1946 Dalton noted that

> the total sum which the Service Departments and the Ministry of Supply would ask the Treasury to find would be in the neighbourhood of £2,000 million. This was a figure which we could not possibly afford . . . the figure of 2 million men should be viewed in relation to the probable figure for peace-time regular strengths of 500,000. The whole picture of defence manpower and expenditure appeared out of scale and if there was no quick drop, particularly abroad, in the expenditure, he could not promise anything but economic disaster.

Dalton was supported ten days later by Morrison and Attlee, who both noted that in view of the alarming manpower deficiences revealed by the Economic Survey, 'a cut in the size of the forces was unavoidable'. Bevin, initially as eager as anyone to cut the resources allocated to defence in his role as chairman of the Manpower Committee, had however begun to shift his position, arguing that in order to strengthen his hand as Foreign Secretary in negotiations with the Soviet Union and the United States, it would be unwise to weaken the armed forces in the immediate future. Attlee, to accommodate this, therefore proposed that the bulk of the manpower cuts should come in the second half of 1946, from 1,900,000 men in June to 1,100,000 in December, and should fall mainly on the Navy and the RAF as the Army 'had a great number of commitments which could not be liquidated'.[7]

The response of the COS was uncompromising and ultimately unsuccessful: cuts on this scale would entail the winding up of certain commitments, chiefly in the Mediterranean and south-eastern Europe, and an acceptance of a reduction of the armed forces to the point where they could not meet an emergency in the next three years. They were unable, however, to put forward a long-term programme to underpin their demands. Attlee and Dalton were equally unyielding in pushing through both the cuts in manpower and a 10 per cent cut in the financial provision to £1,667 million, arguing that the COS provisos would have to be accepted in the interests of national recovery, particularly as there was no real danger of war with the Soviet Union in the foreseeable future. Even so, Attlee warned that although 'the cuts which had been made involved considerable risks . . . the burden of expenditure was greater than the country could bear for long.'[8]

Although these reductions in manpower were disappointing for the COS in that they involved the postponement of the reconstruction plans for the armed forces, they did manage in May 1946 to secure the approval of the Defence Committee to the temporary continuation of conscription pending the introduction of a permanent scheme, even though Attlee and Dalton would make no long-term commitment on numbers.[9] A further ray of hope came in October when the principle of permanent peacetime conscription from 1 January 1949 was accepted. Despite the reservations of Dalton, Cripps and Isaccs about the economic implications of the scheme, the Defence Committee accepted the arguments of the Service Departments and Ernest Bevin that conscription was essential in order to avoid the mistakes of the inter-war period, to fulfil the inescapable short-term commitments of the armed forces and to build up the reserves of trained manpower which would be vital on the outbreak of any future total war with the Soviet Union. This at least held out to the Services the prospect of a continued annual intake of raw recruits, but as the COS pointed out, it did nothing to resolve the fundamental questions of long-term strategy in relation to the role and composition of the armed forces, without which defence policy would continue to drift, nor did it lift the damaging short-term constraints from the shoulders of the armed forces.[10]

The bleak short-term prospect was confirmed in the winter of 1946/7. In November the Defence Committee refused to approve a COS requirement for over 1 million men in March 1948. This refusal was significant because for the first time the COS had tried to justify their figures by reference to the initial conclusions from their long-term strategic review. None the less their report met with a frosty reception. Dalton and Isaacs again queried the economic and industrial impact of such manpower allocations. Attlee, although he thought the report was of some use as a basis for discussion, felt that 'it would be quite wrong for the Committee to reach a decision . . . without further scrutiny.'[11]

The COS initially fared no better with the defence estimates for 1947/8. The newly appointed Minister of Defence Albert Alexander was still unable to present a long-term defence policy and could justify figures of £963 million and 1,094,000 men in the forces by March 1948 only in terms of the continuing occupation commitments demanded by the foreign policy of Bevin. Despite stressing that the Services were doing all they could to reduce their demands by living off war stocks and delaying new production, Alexander was unable to reduce the estimates further. Predictably Attlee, Dalton and Isaacs again stressed the primacy of economic recovery, pointing to a deficiency of 650,000 men in the total manpower budget and arguing that the most that could be allocated to the forces for 1947/8 was £750 million. The estimates were therefore passed to the Cabinet for review.[12]

In a Cabinet that had just considered an Economic Survey for 1947 which highlighted future manpower shortages and balance of payment difficulties, the requirements of the armed forces presented by Alexander were hardly acceptable. Cripps, Dalton and Isaacs argued that

> nothing would be gained by maintaining the strength of the armed forces at the cost of overstraining the industrial resources of the country or reducing the standard of home consumption. Our influence within international affairs and our strength in any future war depended on our industrial and social stability as much as on the size of our peace-time armed forces.

Surprisingly, however, Attlee, much to the chagrin of Dalton, supported Alexander in his bid for 1,167,000 men for the forces and 450,000 in the supply sector by December 1947, pointing to the 'experience after the war of 1914–1918 [which] showed the disastrous effect on British foreign policy of allowing the armed forces to be unduly weakened'.[13]

Moreover, when the Cabinet came to consider the 1947/8 financial estimates for the services of £940.5 million (of which £118.5 million was for terminal charges arising out of war), Attlee again backed the Minister of Defence. Dalton cited the Coalition government figure of £500 million per annum for defence and pointed out that Alexander's scrutiny had resulted in a cut of only £22 million towards the 'acceptable' figure of £750 million: he therefore suggested a 10 per cent cut with the possibility of supplementary estimates if they should be required. However, Alexander felt that there

> was no room for further sweeping reductions. He was satisfied that the provision made in the estimates before the Cabinet was the absolute minimum consistent with the tasks which the Services had to discharge: if further reduction were made of the order now proposed, he would have to consider whether he could assure Parliament that the forces would be maintained in a state of reasonable efficiency.

Although Alexander was instructed to consider the implications of a reduction of £80 million, he received a strong endorsement of his position from the Prime Minister: 'the Cabinet must bear in mind the importance of preserving an armed strength sufficient to support the foreign policy which the Government had undertaken to pursue.'[14]

This temporary shift by the Prime Minister in supporting his Minister of Defence was shaped by the foreign policy difficulties that Bevin had experienced in New York and by a resignation threat from the COS over his disagreements with them about the strategic significance of the Middle East.[15] Pushed by the combined demands of Bevin and the COS, Attlee reluctantly supported estimates on a scale that he had previously condemned. With the continuing support of the Prime Minister, who cast doubt on Dalton's constant referral to the figure of £500 million, and the Foreign Secretary, who thought the estimates 'a very substantial achievement when allowance was made for the abnormal conditions of the present time', Alexander painted the blackest possible picture of the proposed 10 per cent cut, arguing that it would 'have the most serious consequences on the efficiency and welfare of the forces, their ability to undertake . . . commitments and any plan for the establishment of balanced forces in future years'. Consequently Dalton could only express his gratitude at a possible 5 per cent cut to approximately £899 million and assure Alexander that there would be no difficulty about meeting any suplementary estimates that might be necessary.[16]

By the early spring of 1947, therefore, the defence policy of the Attlee government was in disarray. The position reached reflected the worst of both worlds: due to manpower cuts the armed forces were without exception completely disorganized, but they still demanded more resources than the Chancellor of the Exchequer and the Minister of Labour thought that the country could afford. For the military a long-term defence policy within which the reconstruction of the forces could be framed was now urgent but this depended on the long-awaited strategic review to provide a justification for their requirements. The Labour government, too, eagerly awaited this review as it held out the prospect of reducing defence expenditure to manageable proportions. In February 1947, Alexander, after consulting the Prime Minister and Foreign Secretary, took the initiative and laid down the basis on which the JPS should plan future defence policy for the long-term. He stressed that the 1947/8 estimates merely reflected transitional requirements, and that the next estimates for 1948/9 would be the first of a ten-year programme designed to produce definitive peacetime armed forces based on a maximum allocation of no more than £600 million per annum. Within this figure priority was to be given to the development of the deterrent forces of the RAF.[17]

In the spring of 1947 the JPS report on 'Future defence policy' was at last produced, discussed and approved. However, in order to prevent inter-service rivalry and competition for priority from delaying an already prolonged process, the COS had ruled that this should be initially an undiluted strategic appreciation unhampered by any consideration of the thorny problem of resources. This approach simply perpetuated the errors of the previous two years with the result that a defence policy that balanced the economic priorities of the Cabinet and the strategic requirements of the military was as far away as ever.

The aim of the COS in their 'Future defence policy' was to 'refashion our forces and our war potential to meet the needs of the future'. The most pressing threat was the prospect of a Soviet Union equipped with atomic and biological weapons and appropriate delivery systems, and able and willing to launch a premeditated 'hot' war in the mid-1950s, which a Britain without allies would be unable to oppose. According to the military, British defence policy had to be geared to meeting this nightmare scenario. Thus the JPS argued that it was of the utmost importance 'to give us a chance of survival and victory in the event of the war' to be prepared

> to take offensive action from the outset since the war will rapidly reach a climax and the endurance of the United Kingdom cannot be guaranteed for any considerable period against attacks by modern weapons, still less by weapons of mass destruction. The best bases for this offensive action are the United Kingdom, Middle East and if possible North-West India

Moreover, the Services had 'to be prepared, equipped and able to use weapons of mass destruction as part of this offensive action'. The security of the United Kingdom therefore depended above all on the RAF as although 'the possession of a powerful offensive force is essential to our security, the development of our active and passive air defence organisations, in all their aspects, must be complementary to the build-up of our striking force.' In war the RAF would play the primary role in providing the fighter defence of the main base for the war effort, the United Kingdom, and in carrying out the bomber offensive using mass destruction weapons which alone could ensure victory. In peace the RAF was assigned the leading role in British defence policy, as an efficient and prepared Bomber Command and Fighter Command would be 'the only effective deterrent' to either accidental or deliberate Soviet aggression: they alone provided the only 'tangible evidence of our intention and ability to withstand attack and hit back immediately'.[18]

Following the acceptance of this 'three pillar strategy' (so called because it relied on securing the interdependent tripod of the United Kingdom, the Middle East and the sea communications between) as the framework for British defence policy by the Prime Minister at a Staff Conference in June 1947, the COS set in motion the process of turning a paper exercise into a real policy by calculating the forces required to carry it out on the outbreak of war and from this deriving the size of the peacetime armed forces. Not surprisingly this produced a considerable increase in projected cost with Service Department forecasts of long-term defence expenditure, excluding supply, ranging from £873 million in 1948/9 to nearly £1,500 million per annum by the mid-1950s, as the Soviet threat curve and the associated British preparations peaked.

Such estimates were very much at odds with the reductions in manpower and expenditure being demanded of the Services by the Cabinet as a consequence of the convertability crisis: clearly the Services had not learned the lessons of 1945/6.[19] Alexander, with the backing of Attlee, was forced to crack the whip by issuing a directive to the three Services that reaffirmed the figure of £600 million per annum for defence expenditure. As there was held to be little danger of war with the Soviet Union in the next five years, while that country reconstructed its war-torn economy and developed its offensive capacity, and a steadily rising risk of war thereafter, varying according to the offensive strength of British forces, he assigned top priority to the long-term preparation of the deterrent forces of the RAF with only the bare minumum of resources to be allocated to short-term and medium-term commitments. In the event of war before the preparations of the armed forces were completed in the mid—1950s, then British would 'have to fight with what we have'.[20]

However, in the autumn and winter of 1947 the Service Departments proved reluctant to accept this clear ruling by their political masters and tailor their estimates to reflect these priorities, with the result that despite the formal acceptance of the three-pillar strategy, Alexander was unable to place a balanced long-term defence policy before the Defence Committee. Another unseemly budgetary battle therefore ensued over the 1948/9 estimates with the COS giving the Minister of Defence requirements of £662 million and 735,000 men compared with target figures of £600 million and 650,000 men.

The problem was that although the Navy and RAF had based their plans on Alexander's directive, the Army had broken ranks with the other Services and had continued to base its figures of £250 million and 360,000 men solely on 'the provision of forces necessary to meet peace-time commitments'. The result was estimates that exceeded the limit set by Alexander, and moreover, were unbalanced in that the shares of the Navy (£180 million and 150,000 men) and the RAF (£190 million and 225,000 men) were far below what was required. The Chief of the Air Staff and the First Sea Lord were only prepared to accept this position provided it was recognized that from 1949 the provision for the RAF and the Navy would have to be greatly expanded 'if these two Services are to provide any form of deterrent or security as the danger of war increases'. The COS concluded wearily to the minister: 'we therefore want to leave you under no misapprehension. We have not solved the long-term problem.'[21]

Alexander agreed whole-heartedly, and with obvious exasperation noted that 'unless matters are allowed to drift Ministerial decisions are required.' He took the lead by altering the COS requirements to bring them within his targets and to reflect his priorities: £50 million was to be allocated for Research and Development, £140 million for the Navy, £220 million for the Army and £180 million for the RAF, while the COS manpower figures were to be scrutinized to bring them down to his 650,000 total. However, in presenting these requirements he discounted the Coalition government figure of £500 million as being 'a shot in the dark designed to assist the Government in deciding the future trend of expenditure on the social services', and argued that £600 million per annum, 7 per cent of the national income or 20 to 25 per cent of national expenditure, was 'a reasonable figure' that should be guaranteed as the minimum future expenditure on the armed forces. He confirmed his priorities *vis-à-vis* the Services, arguing that the primacy afforded the Army was a short-term measure that would be eliminated as soon as possible.[22]

Although the Defence Committee, spurred on by Attlee, accepted the priorities that underlay the 1948/9 estimates, endorsing the development of deterrent forces at the expense of the Army, Alexander was forced to remind them that implicit within these was the need 'to contemplate heavy additional expenditure on rearmament in the early 1950s'. Predictably this did not find favour with the new Chancellor of the Exchequer, Stafford Cripps, or with Attlee: although both were prepared to accept £600 million as the maximum annual defence expenditure for the foreseeable future, in their view this would have to cover both short-term requirements and any long-term rearmament. The Prime Minister's suggestion was that as the short-term occupation commitments of the Army were wound up, any surplus within the £600 million would be put into 'a reserve fund to help finance . . . the rearmament programme that would have to be undertaken in the 1950s'. Therefore the Minister of Defence, the Service Ministers and the Chiefs of Staff were to make a concerted attempt to work out as soon as possible a long-term co-ordinated plan based on the three-pillar strategy within Alexander's original budget of £600 million and 650,000 men (including 150,000 from the annual national service intake).[23] It seemed that the Labour government was finally beginning to impose order on the chaos of British defence policy. Yet this impression was to prove illusory: by early March 1948 the COS were reporting that the attempt to develop a long-term programme based on the Defence Committee limit of £600 million had been postponed due to the pressure of other business.[24]

One distraction was the possibility of strategic discussions with the French and the Americans on a Western European defence organization, which raised the question of a 'continental commitment' for the British Army in peace and war, something that had not been envisaged in the 'Future defence policy' hammered out in 1946/7. The three-pillar strategy which underpinned the long-term plans of the forces was thus called into question as the War Office, not altogether surprisingly, used this new factor as a lever for an increased role and priority for the Army. Although initially Attlee, Bevin and Alexander were not convinced by the military or political logic of the Army's arguments, to say nothing of the economic questions raised, the long-term strategic debate was back on the COS agenda and remained a running sore throughout the spring and summer of 1948: no long-term programme could be developed until this issue had been resolved.[25]

A second pressure was an acceleration of the Cold War in the spring of 1948 which undermined the attempts of the Defence Committee and Cabinet to control defence expenditure. On 5 March 1948 Bevin reported to the Cabinet that Soviet activities in Czechoslovakia and Finland meant 'that resolute action must be taken to counter . . . [this] threat to Western civilisation'. Amongst the measures approved by the Cabinet was a review of 'the military strength needed to support the diplomatic action under the policy proposed by the Foreign Secretary and of the defence measures needed if that policy was to prevent war'.[26] This shifted the emphasis in the planning of the armed forces from the long-term to the short-term: although it was not believed that the Soviet threat had materially changed, the Service Departments began a lengthy 'stocktaking' exercise in case they had to fight with what they had over the next eighteen months.[27] This raised the possibility of supplementary estimates as such investigations revealed alarming deficiences in manpower and equipment.[28]

This exercise was overtaken by the events of the summer of 1948 as the Berlin crisis focused the attentions of the military and the politicians alike on the immediate emergency. On 26 July 1948 the Cabinet in considering the possibility of 'a firm attitude' over Berlin ordered the Defence Committee to review 'the state of the country's defence preparations and whether any precautionary steps ought to be taken'. However the Cabinet also stressed: 'If we were to undertake a substantial programme of rearmament without special United States aid we should merely hamper the ecomomic recovery on which our capacity for waging war must in the last resort depend.' The precarious balance of military requirements and civil reconstruction had to be maintained: there was no blank cheque for the COS.[29]

The papers laid before the Defence Committee by the military highlighted the parlous condition to which the armed forces had been reduced as a result of the cutbacks of the previous three years. While the Navy was in a fair position to meet any possible maritime threat from the Soviet Union, although short of fuel, the RAF, the mainstay of British strategy, had been reduced to a nominal front-line of less than 1,000 aircraft, and even these were at such a low state of efficiency due to a lack of trained manpower that the air defence of the British Isles and the conduct of a strategic bombing offensive could not be guaranteed. Worse still, the Army, which would take the first shock in the event of a war in Europe, was short of equipment and ammunition, and its forces in Germany and the Middle East were untrained and lacked administrative and logistical support. Alexander put it plainly: 'our forces are not in a fit state to commence a major war.' In order to remedy these deficiencies the release of trained manpower from the armed forces would have to be suspended, reservists recalled and war production restarted, all as soon as possible.[30]

Despite this bleak picture the Defence Committee refused to approve all the COS measures, only agreeing initially to the temporary suspension of releases. Indeed Cripps stressed that there could be no question of increased expenditure until the COS had indicated the tasks and priorities of the armed forces.[31] This provided the COS with the opportunity to widen the debate. The COS presented a comparatively modest programme based on providing the forces to carry out the three-pillar strategy with the addition of a continental commitment in the event of war before 1950. This included a selective call-up of reservists, the revision of mobilization plans, the overhaul of the active and passive air defences of the United Kingdom, the preparation of bomber bases and aircraft and the refitting of naval convoy escorts. However, the Chief of the Air Staff, Lord Tedder stressed that the issue could not be restricted to a consideration of short-term military measures: any steps taken in response to the Berlin crisis had to be seen in the context of British defence policy as a whole, in particular the resources that could or would be allocated for defence over the next ten years. This was essentially a political decision.[32] Although the Defence Committee and the Cabinet approved the COS programme, at an additional cost over and above the 1948/9 estimates of approximately £60 million and 85,000 men, the COS continued to warn the Labour government that it should be under no illusion that these short-term measures did anything for the development of a long-term defence policy.[33]

Alexander was equally conscious of the need to resume long-term planning, and these COS comments led him, supported by Attlee, to ask for the delayed report on the long-term size and shape of the armed forces on a budget of £600 million per annum to be produced by October 1948.[34] A COS examination revealed the same problem that had bedevilled planning in 1947: in order to provide the forces to carry out the three-pillar strategy between 1952 and 1957, the defence estimates would vary from a minimum of £707 million in 1950 to a maximum of £1,380 million in 1957. This was clearly beyond the limits envisaged by the Minister of Defence, and the COS were left with no option but to call for a Staff Conference with Alexander to lay out their difficulties.[35]

At this meeting the COS received short shrift. Alexander categorically stated that the COS figures were out of the question and added:

> It might be that the United Kingdom would find it economically impossible to maintain a first class Navy, Army and Air Force and it might be necessary to consider the priorities on which the provision of these forces should be based . . . he still felt that the provision of Air Defence, including offensive air forces, must be the first priority, the defence of our sea communications being a second priority.

In response to this restatement of the problem, the COS could only reply that they would reconsider the various tasks of the armed forces.[36]

Recognizing the futility of this approach, which would merely repeat the process undertaken in 1947, and under pressure to provide estimates for 1949/50, the COS, with the agreement of Attlee and Alexander, decided to take a fresh long look at the problem of finance and defence policy over the period 1950–3 by setting up an inter-service working party under an independent chairman which would report in February 1949. The aim of this working party was to attempt to define the armed forces 'which could be maintained within an annual framework of £700 million per annum. If this were possible then the whole conception would be built up detail by detail.' The COS were not optimistic about the possibility of the working party reaching a balanced and feasible plan and felt that 'the report . . . was likely to be an unpalatable document.' Time pressures meant of course that the 1949/50 estimates would have to be taken separately and once again would not represent a balanced long-term defence policy.[37]

Provisional costings of the manpower demands of the services for 1949/50, based on a period of eighteen months national service, indicated that they would need an average of 750,000 men, which implied defence estimates of at least £795 million and possibly £833 million. However, a meeting with the Minister of Defence and the Prime Minister confirmed that no more than £700 million would be available for the next financial year. The COS therefore decided that the only way to get down to anywhere near this figure was to base the forthcoming estimates primarily on existing occupation and counter-insurgency commitments; postponing re-equipment and delaying expenditure on improving the welfare services and amenities for the Services would save approximately £60 million.[38]

Before Alexander put these estimates totalling £770 million before the Defence Committee, he asked for a meeting with the COS in order to clarify whether they in fact reflected the priorities that he had set, as 'he was not altogether satisfied that the problem . . . was being tackled in the spirit of emergency which the economic position of the country demanded', especially given the £712 million that the Chancellor of the Exchequer had offered for the forthcoming year. Not surprisingly the COS reassured him that the RAF and the Navy had been given precedence, but claimed that Army expenditure could not be reduced any further as it was 'fully engaged in supporting our position in the Cold War'. Indeed, the disputed sum, representing between 6 and 7 per cent of the defence estimates, would represent 'a good investment for the country'. Any 'overeconomising' would have disastrous effects on the forces' ability to wage the Cold War, meet a Soviet attack in the short term or prepare for war by 1957. In sum it was not possible to carry out all the policies envisaged by the Defence Committee on the resources offered by the Chancellor.[39]

At the Defence Committee Alexander therefore presented estimates for £770 million, stressing that this figure had already been reduced by the COS from £833 million, and that any further cuts in the financial provision would result in a drastic reduction in the readiness of the armed forces and their ability to meet either a cold war or hot war emergency: there would be 'disastrous effects both on all three Services and on national defence as a whole'. Cripps was unmoved: 'he was satisfied that unless the Cabinet were prepared to make drastic cuts in other sections of the budget it would not be possible to devote more than £712 million to the defence services.' He was, moreover, critical of the procedure that the Services had adopted in agreeing their estimates:

> In the present economic position . . . the only proper policy was to decide what total provision could be made for defence and to bring the individual programmes of the Service Departments into line with that figure. These proposals . . . approached the problem from the opposite point of view . . . £770 million seemed to him to be simply the aggregate of the separate requirements of the three individual services. This resulted in the palpably absurd conclusion that the expenditure of the enormous sum of £712 million would nevertheless mean that not one of the services would be an efficient fighting force.

The COS, however, received invaluable support from the Foreign Secretary. Bevin argued that it was vital that Britain should continue to 'make the most effective contribution possible to the Western stand against Soviet pressure': this would both deter the Soviet Union and reassure the countries of Western Europe, thereby fostering the development of the Western Union and the Atlantic Pact, which would, in the fullness of time, ease the defence burden of the United Kingdom. He therefore did not want to see this 'jeopardised by our failure to take the economic steps necessary to make our armed forces an effective military instrument'.

With Alexander and the COS tailoring their arguments to play on the fears of the Foreign Secretary (thus emphasizing the impact of any further cuts on the ability of the Services to support Bevin's foreign policy by highlighting their effect on the Emergency Programme of 1948), the result was a foregone conclusion. After a private meeting involving the Prime Minister, the Foreign Secretary and the Chancellor of the Exchequer, Cripps was forced to surrender, acknowledging that 'a total cost of £760 million was needed if the fighting services were to be effective instruments', and that this 'would not necessarily require a reduction in the estimates for the social services since it was likely that the increase could be met out of the higher national income which was expected in 1949/50'. Cripps did, however, point out the undesirability of any supplementary estimates and the urgency of preparing by May 'a co-ordinated plan which might bring great financial savings'.[40]

With this warning ringing in their ears, the COS awaited the report of the working party on the size and shape of the armed forces. Although this was presented to the COS at the end of March 1949, it was to be October 1949 before a co-ordinated plan could be given to the Defence Committee for consideration. The intervening months were spent by the military attempting to come to terms with the implications that became known as the Harwood Report (after its chairman) had for defence expenditure.

The aim of the Harwood Report was to translate the fixed sum of £2,100 million over three years into armed forces that would be able to carry out the policy to the government. Given that the danger of a premeditated war initiated by the Soviet Union in the late 1950s was the most pressing threat, the working party concluded that only 'a limited premium' should be paid to meet the risk of accidental war in the near future. The emphasis was therefore placed on research and development and production (a total of £515 million over the three year period) to begin to prepare the forces by 1957. Small balanced forces would be maintained to meet the immediate needs of the Cold War and as nucleus for the 1957 defence forces. On a budget of £700 million per annum these priorities therefore inevitably involved severe cuts to forces in being. Although the Army would be able to maintain the bulk of its occupation and counter-insurgency forces while building up a Strategic Reserve in the United Kingdom, the Navy would be reduced to maintaining a small Carrier Task Force and an Anti-submarine Squadron in home waters and small mixed forces in the Mediterranean, while the Air Force would lose all but the nucleus of Bomber Command while attempting to build up Fighter Command. Cuts to the infrastructure of the forces would also have to be made, for example the closing of dockyards and depots. As Harwood put it to the COS, 'His Majesty's Government must realise that either the United Kingdom must shed some of its responsibilities or alternatively the armed forces would cost more than £700 million per year.' Although the COS recorded their 'warm appreciation' for the efforts of the working party, not least because 'it had shown clearly the sacrifices that would have to be accepted if the current financial limit was in fact imposed', it rapidly became apparent that the COS were a long way from accepting the recommendations of the report en bloc.[41]

Notwithstanding the fact that Alexander felt it essential to be able to present agreed inter-service proposals to the Defence Committee within the £700 million limit, the COS reserved the right to examine the proposals of the working party and present 'alternative proposals which need not however necessarily be confined within the financial allocations given in the Harwood Report'. This represented a reversion to the procedure utilized between 1945 and 1949 which had been strongly condemned in the Harwood Report and by Stafford Cripps.[42]

The COS examinations revealed a number of problems with the Harwood Report which made it fatally flawed as a basis on which the COS could proceed to the Defence Committee. The working party had underestimated the cost of the forces it advocated by some £50 million, which would inevitably mean further cuts to come within the £700 million limit. The forces envisaged by the Harwood Report would be unable to sustain the Cold War commitments accepted by the Labour government, and it was therefore 'politically unacceptable'. Further, the sum of money allocated for the long-term re-equipment of the armed forces was inadequate as it would not produce forces able to undertake their tasks on the outbreak of war. Despite the prodding of the Prime Minister and the Minister of Defence, the COS were reluctant to let the Harwood Report go forward to the Defence Committee, as 'until the whole picture had been examined by the COS it would be impossible to say to what extent the Harwood proposals would prove to be acceptable.'[43]

Therefore when the Harwood Report was finally circulated to the Defence Committee at the end of June 1949 it was for information only and parallel COS papers clearly stated their reservations. A summary of the report indicated that although 'there was no insuperable difficulty in producing a balanced modern force . . . such a force may well be deemed insufficient to maintain the position in the world which we desire to occupy.' The COS commentary damned it with faint praise calling it 'a valuable analysis' which could not be accepted as it stood, since the forces provided were 'inadequate to carry out Government policy' in peace and in war. In terms of the three-pillar strategy the Army would be unable to carry out its Cold War tasks or provide forces for Europe and the Middle East on the outbreak of war, the Navy would be untrained and therefore unable to secure vital sea communications, while the RAF would be unable to provide the deterrent bomber forces to prevent war or the fighter forces to protect the United Kingdom.

Alexander felt that the recommendations of the Harwood Report would mean 'our extinction as a first rank power'. In order to support the foreign policy of the government and prepare for war by 1957, he felt that a sum of at least £800 million per annum was necessary in order to maintain the forces in being to meet existing commitments and re-equip them to meet the long-term threat. This expenditure was not a loss but would flow back to the Treasury through taxes and consumption and would have spin-offs in terms of research and development.[44]

Despite all the hopes pinned on the Harwood Report and all the work invested in it, it was never taken by the Defence Committee. The summer recess meant that by the time the Defence Committee reconvened in the autumn, the unacceptable recommendations of the Harwood Report had been superseded by another batch of COS papers on the size and shape of the armed forces. Faced with combined Service forecasts of expenditure totalling £840 million in 1950/1 and an extra £30 million in each subsequent year, Alexander, alive to impending pressure from the Defence Committee for a co-ordinated policy, set up an inter-service Committee under Sir Harold Parker of the Ministry of Defence to report on the implications of defence expenditure of £810 million per annum over the next three financial years. The rationale for this increase in expenditure, well over what was likely to be authorized by the Chancellor of the Exchequer, was that, as the Services argued, 'it would not be possible to make economies of the magnitude originally envisaged by Ministers unless they were prepared to accept a drastic curtailment of our present commitments.'[45]

Initial examinations by the Services indicated that although they could live with £810 million for 1950/1, this could only be done at the expense of deferring re-equipment, which in turn meant increased expenditure in succeeding years. Although it was noted that the Chancellor was unlikely to agree to expenditure on this scale, any deterioration 'in the trend of world affairs' and a consequent expansion of commitments would lead to the Services calling on the government for allocations over and above this figure.[46]

In putting forward proposals for 1950/1 of £201 million for the Navy, £307 million for the Army (declining to £302 million by 1951/2) £233 million for the RAF (rising to £234 million in 1951/2) and £62.5 million for supply, the COS and the InterDepartmental Committee emphasized that British defence policy would have to run serious risks. The Army, in meeting its Cold War tasks, would be unable to meet its commitments under the three-pillar strategy for a hot war, while the RAF, although ostensibly preparing for a major war, would have to leave the conduct of the strategic air offensive to the United States and would be unable to provide reserves for the air defence of Great Britain. All three Services would be forced to keep production to a minimum with the result that they would lack modern equipment and war reserves. To Alexander these proposals represented an acceptable compromise between the demands of the armed forces and the requirements of the Chancellor: unlike the Harwood Report, they would not 'lead to the frustration if not the abandonment of some of the major objectives of our foreign policy', such as the North Atlantic Pact.[47]

In the context of the economic difficulties which led to the devaluation of the pound in September 1949, these requirements were clearly not going to go unchallenged.[48] Indeed, at the Defence Committee in which these estimates were discussed, Alexander was forced to agree to a £12.5 million cut in the current expenditure of the armed forces. In the face of the statement by Cripps that 'there was no possibility whatsoever of finding £810 million in each of the three coming years unless the whole of the present policy of the Government were recast', Alexander stressed that this was the first properly co-ordinated defence policy presented since the war and that the extra expenditure over Cripps target 'flowed from the decision to prosecute the Cold War'. With the COS and the Service Ministers arguing that any cuts in the estimates would mean an abandonment of overseas commitments, it was no surprise to find Bevin once again supporting the military, as such a course in the Far East, the Middle East or in Western Europe 'could hardly fail to lead to an intensification of the Cold War and this he was not prepared to contemplate'. Moreover, the Foreign Secretary felt it invidious 'to be called upon to choose between foreign policy and defence on the one hand and social services on the other.'

Cripps none the less continued to press for a reduction to at most £760 million, and emphasized that any expenditure over that figure would have to be found by corresponding cuts in the social services, as the government could not raise any further income by taxes. While he acknowledged that 'the strength of this country in the diplomatic field depended to a considerable extent on the military strength behind the policy pursued by the Foreign Secretary', it was clear 'that in the last resort the defence of the country depended on the soundness of its economic position and that might be adversely affected by a Budget swollen with additional defence expenditure'.

Faced with this impasse amongst his senior ministers, Attlee therefore forced a compromise: 'in his view the case had been made out for some increase in expenditure over £760 million', and it was agreed that the allocation for 1950/1 would be £780 million with the possibility of supplementary estimates being made available after scrutiny by the Defence Committee to meet the immediate re-equipment needs of the Army and the RAF. Priority was to be given to the Cold War tasks of 'the forces stationed throughout the world for the purposes of deterring any potential aggressor', which implied more emphasis being placed on the Army than had been envisaged by the COS. The long-awaited long-term defence policy that the COS had spent much of 1949 working on disappeared without trace, and Alexander was merely invited 'to bring forward on some future occasion his proposals for a three year defence budget'.[49]

This compromise, which continued the policy of drift in British defence policy by emphasizing short-term Cold war commitments and making little or no provision for the medium term, was to be brutally exposed in 1950. The Services found it increasingly difficult in the spring of 1950 to balance their short-term and long-term commitments within the £780 million budget authorized by the Cabinet and Defence Committee, largely due to developments in the Western Union including the adoption of a formal Continental commitment of two divisions in the event of war.[50] When Alexander was replaced by former Secretary of State for War, Emanuel Shinwell, as Minister of Defence, Shinwell took the opportunity of instituting a further review of defence policy, calling for a report from the COS to enable him 'to explain to his colleagues the hard facts of the situation'. He was particularly concerned that in the absence of an agreed defence policy, the Services were falling between two stools, as the emphasis by the Cabinet on meeting short-term cold war commitments left them uprepared for a hot war, whether in the short term, the medium term or the long term. The COS were in complete agreement; exasperated by the failure of the Defence Committee and Cabinet in December 1949 to support their three-year programme they felt 'it was time the Chiefs of Staff Committee made the position quite clear to Ministers.'[51] However, hardly had the COS and the JPS begun work on this than the outbreak of the Korean War made their case for them by laying bare the state to which the armed forces had been reduced and the bankruptcy of British defence policy.

While the Defence Committee was concerned with the immediate implications of the Korean War, including the dispatch of British forces to assist the United States, the COS believed the North Korean invasion provided a suitable opportunity for the military to put before the Defence Committee both a package of emergency measures comparable with those of 1948 to rectify the short-term deficiencies of the armed forces and a long-term programme to improve the readiness of the forces by instituting the deferred re-equipment of the services.[52] For Shinwell and the COS the issue was simple: a restitution of the £30 million cut from the 1950/1 estimates, and an additional £100 million per year over the next two financial years would enable the COS to make a start on rectifying short-term weaknesses such as a lack of modern weapons for the Army and a general shortage of stocks and reserves, but 'would not of course put the Services on anything like a war footing'.

In the crisis atmosphere engendered by the Korean War, these emergency measures met with little difficulty in the Defence Committee, with Attlee and Cripps agreeing to the provision of £100 million for the Services over the next year, and £30 million guaranteed before December 1950, subject to a review when the annual defence estimates were considered. Although doubts were expressed about the impact of increased defence expenditure in the next financial year, the Cabinet approved the interim instalment of £100 million and agreed to consider the additional expenditure in subsequent years which 'would enable this country to play its full part under the North Atlantic Pact'.[53]

The Cabinet were, however, not to be allowed the luxury of once more deferring consideration of an increase in defence expenditure. Ministers' hands were forced by an enquiry from the United States administration about

> the nature and extent of the increased effort which they were willing and able to undertake in increasing their armed forces and their military production and of the further military production programmes which they could meet with United States financial assistance.

This offer of aid forced Cripps and the Cabinet to look seriously at the defence programme which they had hitherto postponed. Given the short notice of the American initiative, the programme put before Cabinet did not represent any new thinking but rather it took the cost of the 1950/1 programme with its £100 million supplementary estimates, added a further £100 million over the following three years to cover any small increases in the size of the armed forces, and added to that the production programmes envisaged by the COS in 1949. This produced a forecast of total defence expenditure for 1951–4 of £3,400 million: compared with the 1950/1 estimates projected over three years, the extra expenditure produced by rearmament measures was in reality only some £1,100 million.

Cripps felt that 'on general economic grounds' the most that Britain could afford to spend on defence over the next three years was £950 million per annum, and even this 'could not be provided without some reduction in government expenditure, some additional taxation, or some reduction in capital investment or a combination of all three'. The shortfall to be made up by the provision of aid in dollars from the United States was therefore in the region of £550 million. Despite the misgivings of Bevan about the impact of this expenditure on the government's civil programmes, the proposals put forward by Cripps were approved by the Cabinet in the belief that 'the fact was that our forces were insufficiently equipped to meet the dangers with which we were now faced. It was abundantly clear that we must spend substantially more on defence.'[54] With the Korean War rearmament programme, the Labour government had finally grasped the nettle and recognized that in the order to carry out its foreign and defence policy obligations, a sustained rearmament programme had to be instituted, whatever the economic and political cost.

In the final analysis the refusal of the Attlee government to 'face the facts' and meet the requirements put forward by the COS until the realities of the Cold War in the summer of 1950 forced them to do so rested on the belief of successive Chancellors of the Exchequer that this would court economic disaster. For the COS, military logic and the foreign policy laid down by the Labour government entailed the maintenance of armed forces which could meet their short-term commitments while reconstructing the Services to meet the long-term threat. This, however, entailed expenditure in the short term which exceeded what the Treasury were prepared to make available: moreover, the COS consistently informed the government from the end of the Second World War that an additional long-term rearmament programme was essential. For Dalton and Cripps, an equally compelling assessment of 'the facts' persuaded them that the demands of the COS would retard economic recovery while not necessarily adding to British security.

The constraints on the evolution of a settled long-term defence policy by the Attlee government were therefore twofold, strategic and economic, each endorsed by an influential and powerful section of the British policy-making establishment. The ensuing deadlock between 1945 and 1950 led to a growing gap between British commitments and the wherewithal to meet them, an uncomfortable position that could only be justified while the risk of 'hot' war was slight. In the face of this the Labour government sought to postpone hard choices until the Korean War, and only the attendant risk of a general war forced them to accept the arguments of the COS and put military preparations ahead of economic recovery. Attlee and his colleagues were not the first British government to face this dilemma, nor were they to be the last.

Notes

1. DEFE 4/31: COS(50) mtg 74, 11 May 1950.
2. Cmd 6743 and Cmd 7042 .
3. FO 800/351: Bevin to Attlee, 3 September 1945; and Attlee to Bevin, 5 September 1945.
4. See A. Gorst, 'British military planning for postwar Defence, 1943–5', in A. Deighton (ed.) *Britain and the First Cold War*, 1990.
5. A. Gorst, 'We must cut our coat according to our cloth': the making of British defence policy 1945–1948', in R. Aldrich (ed), *British Intelligence, Strategy and the Cold War*, forthcoming; and J. Lewis, *Changing Direction: British military planning for post-war strategic defence, 1942–1947*, 1988, chs 5 and 6.
6. See for example, CAB 69/7: DO(45) mtg 6, 14 September 1945; DO(45) mtg 7, 3 October 1945; DO(45) mtg 11, 29 October 1945; and DO(45) mtg 13, 7 November 1945; and Gorst, op. cit., 'We must cut our coat'.
7. CAB 131/1: DO(46) mtg 1, 11 January 1946; and DO(46) mtg 3, 21 January 1946.
8. CAB 131/2: DO(46)20, 13 February 1946; CAB 131/1: DO(46) mtg 5, 15 February 1946; CAB 129/7: CP(46)65, 15 February 1946; and CAB 128/5: CM(46) mtg 16, 18 February 1946.
9. CAB 131/2: DO(46)52, 11 April 1946, and DO(46)66, 10 May 1946; CAB 131/1: DO(46) mtg 12, 15 April 1946, and DO(46) mtg 16, 17 May 1946.
10. CAB 131/3: DO(46)117, 9 October 1946; CAB 131/1: DO(46) mtg 27, 16 October 1946, and DO(46) mtg 28, 17 October 1946.
11. CAB 131/3: DO(46)135, 8 November 1946; CAB 131/1: DO(46) mtg 33, 20 November 1946.
12. CAB 131/4: DO(47)4, 7 January 1947, DO(47)9, 13 January 1947; CAB 131/5 DO(47) mtg 2, 14 January 1947.
13. CAB 128/9: CM(47) mtg 7, 17 January 1947, and CM(47) mtg 9, 17 January 1947.
14. CAB 128/9: CM(47) mtg 10, 21 January 1947.
15. R. Smith and J. Zametica, 'The Cold Warrior: Clement Attlee reconsidered, 1945–7', *International Affairs*, vol. 61, no. 2 (1985) 251.
16. CAB 128/9: CM(47) mtg 13, 28 January 1947.
17. DEFE 5/3: COS(47)33(0), 18 February 1947.
18. CAB 21/1800: DO(47)44, 22 May 1947.
19. CAB 128/10: CM(47) mtg 65, 29 July 1947, CM(47) mtg 67, 1 August 1947, and CM(47) mtg 69, 5 August 1947.
20. DEFE 5/5: COS(47)173(0), 23 August 1947.
21. CAB 131/6: DO(48)3, 5 January 1948.
22. CAB 131/6: DO(48)2, 5 January 1948.
23. CAB 131/5: DO(48) mtg 2, 8 January 1948 and DO(48) mtg 3, 14 January 1948.
24. DEFE 4/11: COS(48) mtg 34, 9 March 1948.
25. DEFE 4/10: COS(48) mtg 16, 2 February 1948, and COS(48) mtg 18, 4 February 1948.
26. CAB 128/12: CM(48) mtg 19, 5 March 1948.

27. DEFE 4/11: COS(48) mtg 35, 9 March 1948.
28. DEFE 5/10: COS(48) mtg 76, 7 April 48, COS(48)77(O), 7 April, 1948, and COS(48)90(O), 9 April 1948.
29. CAB 129/13: CM(48) mtg 54, 26 July 1948.
30. CAB 131/6: DO(48)46, 26 July 1948, and DO(48)49, 29 July 1948.
31. CAB 131/5: DO(48) mtg 13, 27 July 1948, and DO(48) mtg 14, 30 July 1948.
32. CAB 131/6: DO(48)53, 11 August 48; and CAB 131/5 DO(48) mtg 16, 13 August 1948.
33. CAB 131/6: DO(48)55, 19 August 48; and CAB 131/5 DO(48) mtg 16, 13 August 1948; CAB 128/13 CM(48) mtg 57, 26 August 1948, and CM(48) mtg 58, 3 September 1948.
34. DEFE 4/16: COS(48)209(O), 16 September 1948, considered at COS(48) mtg 133, 21 September 1948, and COS(48) mtg 136, 24 September 1948.
35. DEFE 4/16: COS(48)223(O), 1 October 1948, COS(48)226(O) 1/10/1948, and COS(48)227(O), 2 October 1948, considered at COS(48) mtg 143, 6 October 1948.
36. DEFE 4/16: COS(48) mtg 146, 13 October 1948.
37. DEFE 4/17: COS(48) mtg 159, 9 November 1948; and DEFE4/18: COS(48) mtg 176, 9 December 1948.
38. DEFE 4/17: COS(48) mtg 155, 3 November 1948, COS(48) mtg 156, 4 November 1948, and COS(48) mtg 159, 9 November 1948.
39. DEFE 4/18: COS(48) mtg 174, 7 December 1948.
40. CAB 131/5: DO(48) mtg 23, 8 December 1948; and CAB 128/15: CM(49) mtg 6, 24 January 1949.
41. CAB 131/7: MISC/P(49)6, 28 February 1949, circulated under cover of DO(49)47, 21 June 1949; and DEFE 4/20 COS(49) mtg 48, 28 March 49.
42. DEFE 4/21: COS(49) mtg 61, 27 April 1949.
43. DEFE 4/21: COS(49) mgt 68, 10 May 1949, and COS(49) mtg 69, 10 May 1949.
44. CAB 131/7: DO(49)47, 21 June 1949, DO(49)48, 21 June 1949, DO(49)50, 22 June 1949, and DO(49)51, 27 June 1949.
45. DEFE 4/23: COS(49) mtg 110, 28 July 1949, and COS(49) mtg 123, 24 August 1949.
46. DEFE 4/24: COS(49) mtg 127, 31 August 1949, COS(49) mtg 132, 9 September 1949, and COS(49) mtg 136, 15 September 1949.
47. CAB 131/7: DO(49)65, 15 October 1949, and DO(49)66, 18 October 1949.
48. CAB 128/16: CM(49) mtg 50, 28 July 1949, CM(49) mtg 51, 29 July 1949, and CM(49) mtg 53, 29 August 1949.
49. CAB 131/8: DO(49) mtg 19, 19 October 1949, DO(49) mtg 20, 15 November 1949, DO(49) mtg 19, 21 November 1949, and DO(49) mtg 22, 25 November 1949; and CAB 126/16: CM (49) mtg 72, 15 December 1949.
50. CAB 131/8: DO(50) mtg 1, 9 January 1950, DO(50) mtg 4, 15 March 1950, DO(50) mtg 5, 23 March 1950, and DO(50) mtg 7, 14 April 1950.
51. DEFE 4/31: COS(50) mtg 74, 11 May 1950, and COS(50) mtg 77, 17 May 1950.
52. CAB 131/8: DO(50) mtg 11, 28 June 1950, DO(50) mtg 12, 6 July 1950, and DO(50) mtg 15, 24 July 1950; and DEFE 4/33: COS(50) mtg 102, 5 July 1950.
53. DEFE 4/33: COS(50) mtg 113, 19 July 1950; CAB 131/8: DO(50) mtg 15, 24 July 1950; and CAB 128/18: CM(50) mtg 50, 25 July 1950.
54. CAB 128/18: CM(50) mtg 52, 1 August 1950.

Index